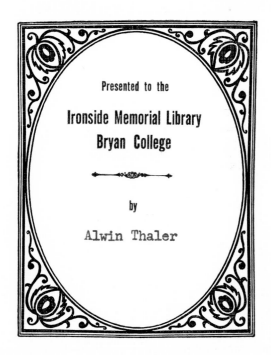

Short Histories of the Literatures
of the World

Edited by Edmund Gosse

A HISTORY OF

GERMAN LITERATURE

BY

CALVIN THOMAS, LL.D.

PROFESSOR OF GERMANIC LANGUAGES AND LITERATURES
IN COLUMBIA UNIVERSITY

NEW YORK
D. APPLETON AND COMPANY
1909

Published March, 1909

PREFACE

In writing this volume, it was my task to compress more than a thousand years of literary history into a volume of about four hundred pages. The book was not to be a collection of sheaves garnered here and there in favorite fields, but a real history, dealing with the whole subject coherently and with due regard to the relative importance of periods, writers, and writings. As it was evident that I should be obliged to omit freely and boldly, I decided, first of all, to omit the scholars, philosophers, and men of science; that is, to confine myself pretty closely to " literature " in the restricted English sense of the word. The broader conception of literature is no doubt the more philosophic, but it is less convenient for a writer who must economize space at every step. The German genius has done much of its best work in scholarship, philosophy, and science, but I was not writing a history of the German genius.

I had, then, to apportion my space among the centuries, and to settle many a perplexing question of inclusion or exclusion. Most difficult of all was to decide, in connection with each new topic taken up, what was on the whole best worth saying when so little could be said of all that one would have liked to say. As these are matters about which no two experts would agree, it will not be strange if I am taxed with sins of omission and disproportion. I hope, however, that such shortcomings will not seem very grave to anyone who has ever tried to write a brief account of any large and complicated matter. There are, in the main, two ways of condensing history. One is to reduce the manifoldness of the facts to a more or less abstract formula, and dwell at length on the "interpretation," treating the facts briefly as so much illustrative material. The other way is to select from the manifold concrete facts those which seem to be most representative and most pregnant, and to dwell on those at some length, leaving the minor phenomena unnoticed. In general, I have preferred the latter method.

Of the numberless writers whom I have drawn on for help, I owe most, probably, to the various editors of the great modern collections which are enumerated in the bibliographic note at the end of the volume. Of the many historians whose works have been accessible, I owe most to Goedeke, Scherer, Koenig, Francke, Meyer (for the nineteenth century), Hettner (for the eighteenth), and Vogt and Koch. The work of Vogt, in particular, has been laid under contribution more often than the foot-

notes—intentionally sparse—would indicate. While I
have tried to deal independently with my subject, so far
as critical appreciation is concerned, I am under great
obligation to these predecessors for data of fact, points
of view, and helpful hints of one kind and another.

Finally, I desire to thank my Columbia colleagues,
Prof. A. F. J. Remy and Mrs. Juliana Haskell, Ph.D.,
for assistance rendered in the way of proof-reading.

CALVIN THOMAS.

NEW YORK, November, 1908.

CONTENTS

A HISTORY OF
GERMAN LITERATURE

CHAPTER I

THE LEGACY OF PAGANISM

THE history of German literature, as a connected account of writings that have literary interest and are extant in the German language, begins about the year 800. It is true that for many centuries prior to that time Germans had been producing poetry in abundance, but it was not written down, and only one late fragment of it has been preserved. A system of alphabetic writing, the so-called runes, may possibly have been in use among the High Germans, but if so the letters were always cut on wood, metal, or stone, and were not employed for what would now be called literary purposes. It was not until Christianity came in, bringing the Latin alphabet and a class of men acquainted with the use of pen, ink, and parchment, that anything of literary value was written down in German.

When Karl the Great died, in the year 814, that part of his vast dominion which was to be known to its inhabitants as Deutschland was all nominally Christian, albeit less than sixty years had passed since the death of Boniface, the great English missionary who had found

much of the German territory virtually untouched by the
religion of the cross.   Let it be remembered, however,
that what the Germans had so quickly accepted under the
name of Christianity was neither the ethics of Jesus, nor
the theology of St. Paul, nor any species of asceticism.
They continued to be, as they had been, a people for
whom fighting was the most important of occupations,
vengeance a matter of course, and fidelity to a chief the
most exigent of social duties.   There had been nothing
like a right-about-face in their ideals or their mode of
living.   What they had accepted was, in its most important aspect, a church organisation which looked to Rome
as its centre of authority and was felt to be closely connected with the imperialistic pretensions of the Frankish
monarchy.   The Saxons had lately been brought into the
church by wholesale at the point of the sword.

In the domain of religion proper, as distinguished
from the machinery of the church, a process of adaptation
had been going on.   The old gods had not been forgotten, nor did the clergy teach that they were unrealities.
As devils, witches, *Unholde*, they continued for a while
to be as real, perhaps, as they had ever been.   Meanwhile there was much in the new system which a German
could use without any bouleversation of his ideas.   The
magic of the church was not so very unlike that to which
he had been accustomed, and its doctrine of a life after
death was in the line of his own beliefs.   So he readily
learned to swear by Christ and the saints, instead of
Donar and Ziu, and to substitute holy for interdicted
names in his incantations.   For some time the lines were
not very distinctly drawn, and there was much friendly

comity between the old order and the new. A Christian
church might be erected on the spot where a pagan altar
had stood, and the old rites continued, with some modification, as a part of the new worship. Pagan festivals
were transferred to the Christian calendar, and pagan
offerings were converted to the use of the church.

Who were the old gods, and what was the nature of
their cult?

This question is pertinent to a history of German
literature, because among the Germans poetry was at first
in large measure an expression of the religious instinct.
One may say that their gods, including the numerous
minor divinities with which their imagination peopled
earth and sky, forest and stream, mountain and cave,
were their earliest poetic creations. This being so, it
is regrettable that we know so very little of their religion
as it had shaped itself just before their acceptance of
Christianity. Hardly a glint of light is thrown on the
subject by the Old German documents. The priest or
monk, who alone could write, was no anthropologist.
For him the old gods were anathema; to write out a
calm description of their damnable rites was not his
affair. So we are left to rely mainly on the *Edda* and
Tacitus, with here and there a hint from other sources.
But Norse mythology, as known to us, is the result of
a long evolution in which, for many centuries, the continental Germans had had no part. We cannot identify
Donar with Thor, for example, except for the purposes
of etymology. Far back in time they had been of course
identical; but what Donar had come to be in the eighth
century A.D. we simply do not know. We only know

about Thor. It is a persistent error inherited from the eighteenth century to suppose that the religion of the Norsemen, as known to us, was at one time the religion of the continental Germans. And as for the priceless little book of Tacitus, the *Germania*, let it be remembered that seven centuries of upheaval and readjustment had intervened since it was written, in the year 98 A.D.

In general the great gods are of small importance in literary history. With the advent of Christianity they drop quickly out of sight, and no poetry of the ensuing centuries is vitally connected with them. It is quite different, however, with regard to the lower mythology of dwarfs, elves, kobolds, wood-sprites, nixies, and so forth, with the concomitant ideas of magic, monsters, metamorphoses, quasi-human souls inhabiting the bodies of beasts, and all that. Such conceptions, rooted in a deep subsoil of ancient superstition, have proved wonderfully tenacious of life and have furnished an element of mysterious fascination to countless folk-songs, ballads, and *Märchen*. In all ages, German poetry in some of its most appealing aspects has drawn nourishment from a supernaturalism that is in part older than Christianity. The progress of science in the fields of anthropology and mythology is making it increasingly evident that these products of primitive superstition are everywhere much the same, and that everywhere the higher mythology is to a large extent a development from them. It is probable, if not yet proved, that imaginative men have made the gods, very much as gardeners have made the jacqueminot. And this supernaturalism is indestructible. It

changes form with the lapse of ages, but it does not die
or lose its zest for the imagination. Hence it is that such
a play as Hauptmann's *Sunken Bell,* with its elfish heroine, its faunish Waldschrat, and its croaking Nickelmann,
could leap into instant favour without much need of commentary. Every German whose childhood had fed on the
folk-lore of the fatherland understood him readily.
When Heine, wishing to explain the Germans to Frenchmen, wrote first a book on religion and philosophy, and
then a book on elemental spirits and demons, he was quite
on the right track.

An Old German charm presents Wodan, whose name
is preserved in our *Wednesday,* as wiser than the other
gods in the ways of magic healing. As he is riding
through the woods with certain other divinities, a horse's
leg is sprained. The others " bespeak " the injury in
vain, but Wodan, who " well knew how," effects a
cure. Another alliterative charm tells of *Idises,* female
divinities similar to the Norse valkyries, who take part
variously in a battle: some fastening fetters, others breaking bonds, others fighting the foe. The *Lay of Hildebrand*, sole surviving relic of heroic song, appeals to a
" mighty god," perhaps Ziu, whose name we have in
our *Tuesday*, as witness to the truth of an assertion.

This is all there is to be learned from Old German
sources about the gods. How they were worshipped, how
they looked in the mind's eye of their worshippers, what
ethical qualities were ascribed to them, we do not defi-
nitely know. If we go back to Tacitus, however, we do
get an interesting glimpse of the worship of Nerthus,
a Low German goddess of fecundity. At the appointed

time her veiled image was placed in a cart and drawn
about the country by cows. At the end of this solemn
procession, which was doubtless accompanied by litur-
gical rites—one may imagine hymns of thanksgiving for
past favours, and prayers and offerings for the further
bestowal of increase,—the symbol of the goddess was
returned to her sacred island grove. Other sacred groves,
in which a tribal divinity was worshipped, are known to
have existed in different parts of Germany. Thus we
hear of one which was held in such awe by the Semnones,
a branch of the Suevi, that it might not be approached
save with fettered limbs. The cult of the god—probably
Ziu—included occasional human sacrifices.

From what is known of other peoples, it is fairly
certain that these religious rites consisted partly in choral
processions, with measured chant and rhythmic movements of the body. Such was the use, probably, of those
" ancient songs in which," says Tacitus, " they celebrate
the earth-born god Tuisto and his son Mannus as the
original ancestors of their nation." We have to think,
evidently, of solemn hymns, with more or less of epic
recital, involving a tribal myth. Tacitus observes that
these songs were the only kind of traditionary annals
that the Germans possessed. He also speaks of their
singing heroic lays when about to go into battle. From
other sources we know that the funeral of a chief was
likewise an occasion for commemorative song. Tacitus
does not mention the singing of songs for entertainment,
but the custom may well have existed in his time, as it
certainly did later.

The existence of hymns and heroic lays, thus clearly

attested for the end of the first century A.D., presupposes
a class of men who may best be called by the Greek name
poet, or *maker*,—the predecessors of the Old English *scop*
and the Scandinavian *skald*. What the art of these men
may have been like, in the centuries that precede the first
records, can only be divined in a general way. Very certainly it was based on alliteration, as it is somewhat
inaptly called. The verse, or " turn," consisted of two
parts bound together by a scheme which required—to
take the normal case—that two strongly stressed syllables
in the first part should begin with the same sound; and
that this sound should then be repeated at the beginning
of a stressed syllable not too far along in the second
part; thus:

> *Grimly they gird on   their gear for the fray.*

The alliteration always fell on important words such as
could fitly bear the stress. Any vowel might alliterate
with any other vowel, and the number and arrangement
of the unstressed syllables and non-alliterating elements
might vary. Indeed, the number of alliterations was not
rigidly fixed; while the norm was three, as in the example given, there was often but one in each half verse,
and there might be two. If it be a sound theory which
traces the origin of versification back to primitive choral
movements, we may suppose that, in the early stages of
Germanic alliteration, the utterance of the stressed syllables was attended by some sort of rude metronomic
action, which in time developed into a musical accompaniment.

2

But this is speculation. What is certain, and at the same time important, is that the Germans, a thousand years before they commenced making literary records, had developed an indigenous poetic art which served the purposes of religious worship and of ethnic annals, very likely also the purpose of social entertainment. There is a lost and irrecoverable German literature, the extent and value of which can never be known. We have no reason to believe that a German Homer may have missed immortality through lack of a scribe, but there may well have been poets whose fame flew far and wide and endured for generations. There may have been hymns comparable to those of the Veda and the Old Testament. There may have been heroic poetry superior to any that was afterward produced in Christian times. We do not know; but the attentive reader of the *Edda* and *Beowulf* will be inclined to imagine rather large possibilities for this extinct German poetry.

Especially rich in poetic creation, or in the mythopœic beginnings which formed the raw material of poetry, was the epoch of the great migrations. A large body of heroic saga, on which the Germanic imagination was destined to feed for centuries to come, originated in the fifth and sixth centuries. As these tales, more or less modified and incrusted with new matter, will meet us in the poetry of the Middle Ages, it will be in order to glance at them here. And first let it be remarked, in a general way, that they are stories of persons. The great fighter is the one interesting object. The mighty events that destroyed the Roman Empire and completely changed the course of European civilisation are reduced in Germanic saga to a mass of personal narratives, in which history is strangely perverted and mixed up with fabulous invention. Patriotism, tribal instinct, religion, play no part of any importance. There is no feeling for the pathos of national calamity, or for the larger import of national triumph, save as these may be reflected in the fate of persons.

Thus, for example, the terrific collisions of Goth and Hun in the East left no trace in saga-lore, nor is the important relation of Goth and Roman anywise reflected in it. For some three hundred years, counting from the middle of the fourth century, the Goths played the leading part among the Germanic tribes. They were the first to come under the influence of Christianity and of Roman civilisation. During the fourth century a large community of them was converted to Arianism by their gifted bishop Wulfila, or Ulphilas, whose partly preserved translation of the Bible into Gothic is the earliest literary record in any Germanic language. From this time on the Goths were constantly in contact with the superior civilisation of southern Europe. Driven from their home on the lower Danube, they surged westward in successive waves of migration, overthrew the Roman Empire and established powerful kingdoms in Italy, Gaul, and Spain. But of all this, in its momentous political aspect, the sagas have nothing to say. We do hear, indeed, of Odoacer, and of his adversary, Theoderic, who, under the name of Dietrich of Bern, towers above all the other saga-heroes. But the relations of the two men are curiously perverted. The real Theoderic waged war against Odoacer in Italy, finally prevailed, and then treacherously

murdered his antagonist; but the saga, seizing, it would
seem, upon some temporary reverse, makes Dietrich flee
eastward from the wrath of Otacher (sometimes it is
Ermanric from whom he flees), and spend thirty years
in exile at the court of Etzel (Attila), who in reality died
long before Theodoric became king. There he appears,
at the end of the *Nibelung Lay*, as the mightiest man of
all the fierce and doughty rout.

In barest outline the genesis of the complicated Nibelung saga was somewhat as follows.[1] Long prior to the
fifth century A.D. there arose gradually, in Westfalia and
the neighbouring Denmark, a saga of greed, murder,
and vengeance among kinsmen by marriage. The story
told of two Low German kings, Siegfried and Hagen.
Siegfried is married to Hagen's sister, whose name is
Grimhild or Gudrun. Hagen covets a treasure possessed
by his brother-in-law, and murders him to get it. The
widow marries a king of the Hûnen living at Soest
(Hûnaland is an old name of Westfalia). This king,
whose original name is lost, but who was conceived as a
monster of cupidity, cruelty, and treachery, covets the
treasure, invites Hagen to his court, and murders him.
Grimhild is on the side of her blood-kin, and when Hagen
is killed she takes horrible vengeance on her husband.
But neither Hagen nor Siegfried is a natural human
being. The great antiquity of the story appears in the fact

---

[1] In the main I here accept the conclusions of R. C. Boer in his
exhaustive *Untersuchungen über den Ursprung und die Entwickelung
der Nibelungensage*, Halle, 1907. I am also much indebted, here as
in other places, to the admirable work of Friedrich Vogt in his part
of Vogt and Koch's *Geschichte der deutschen Literatur*, 2d ed., 1904.

that it is mixed up with ideas of magic, monsters, talking animals, and other elements of primitive superstition.[1] Hagen is the son of an elf. Siegfried is of divine lineage, and as a boy receives instruction from a wonder-working smith, who gives him magic weapons. With these he kills a dragon and thereby captures a treasure which the dragon has taken by force from the black dwarfs. These gold-gathering dwarfs, who live underground, are the original Nibelungs or Darklanders. Possessed of the treasure, on which a curse now rests, Siegfried makes his way, by an act of supreme daring, to a bewitched maid (sleeping beauty), whom the Scandinavians came to think of as a valkyr. He wakens Brynhild from her trance, loves her, leaves her, and marries Grimhild.

In the fourth century the Burgundians, who had been living on the banks of the Vistula, were driven westward and found a new home on the Middle Rhine. This country, that about Worms, was reputed to be very rich, and gold in small quantities was actually found in the bed of the stream. The idea became current that the Burgundian kings possessed a wonderful Rhinegold. In 437 the Burgundians were attacked by the Huns and almost annihilated. Twenty thousand of them, including their

---

[1] It is still a favourite theory of German writers, following Lachmann, that the Siegfried story was originally a nature-myth, and the hero himself either a dawn-god or a spring-god. In that case his enemies, the original Nibelungs or Darklanders, would be the demons of the night or of the winter clouds. The reader must take this speculation for what he thinks it worth. Personally, I incline more and more to the opinion that celestial allegory had little to do with the origin of the Aryan hero-tales.

king Gundicarius, says the Latin chronicler, were slain. Saga said that the Huns coveted the Burgundian treasure. In 452 Attila, the Scourge of God, was found dead in his bed, and the suspicion arose that he had been murdered by his wife, a German princess named Ildico (diminutive of Hilde). What now happened was that the old Low German saga of Hagen and Siegfried and Grimhild, and the King of the Hûnen at Soest, was attached to and mixed up with the historical saga of the Burgundian defeat and the death of Attila, whose wife had killed him to avenge the death of her Burgundian kin. The King of the Hûnen at Soest became the King of the Huns at Ofen. Hagen was transferred to Worms, but on account of Gunter's kingship could not remain an independent prince. He became the vassal of the Burgundian princes, but retained his essential primacy over them in the story. His sister Grimhild became his liege mistress Kriemhild, the Burgundian princess who had married Attila. But as the story developed on German soil the characters of Kriemhild and Attila underwent a great change. Attila was no longer thought of as a depraved monster, but as a benevolent and high-minded monarch, in no way privy to his wife's vengeful plans. And Kriemhild, originally the avenger of her blood-kin upon her husband, became, perhaps in consequence of changing conceptions of wifely duty, the avenger of her murdered husband upon her blood-kin. In the Scandinavian versions of the story, Atli and Grimhild, or Gudrun, as she is there called, retain more of their original characteristics.

These are but examples of a saga-lore that sprang up abundantly on German soil during the migration period.

A large part of it has perished utterly. Some of it got recorded, imperfectly and with complete loss of its poetic form, in Latin. Some of it was carried to the far North, where it was worked over into poems that have reached us in other languages than German. In Germany it continued, after as before the introduction of the Latin alphabet and the art of writing, to be propagated orally among the unlettered folk. The usual form was that of alliterative verse, which was used also for incantations, riddles, and wise sayings. The existence of sagas in prose, or in a mixture of prose and verse, is quite thinkable, but cannot be proved from German sources.

What has survived of pagan poetry in the German language consists of two charms—the so-called *Merseburg Incantations*—and the fragmentary LAY OF HILDEBRAND. This last comprises sixty-nine verses which were written down early in the ninth century on the first and last pages of a Latin manuscript now preserved at Cassel. The language shows a mixture of High and Low German, there are breaks in the sense, and the versification is defective. The subject-matter is an episode of the Dietrich-saga. Hildebrand, Dietrich's doughty old retainer, being on the way home from his long exile at the Hunnish court, is met by his son Hadubrand, whom he has not seen for thirty years. The two leaders hold parley between their armies. Hildebrand quickly comprehends the situation, declares himself and tries to make peace; but the younger man is sceptical and replies with taunts. Hildebrand sees that he must fight. "Woe now," he exclaims,

> *Woe now, Wielder above,   woe-weird cometh!*
> *I have wandered summers and winters   sixty abroad,*
> *And ever have found me   where fighters foregathered,*
> *Yet before no burg   did bane befall.*
> *And now my son with sword   shall smite me,*
> *With battle-axe brain me,   or a bane must I be to him.*
> *Now easily mayst thou,   if thy arm suffice,*
> *Get thee the gear   of such a graybeard,*
> *Rob him of booty,   if thou hast a right to it.*
> *He were the meanest   of the men of Eastland*
> *Who should refuse thee   the fight thou cravest,*
> *The close encounter.   Let combat decide*
> *Who fares from here   with his foeman's armour*
> *And boasts of the byrnies   both hereafter.*

With the beginning of the duel the fragment breaks off. One may surmise that the end would have been the death of the headstrong son, as in the parallel story of Sohrab and Rustem. In a later version, however, the far-famed encounter is made to end happily, the son becoming convinced by the terrific blows dealt him that his redoubtable father has indeed returned.

With all its imperfections in the form that has reached us, this little remnant of the old pagan art is extremely interesting. While the most of the lines now sound rather tame, there are some that carry the day by their rugged force and laconic directness. The salient feature of the technic, apart from the alliterative form, is what is usually called " parallelism," though it is not exactly the familiar parallelism of Hebrew poetry. It consists in repeating the essential content of a clause, but with a different turn of phrase; for example, " looked to their armour " is varied as " got ready their war-gear "; " the fight thou cravest " as " the close encounter." The effect of these constantly recurring appositions is to throw a strong emphasis on the elements thus repeated and to make the verse fluctuate instead of flowing steadily.

The incantations above mentioned hardly belong to literature in the restricted sense of the word, but they are interesting because, while preserved in a manuscript of the tenth century, they are pure products of paganism and afford proof positive of the antiquity of the type to which they belong. The type, which is found also in English, Danish, and other languages, consists of two parts: first, a short narrative, in which it is told how the spell was first employed by some divine being; secondly, the potent formula itself. The first of the Merseburg charms is a cure for the sprained leg of a horse, the second a charm to effect the liberation of a fettered prisoner. The first may be roughly Englished thus:

> *Phol and Wodan*   *fared through the woods,*
> *Of Phol's horse*   *the foot was sprained.*
> *Sinthgunt bespake it*   *and Sunna, her sister;*
> *Frija bespake it*   *and Volla, her sister.*
> *Then Wodan bespake it,*   *who well knew how:*
> *Bone to bone,*   *blood to blood,*
> *Part to part,*   *as if pasted together.*

CHAPTER II

QUITE apart from his military achievements, the statesmanship of Karl the Great was marked by a truly imperial breadth of view and energy of initiative. For ages after his time there is no German ruler who can compare with him in far-sighted intelligence. Soon after his accession to the throne, in 768, he entered upon an educational reform the primary object of which was to banish gross ignorance from the priesthood. Candidates for the clerical life were required to pass an examination of specified scope, and schools in which the necessary knowledge could be obtained were established. It was provided also that these schools might be attended by boys who were not intending to be churchmen. The king's personal example supported his official measures. He called about him eminent scholars, such as Alcuin of York, and Paulus Diaconus of Pisa, established a school at his court and took part in it himself. There was something like a royal academy, the members of which devoted themselves assiduously to reading, discussing, and imitating the Roman poets.

The influence of the king gave to scholarship an

impulse that was felt throughout his dominions. Important centres of monastic learning soon developed at several different points in Germany, and a new race of scholars took to glossing Latin texts in the dialect of the locality, or rendering into it the creed, catechism, paternoster, monastic rule, baptismal vow, or such other documents as the Church had use for. And thus German literature begins. The glosses, which are very abundant and date farthest back, exhibit the first groping attempts at lexicography. The other earliest records, some of them referable to the last quarter of the eighth century, and representing the beginnings of German prose, have in general only a linguistic interest. Their total bulk is small, and they are largely fragmentary. Aside from specimens, in different dialects, of the species just enumerated, we have some parts of sermons, a version of Matthew's gospel, and a version of the *De Fide Catholica* by Bishop Isidore of Seville. The last is a work of considerable literary skill—the most important piece of German prose that has come down to us from the time of Karl the Great.

Of the monastic schools, which for more than five hundred years were destined to take the place of the modern university with its preparatory school, as well as of the printing press, the most noteworthy on High German soil were those at St. Gall on Lake Constance, and at Weissenburg in Alsatia. On the Low German border was the important school of Fulda, whose learned abbot, Hrabanus Maurus, was the most eminent German scholar of the ninth century. At the date of the beginning of literary records the South German dialects were already undergoing the process of phonetic change which was to result finally in a broad differentiation of High German from Low. The change consisted, in part, in the conversion of an earlier *d, t, p*, into *t, ts* or *s, f* or *pf*; thus, for example, the old words which appear in English with the original consonants as *day, heart, deep*, became in High German *tag, herz, tief*, but in Low German *dag, hert, dêp*. As this change of pronunciation affected a large number of words, the result was to sunder the north from the south in the matter of language —a condition which, of course, has its bearing on literary history.

Karl the Great's interest in learning did not end with the encouragement of clerical scholarship, but extended to the language and traditions of his eastern subjects. According to his biographer, Einhard, he wrote or began to write a German grammar, and tried to introduce, among the Franks of his entourage, the German names of the months and points of the compass. He also directed the writing down, says Einhard, of " the ancient barbarian songs in which the warlike deeds of the old kings were celebrated." This has almost a modern sound. It was certainly a great thought to have found lodgment in the mind of a most Christian king of the eighth century, to collect, while it was still possible, and preserve for posterity the national poetry of his German-speaking subjects. But his son and successor, Ludwig the Pious, was a man of different temper. His " piety " was of an intense and narrow kind such as left no room for an interest in pagan poetry. Under him and his successors, whether through the indifference of the clergy or through their active opposition, the fine enterprise of King Karl came to naught. No trace of his collection has been preserved.

On the other hand, it is certainly a point in the pious king's favour if he really instigated, as tradition avers, the writing of the Old Saxon HELIAND, the most interesting religious poem of the early Christian centuries in any Germanic dialect. The title, which is Old Saxon for *Saviour*, is of modern origin. The poem was written about 830 and consists of between five and six thousand alliterating verses, which perpetuate the old epic art and present the Christ from a thoroughly German point of view. Contemporary data concerning the author are wanting, but the lack is supplied, in a way, by a Latin preface and some Latin hexameters which are usually printed with the poem. The preface and the verses cannot be traced farther back than the sixteenth century, but are believed to rest upon authentic tradition. According to this authority, the author of the *Heliand* was a poet of some repute among his own people—*apud suos non ignobilis vates*—who was instigated by King Ludwig to write a poem on the Saviour for the edification of the newly converted Saxons. The author did not draw directly from the New Testament, but from a harmony of the gospels by the Syrian bishop Tatian. He also made some use of learned commentaries by Hrabanus Maurus and others—was, therefore, a scholar. But, speaking broadly, there is in the *Heliand* very little of theological abstraction or lean scholasticism. It is indeed didactic, and for long stretches the author can be as prosy as any metrical preacher; but on occasion the language throbs

with real poetry and the scenes come out vividly before
the mind's eye.

Christ is represented in the *Heliand* as a powerful
duke, rich in lands and treasure, and of a benignant disposition. The disciples are his vassals, who serve him
because he is a kind and munificent lord. They are
"swift thanes"—*snelle thegnos*—and he is "the holy
Lord," "the shepherd of the land," "the ruler," etc.
Matthew has left another master to follow the more gen-
erous Christ. The Palestinian villages become *Burgen*—
Nazaretburg, Galiläaburg, etc. The storm on the Lake
of Galilee is depicted in the local colours of the German
lowlands. The marriage at Cana becomes a hilarious
drinking-bout, the sermon on the mount the discourse of
a wise prince before the assembled people. The action
of the Master just before uttering the beatitudes is thus
portrayed:

> Sat he there silent   and searchingly gazed at them;
> Gracious and good to them   was the godly Master,
> Mild in his mind;   then his mouth he opened
> In words of wisdom,   the Wielder's son,
> And many a marvel   to the men spake he
> In sapient speech for them that   to the assembly yonder
> Christ the almighty   had called and chosen;
> Showing whom, in the hosts   of human kind,
> Of all on earth   God honours chiefly.

The idea of loyalty to a leader was one which the
Saxon could easily assimilate; not so easily the ideas
of humility and non-resistance. In dealing with this
phase of his subject the poet of the *Heliand* is discreet;

he omits the command to turn the other cheek, and in describing the arrest and manacling of Christ he explains:

> *Need he had none*
> *To suffer shame   in silence, the Saviour,*
> *And meekly to yield.   For men he did it,*
> *Choosing to save   the children of earth,*
> *To help them from hell   to the heavenly kingdom,*
> *The wide estate of weal.*

The one incident of the story which has a suggestion of fighting—the attack on Malchus by Simon Peter—is elaborated into a grim picture of fierce wrath and flowing blood:

> *His weapon he drew,*
> *His sword from his side,   and smote to defend him*
> *The foremost foe   with the force of his arm.*
> *And the sharp edge   shore the cheek of Malchus,*
> *Cutting full deep   and cleaving his head*
> *In a gaping gash   whence gushed the blood.*

There is no reason to doubt that the *Heliand* preserves the essential characteristics of the old epic art. The modern reader may perhaps be repelled at first by its parallelism. The repetitions and recurrent phrases have an effect of padding out the verse with vacuous matter. But we may be very sure that they never suggested poverty of thought to the ancient listener. To him the variations of phrasing and the recurrent formulas, which required no new effort of comprehension, were welcome resting-places for the mind. And they facilitated verse-making, just as did the stock epithets and formulas of Homer, by supplying ready-made parts which could be used at pleasure.

In comparison with the *Heliand* the other remains of Christian alliterative verse are of minor importance. A few years ago (1894) a neglected Vatican manuscript of the ninth century was found to contain, along with an extract from the *Heliand*, a number of poetic fragments in the same style and dialect, but relating to the fall of Adam, the murder of Abel, the visit of the Lord to Abraham, and the destruction of Sodom. This *Old Saxon Genesis,* as the find was called for convenience, was at first believed to be part of a lost poem by the author of the *Heliand,* whom the Latin preface above referred to credits with having poetised portions of the Old Testament as well as the life of Christ. It now appears probable, however, that the *Old Saxon Genesis* is by another hand, perhaps that of a pupil. Of the recovered fragments, that relating to the crime and curse of Cain is poetically the most vigorous.

Then there are the *Wessobrun Prayer* and the *Muspilli*. The former, which derives its name from the Bavarian convent in which the manuscript originated, consists of a prayer preceded by a number of defective verses on the primordial void out of which God created the world. The sense of the verses is as follows: " I have heard of it as the greatest of marvels among men that there was (once) neither earth nor sky, nor tree nor mountain, nor shining sun, nor bright moon, nor mighty sea. And when there was naught anywhere of ends or bounds, there was the one almighty God, the most gener-

ous of men, and with him were many divine spirits; and
God is holy." Then follows a prayer for divine grace,
the prayer being in prose, but with traces of alliteration
and of a single attempt at rhyming. It was at one time
supposed, on the strength of a passage of like import
in the *Edda,* that the verses had belonged to an old poetic
cosmogony; that is, had been taken over from paganism
and applied to Christian uses. And it is quite probable
that the language preserves old epic turns of expression.
But the substance is Christian without alloy. It seems
to be a poetic fantasy on the theme of Psalm xc, 2, the
creation of the world out of nothing being regarded as an
earnest of God's power to answer prayer.

Of Bavarian origin, too, is the fragment called *Muspilli,* that is, destruction of the earth. It was found at
Regensburg, written on vacant space in a Latin manuscript which once belonged to Ludwig the Pious. Possibly the verses were written by the king's own hand.
The beginning and the end of the poem, which must
have been a sort of *memento mori,* are missing. The
extant verses first describe the fate of the soul after death :
angels and devils do battle for it and carry it away to
heaven or hell, where it must await final judgment. The
joy of paradise, where there is " life without death and
light without darkness," is contrasted with the horror
of bondage to Satan in the lake of burning pitch. Then
comes an account of the last things: the fight of Elijah
with Antichrist, the world-conflagration, the awful day
of doom. The world-fire is thought of as kindled by the
blood of Elijah, as he is wounded in the fight with Antichrist:

3

> As Elijah's blood   then leaps to the earth,
> The fells take fire,   the forests burn,
> Not a tree remains,   nor trace of water,
> The sea is consumed,   the sky aflame,
> The moon falls,   midgard blazes,
> Not a wrack is left.   'Tis the wrathful day,
> That draweth near   to doom the sinner.

The vision continues with a question and answer: " When the broad earth is all burnt up, . . . what then will have become of the boundary-marks that kinsmen fought over? The fire has consumed the boundaries, the soul stands filled with fear; it knows not how to pay its debt and goes away to eternal torment." It has been conjectured that these last lines allude to the quarrel of King Ludwig's sons over the division of the kingdom.

We come now to OTFRIED, the pioneer of rhyme and the first German author whose name and local habitation are known to history. Otfried was a learned monk of Weissenburg who was impelled by religious and patriotic motives to write a Messiad in the language of his countrymen, the Rhenish Franks. In his earlier years he studied under Hrabanus Maurus at Fulda and he may have studied at St. Gall. His poem, which he called the *Book of the Gospels,* was completed after some forty years of toil about 868. Upon finishing it he sent a copy to Bishop Liutbert, of Mainz, and another to King Ludwig, accompanying the gift in each case with a German poem which formed a double acrostic on the Latin name of the recipient. If this feat suggests patient ingenuity rather than genius, the idea will not be seriously wrong; for the interest of Otfried lies mainly on the formal side of his work. His style is much less forceful and sensuous than that of the *Heliand*.

Why did this devout Alsatian monk, in setting out to make a German poem on the life of Christ, choose to employ rhyme instead of the traditional alliteration? Probably because the old form was associated in his mind with paganism, whereas the new might count on the favour of holy men. It is reasonably certain that rhyme was first systematically employed in Latin church hymns, passed thence to songs composed in the *lingua romana* and came thus to the knowledge of neighbouring Germanic peoples. There is reason to believe that Otfried, living on the borders of West Francia, which had long been Christian, was familiar not only with rhymed hymns in church Latin but also with rude attempts at rhyming in his German vernacular. This is fairly inferable from a passage in his poetic epistle to Bishop Liutbert. At any rate, what he did was to take over the favourite Latin metre—a four-line stanza with sequent rhymes and lines consisting normally of four iambic feet—and accommodate it, so to speak, to the old alliterative verse. The Latin stanza of four short lines became a German strophe of two long lines, each divided into two parts; but the parts were bound together by final, instead of initial, identities of sound. This gave a verse which was based, like the older verse, on the natural accent of words. With respect to the number of accents in the half-line and the treatment of the unaccented elements, Otfried allowed himself the same freedom that the older poets had always used. His half-line tended to become a regular iambic tetrameter; but the exigencies of the new art, for which there were no literary precedents, gave rise to much difficulty and many compromises. He laboured hard over his metrical form, marking accents and elisions, and even supplying neumic notes as an aid to the vocal rendering of his lines. As for his rhymes, many of them would not now count as such, or even as half-rhymes. In general he was content with a homophony affecting only the final syllable, even if it was unaccented; as if *going* were to be regarded as a rhyme to *living*, or *populous* to *serious*. Yet he often hit on real rhymes in the modern sense of the word; and as he proceeded with his task, gaining in insight and dexterity, the proportion of these increased.

These characteristics of Otfried make it very difficult to give a correct idea of his form in English or even in modern German. To render him into smooth verse of any kind is to credit him with a regularity which he never attained and would not have thought important. On the other hand, an attempt at close imitation of his peculiarities results in something which has no melody for the modern ear and only a feeble suggestion of poetry. For example:

> *Now is our life wanting   in all that is joy-giving,*
> *And we must here e'en suffer   a destiny full bitter.*
> *Mourning we must tarry   in this doleful country,*
> *In multifarious sadness   because of all our badness.*
> *Many a trouble sore   besets us evermore;*
> *Our home we may not see,   wretched exiles we!*

These lines are from a part of the poem in which Otfried, having narrated the visit of the Magi to the manger at Bethlehem, proceeds to explain the symbolic meaning of their homeward journey. It is an emblem of man's return from the bitter exile of the earthly life to the heavenly home. Such allegorical interpretations of Scripture abound in the poem, and some of them are far-fetched to the degree of absurdity. Thus the ass on which the Saviour rides into Jerusalem becomes a symbol of sin-laden man. The raiment which the disciples place on the animal is their doctrine and example. Jerusalem is heaven. The people who cast their garments in the Lord's path are the martyrs who have thrown away their lives. And so on.

Otfried relates that he undertook his poem at the urgent request of two friends, one of them a woman, who complained that their devotions were disturbed by the singing of unholy songs. The problem was to wean the people by giving them something better—something with the ancient charm of poetry, yet at the same time safe and edifying. That the continued popularity of the old songs was a sore trial to other devout men of the time appears from a passage in which Hrabanus Maurus castigates the German Christians who got drunk and danced and leaped and sang all sorts of amorous and voluptuous nonsense. The antidote which Otfried provided for this annoying secularity was a poem of some fifteen thousand lines, in five books, wherein he told the story of Christ's life, as he had been able to gather it from the gospels and from various works of clerical erudition. He, too, Germanises the story and the actors, yet not to the same extent as the author of the *Heliand*. The Low German Messiad is more imaginative, the High German more erudite. The *Heliand* poet, when at his best, seems to be reporting what he had seen with his mind's eye; Otfried to be reporting what he had read about in divers books.

The best part of the *Book of the Gospels* is the introduction, in which Otfried explains why he wrote in German. It is in effect a patriotic encomium of the Franks; a glowing eulogy instinct with the new imperialism. Other nations, says Otfried, have had their famous poets whose cunning works have increased the renown of their countrymen. In particular the Greeks and Romans have thus distinguished themselves. Why not, then, the Franks? Are not they the equal of any people that ever lived—as brave, as enterprising, as intelligent? Are they not descended from Alexander the Great? Have they not subdued the world to the borders of the sea? Have they not a rich and fertile land? The conclusion is that such a wonderful people should no longer lag behind in literary production. And before all things else it should be made possible for them to read the praise of God— most important of all subject-matters—in their own tongue and in a form made attractive by the lures of verse.

One sees that the cloistered monk of Weissenburg was not entirely dead to the pressure of life in the outside world. He gloried in the prestige of the Franks and was eager to serve his country in serving God. Whether his ambitious effort exerted any substantial influence either literary or religious, in the monasteries or without, is a question which cannot be answered from the extant data. All that can be said is that before him nothing poetic is known to have been written in rhyme, and after him nothing in the alliterative form. Several scraps of

rhymed religious verse have been found in manuscripts
of the ninth century, but they have no literary interest
and are not precisely datable with reference to Otfried.
Of non-religious literature there is nothing whatever.
With a single exception presently to be considered, the
great events of the century, which were no doubt sung
by unlettered poets as great events had always been sung
from time immemorial, left no record in any German
writing that has been preserved. The bitter quarrel
among the sons of Ludwig the Pious; the division of the
empire; the battle and treaty of Verdun, with the final
separation of what was to be France from what was to
be Germany; the struggles of the new German kingdom against Magyar and Slav in the east and viking
in the north—all this is known to us only from books
written in Latin. What is strangest of all, the career
of the great Karl himself left no trace on any German
poetry that has survived. His campaign of the year 778
against the Moors in Spain gave rise among the Western
Franks to an elaborate saga which some three centuries
later took artistic form in that precious epic of " sweet
France," the *Chanson de Roland*. But the Charlemagne
legend is entirely French, and when it finally found its
way into Germany it was as an importation from abroad.

The one exception above referred to is the LAY OF
LUDWIG, a late example of what Tacitus had in mind
when he wrote of songs that took the place of annals. It
is a rhymed poem of fifty-nine verses celebrating the
victory of King Ludwig over the Norsemen in the year
881. In that year a large horde of the hardy sea-rovers
who were just then founding the colony that was to be

Normandy, penetrated inland to a point between Abbe-
ville and Eu. Here they were met by Ludwig, at the time
but eighteen years old, who cut off their retreat to the sea
and slew a large number of them. It was an achievement
to touch the imagination and be long remembered—
almost a repetition, it may have seemed, of the delivery
of Christendom by Charles Martel. The song begins:

> *Einan kuning uueiz ih,*   *Heizsit her Hluduîg,*
> *Ther gerno gode thionôt.*   *Ih uueiz her imos lônôt.*

That is: " I know a king, he is hight Ludwig, who
gladly serves God. I know that He will reward him for
it." An attempt to imitate the form in English would
meet with the same insurmountable obstacle as in the
case of Otfried. The singer is very religious and has
something of the divine afflatus. Ludwig is described as
losing his father in childhood and being thereafter taken
in charge by God in person. In time God sends heathen
men from over the sea to afflict his people for their sins,
at the same time summoning Ludwig to fight them. The
king responds with alacrity, and his Franks go into the
fray singing *kyrie eleison*. "The song was sung, the
battle began, blood shone in their cheeks, the Franks were
furious. Every warrior fought, but none like Ludwig.
One he thrust through with his sword, another with his
spear; he poured out a bitter draught for his enemies.
Woe to them evermore! Praised be the power of God!
Ludwig won the victory."

As Ludwig III died in 882 and the poem speaks
of him as still living, it must have been composed very

soon after the battle. The author would seem to have been an East Frankish cleric who in some way stood close to the West Frankish court. It is natural to suppose that an event of such thrilling interest as the repulse of the Norsemen in 881 must have been sung about in the language of the people whom it most nearly concerned, that is, in the Gallic *lingua romana* of which we get a glimpse in the Strassburg Oaths. That there were cantilenes in this early French of the ninth century is certain, since the Charlemagne legend must have been propagated by means of them. In the absence of any examples the German *Lay of Ludwig* is doubly interesting as the one extant specimen of a type of poetry that flourished on both sides of the Rhine.

CHAPTER III

FROM MONASTICISM TO CHIVALRY

On the whole, the ninth century was a period of excellent promise for the growth of a new national literature in Germany. When it is remembered that the men of action and the gleemen could not write; that the clerics who were moved to write in German led cloistered lives in widely separated places, and that paganism was under a strict ban, the volume and the merit of the extant production become rather impressive. In the rest of Europe, north and west of the area of Byzantine Greek, it is only in England that letters are known to have been cultivated at all during this period in any vernacular language. But there was Latin. Amid the decay of ancient Rome's political greatness her language had retained its prestige, largely because its use was fostered by the Roman Church. Latin was the one medium whereby a writer in any Christian land might hope to exert large influence. To write in any vulgar tongue was to court a restricted audience and, what is still more important, to use an instrument that was felt to be barbarous and uncouth. This feeling seems to have been strongest in those countries where the vernacular itself had the appearance of bad Latin; but it was strong enough in

Germany also. Even in the time of Karl the Great, what lay nearest the king's heart was the promotion of Latin rather than German scholarship. His biographer Einhard, himself an Englishman of Germanic stock, speaks of the Germans as " barbarians " : one sees that from the high vantage ground of Latin erudition their jargon was still regarded very much as it would have been by Cicero or Quintilian.

It is not so very surprising, then, that the earliest German writings were such as grew out of the pioneer effort of the church to propagate the faith; or that, as the church became more firmly established and the missionary motive less exigent, the Latin tradition resumed its sway over the minds of men who could write. At any rate, that is what happened. The work so well begun under the Karlovingian kings was not continued under their immediate successors. From the end of the ninth century till near the beginning of the twelfth nothing of literary importance was written in the German language. There is no poetry whatever, and no prose except a few translations, commentaries, and other productions of monkish scholarship. The schools were occupied with the study and imitation of Latin authors, and they went their way without much encouragement from kings. After long continued convulsions, due to the repeated divisions of the empire and the never-ending encroachments of Magyar and Slav, Dane and Norman, the crown passed, in 918, from the exhausted line of Karl to the more vigorous and masterful dukes of Saxony. But the Saxon kings were at first soldiers who gave little thought to the quiet wielders of the pen. Heinrich I could not read or write, and Otto the Great learned these arts late in life. Under some of the later Saxon monarchs, it is true, and notably under Otto the Great, letters enjoyed a measure of royal favour; but here again it was Latin scholarship, and not German literature, that mainly interested the emperor and his entourage.

In this short history but little attention will be paid to Latin writings of any period, unless for some special reason they really belong to German literature. Such is the case with a poem WALTHARIUS MANU FORTIS, which is altogether German in spirit, and preserves an old Hunnish-Burgundian saga that is nowhere else so fully recorded. It was composed about the middle of the tenth century by a young monk named Ekkehard, a pupil of the school at St. Gall, and afterward revised by another man of the same name. The form is the Vergilian hexameter, and the imitation of Vergil is decidedly good for a school exercise. There is no telling whether the author versified his German original from oral tradition or from a manuscript. At any rate, his smooth-rolling hexameters counterfeit the style of the old sagas very successfully. Especially readable is the account of the great fight in the Vosges Mountains, where the doughty Walter is compelled to do battle with twelve Burgundians in succession, while the fair Hiltgunt sits by and guards the treasure that she and her lover have stolen from Attila the Hun. One after the other, eleven Burgundian champions are disposed of by him of the strong hand, each one of them, just as in the *Æneid,* being given something appropriate to say before he bites the dust. King Gunter is quickly retired with a lost leg, and then

comes the terrific duel between Walter and his old friend
and fellow-exile Hagen.   Hagen cuts off Walter's arm,
Walter gouges out Hagen's eye and six teeth.   Then they
perforce quit fighting and Hiltgunt is called in to dress
the wounds, while the grim fighters chaff each other over
their respective mutilations.

The spirit of monastic life in the tenth century was
extremely liberal—so much so that Scherer was led to
group the Latin writings of the period under the head
of "mediæval Renascence."   The clergy, some of them
at least, were not averse to taking note of the life of mankind and describing it in terms of bluff realism.   Terence
and Ovid, as well as Vergil, were studied in the convent
schools, and there was a disposition to deal frankly with
secular passions and pursuits.   HROTSVITH, a learned *Roswitha*
nun of Gandersheim, attacked with holy boldness the
endlessly difficult problem of providing a wholesome
Christian substitute for the immoral comedies of Terence.   She also versified a number of church legends
and a life of Otto the Great in leonine hexameters, but
her plays were written in prose interspersed with occasional rhymes.   She is the first German woman, and
with an unimportant exception the last for many centuries, who is known to have concerned herself with
literary production.   Such loneliness on the banks of
the long river of Time is in itself a distinction.   Her plays
are interesting, too, in their way, but there is nothing dis-
tinctively German about them either in form or substance.
Her main purpose was to glorify woman's chastity and
portray its triumph over the wicked wiles of the flesh.
She decks out her dialogues with scholastic erudition, and

makes her villains act like horrid puppets. Now and
then, as in *Calimachus*, a heroine soliloquises convin-
cingly in language which tells a real agony of soul; and
then comes a miracle to relieve the tension and shed a
divine light over conquering virtue.

Not long after the nun of Gandersheim formulated
her ascetic ideal of womanhood a nameless monk of
Tegernsee wrote the poem *Ruodlieb* (about 1030), a realistic novelette of the times. The form is the leonine hexameter, and much of the text has been lost; but the extant
fragments contain interesting and surprisingly dispassion-
ate pictures of every-day life. Young Ruodlieb leaves
home to seek his fortune, gets on brilliantly in the service
of a king, and then returns to his lonely mother. For
the journey the king fits him out, Polonius-like, with
rules of life which he soon has occasion to put to the test.
The scheme is not fully recoverable from the fragments,
but we get glimpses of the secular life of the day, both
high and low, in almost every imaginable phase. There
is no satiric or ascetic animus apparent. Even in dealing with sexual depravity the author is singularly cool.
He evidently thought the motley spectacle of life an
interesting thing worth describing for its own sake.

An age in which the monastic cell gave forth such
products as *Waltharius* and *Ruodlieb* was evidently not
altogether committed to a denial of the will to live. And
there are other evidences that a wholesome secularity was
rife. The form of the "sequence," originally an exten-
sion of the church ritual, became semi-popular and was
used for all sorts of themes. The Ottos had relations
with the Eastern emperors, and intercourse with By-

zantium began to bring in Oriental tales which may have had their origin on the Ganges, in Persia, in Arabia, or in the folk-lore of the Levant: tales of animals reasoning and acting like men; of disguised princes and wonderful wooings; of magic and strange adventure; of encounters with griffins and dragons and other fabulous beasts. Such stories, written down at first in Latin and accumulating rapidly after the crusades began, formed the raw material of a coming literature of entertainment. The gleemen continued, of course, to ply their ancient art in the vernacular, but no one thought it worth while to write down one of their songs. During the long eclipse of German poetry there was, however, one eminent scholar who did good work as a translator from the Latin. This was NOTKER of St. Gall, surnamed Teutonicus for his laudable efforts on behalf of the vernacular. He died in 1022 at the age of seventy, recalling on his death-bed as his gravest sin the fact that he had once wantonly killed a wolf. Of his surviving translations the most important are his versions of the Psalms, of Boethius' *De Consolatione Philosophiæ*, and some bits of Aristotle.

In the eleventh century a wave of reform swept over the German monasteries and put an end to their dabbling with the poets of pagan Rome. What had these to do with salvation? The stern old fanatic who sought to rule the world from the chair of St. Peter, and who inflicted the awful humiliation on Heinrich IV at Canossa, was resolved to force his ascetic views of religion on mankind everywhere. The church, with its dogmas and traditions, its hagiology and sacred books, its worship and promises, was to fill up and dominate the minds of men. And so the life of the only literary class in Germany became narrower and more rigid than it had been. The influences that had begun to make for a freer and ampler view of existence were cut off, and nothing remained but the straight and narrow path through a world of woe, with the veiled prospect of the celestial city at the end. The only things worth attending to were the things connected with man's fall and redemption. Antiquity was a vague stretch of time whose happenings were of importance only as a preparation for Him that should come to break the curse.

In the latter half of the eleventh century the clergy began again here and there to write German verses; and what they wrote reflects at first the view of life just described. It is a poetry, if one may apply that name to a body of verse which in the main does not deserve it, of intense and narrow other-worldliness. We find rhymed paraphrases of Genesis and Exodus, with the story carried back to the creation of the angels and the fall of Lucifer; poems of Christ and the redemption; pictures of heaven and hell; castigations of earthly vanity. The form is the short couplet, with very imperfect rhymes and a variable number of accents to the line. The style is generally dry, straightforward, matter-of-fact, but sometimes becomes impressive by its very simplicity and directness. Such is the case, for example, with some of the stories of the patriarchs in the so-called *Vienna Genesis,* and still more with Ezzo's terse and rapid *Lay of Christ,* a poem of some four hundred verses written at the instigation of the Bishop of Bamberg by one of his clergy. The introduction says that when it was done

" all hastened to become monks "—which means no more, according to Vogt, than that the Bamberg clergy joined the ascetic movement and adopted a monastic rule of life. The poem opens with a jejune epitome of world-history and then leads up quickly to its central theme, the miracles and death of the Saviour. One might call it a primer of Christology.

The most original in conception of all these clerical productions is the *Lay of Anno,* an epopee of a contemporary Christian prelate. Archbishop Anno of Cologne (died in 1075) was a leader of the papal party in the war on Heinrich IV. The poem begins with a world-history, dilates at some length on the four ancient monarchies, and then describes the founding of Cologne and the life-work of Anno. One gets an impression that the author had been somewhat influenced by the popular poets and wished to do for a hero of the church what they did for the heroes of saga; that is, to glorify him by singing of him in ambitious strains and connecting him with a great and divine past. For all along the clergy had employed two methods of warfare: first that of preachments on the vanity of life, the certainty of death, the joys of heaven and the horrors of hell; and secondly that of attempts to turn the powerful lures of minstrelsy to the service of the church by the poetisation of sacred themes. What especially drew the fire of the churchmen at this time was the increasing prestige of the knights, who seemed to represent the spirit of this world gone mad in the pursuit of vanity and folly. The most powerful preacher of the wrath to come was the Austrian HEINRICH VON MELK, whose *Meditation*

4

of Death savagely contrasts the glamour of knighthood
with the ghastliness of the mouldering corpse and the horrors of infernal torment. In a similar vein is the *Discourse on Faith* by the Rhinelander Hartmann, who pictures knighthood as a destroyer of the soul. And then
there is a curious prose poem called *Heaven and Hell,*
which fairly racks the language in picturing the tortures
of the damned.

But these lugubrious voices of a life-hating clergy
died out rapidly after the crusading spirit began to sweep
over Germany. From the end of the eleventh century the
imagination of Christendom was fired by a new ideal,
that of the Christian warrior battling against heathendom for the holy cross. This was an ideal which the
churchmen had no ground to assail, every reason to exalt.
The purely literary effects of the crusades soon became
manifest in the form of a quickened interest in the marvels of the Orient and in fabulous tales of fighting and
adventure in far-away lands. With the crusades came
also an increased intercourse between the Germans and
their western neighbours, who, with their *chansons de
geste*, their poems of antiquity, and the splendid flowering of the love lyric in Provence, had entered, in advance
of the rest of Europe, on an era of brilliant literary production. There was much to be borrowed, and the Germans now proved, for the first but not the last time, that
they were good borrowers.

The first fruits of the new spirit were the *Lay of
Alexander* and the *Lay of Roland,* both translations from
the French. The former is the work of a priest named
LAMPRECHT, who seems to have lived somewhere in the

Middle Rhine country, and to have written about 1130. As his French original is lost, with the exception of 105 verses discovered by Paul Heyse and published in 1856, one cannot judge the translation as such. It is tolerably clear, however, that he did not follow the French closely, and that he had at hand some other source, perhaps the Latin *Historia de Præliis*, that curious accretion of wild fables that had gathered in the course of ages about the name of Alexander. In a poem of over 7,000 verses Lamprecht tells the story as the saga, often silly enough, had worked it out, dwelling at length on the siege of Tyre and the battles with Darius, and devoting some 1,500 verses to the reminiscent letter wherein the conquering hero is made to describe the wonders of the Orient for the edification of his mother Olympias and his teacher Aristotle. It is in the main a matter-of-fact narrative notwithstanding the wonderfulness of the things narrated; but it takes on something of a romantic glow in the passage where Alexander tells of his summer's sojourn in the shady wood among the bewitching songstresses that bloomed in maidenly beauty from the spring flowers and died with them in the autumn. Though a priest, Lamprecht writes with evident zest of matters that lie far outside the Christian scheme of salvation. For him at least the world reprobate has become the world interesting. In the end he gives the tale a moral turn by making Alexander repent and reform after being turned away from the gates of Paradise.

The *Lay of Roland* was also written about 1130 and was the work of a priest named KONRAD. It is essentially the famous *Chanson de Roland*, albeit the German text does not conform closely to either of the French versions now known. The differences are by no means inconsiderable, but whether they point to an independent conception of the theme by the German cleric, in other words to a modicum of poetic originality, is a debatable question. So good an authority as M. Gaston Paris was of the opinion that Konrad changed the spirit of the French poem—deliberately, one must suppose—by eliminating its patriotism.[1] But the French *Chanson* is itself essentially a glorification of the Christian warrior. Roland and his men are not so much Frenchmen who happen to be Christians as Christians who happen to be Frenchmen. After all but little is made of their devotion to " sweet France," and that little is not entirely effaced in the German poem, where the dying Roland also bethinks him of the " sweet land of the Karlings." For Konrad and his readers Kaiser Karl was a German, just as, for the author of the *Chanson*, Charlemagne was a Frenchman; and neither poet was greatly concerned to exalt one region of the Christian world over another. It is characteristic of the mediæval crusading spirit that it brought Western Europe under the dominion of a pas-

---

[1] The words of M. Paris, *Histoire poétique de Charlemagne*, p. 121, are as follows: Le trait le plus remarquable de Conrad est la modification qu'il a fait subir à l'esprit du poëme français: cette modification est toute religieuse. . . . Le poëme français portait déjà l'empreinte bien marquée d'une dévotion guerrière qui faisait croire aux héros qu'ils gagnaient le ciel en mourant; mais ce sentiment n'était pas le seul mobile de leurs actions: ils étaient poussés par l'amour de la patrie, de l'empereur leur seigneur, de leur famille, et surtout de la gloire. Tout cela est effacé dans le poëme de Conrad pour faire place à la seule piété et au désir du martyre.

sion that was stronger than patriotism and took little
note of the national boundaries that are so immensely
important to the modern mind.

As poetry the *Lay of Roland* is easily the best production extant in the German language, except perhaps
the *Heliand,* down to the middle of the twelfth century.
The form—a short couplet with rhymes still very imperfect—has the crudities of an inchoate art, and there are
iterations that disturb the modern reader. But the story
is told with fine effects, and its naïve acceptance of the
incredible is at times magnificent. The fiery eyes of
Kaiser Karl, that dazzled like the noonday sun; the splendid nerve of the traitor Genelun in the presence of King
Marsilie; the tremendous prowess of the doomed Roland
at Roncesvalles; his desperate winding of his horn Olivant
to call the far-away emperor to his aid; and especially his
glorious death, taken note of by heaven and earth—all
these are passages in which the most jaded of readers will
still feel the heart-beat of the crusader.

Such poems as the *Lay of Alexander* and the *Lay
of Roland* by no means presuppose the sudden coming
into existence of a reading public in the modern sense,
with the separate units poring over the manuscript each
for himself. We must rather think of them as read, by
some one in possession of the art, to a company of listen-
ers. In this way the more wide-awake clergy were able
to provide a sort of entertainment which combined religious edification with fighting, adventure, and the other
exciting lures of secular minstrelsy. This is what one
of them undertook to do, about 1150, in the *Chronicle
of the Emperors*, a huge affair in very artless rhymes,

purporting to recount the history of the " Roman "
empire from Romulus to Konrad of Hohenstaufen. It is
very mediæval in its lack of perspective and proportion,
its boundless credulousness, its hospitality to all sorts of
trash. But there is good evidence of its great popularity.
It played a part in whetting the general appetite for literary entertainment and preparing the way for caterers
who should not be of the clergy or inclined to exalt the
religious life. The time was at hand when poems such
as had long been composed and recited by illiterate gleemen began to be written down with a view to reading.
In the course of the twelfth century there was to be a rich
development of this minstrelsy turned into literature.

Meanwhile the quickening of religious life in the
monasteries, which was spoken of a few pages back,
united with the new chivalrous feeling for womanhood
to produce a fervid poetic cult of the Virgin Mary. The
imagination of the time was prone to picture Christ as
the awful judge who could be moved to compassion only
by the pleadings of his tender human mother. She
became, therefore, the more important object of devotion,
the more effective symbol of infinite pity and love. It
was a beautiful symbol, combining the human charm of
ideal womanhood and motherhood, the pathos of inef-
fable sorrow and the majesty of a queen of heaven.
The mediæval religious spirit is at its best when it is
dreaming of the mystic Mother of God, the unfailing
Star of the Sea, who guides the anxious mariner to home
and safety. Of the narrative poems on the life of Mary
the best is the *Three Lays of the Maid*, written about
1170 by a South German priest named Wernher, of whom

nothing definite is known. It is noteworthy for its fine blending of religious symbolism with chivalrous sentiment. The Virgin was also the theme of much lyric verse in the form of the *Leich*—a longish tribute of praise, divided into strophes of unequal length and varying meter. The best production in this kind, down to the time of Walter von der Vogelweide, is a *Marienleich* which seems to have been composed for the use of the nuns in the Hessian convent of Arnstein. It is very uneven in poetic quality, but has passages of noble and delicate beauty.

CHAPTER IV

THE INDIGENOUS EPIC OF THE MIDDLE AGES

Soon after the middle of the twelfth century the long clerical monopoly of letters came to an end. The literary art began to be practised by knights of the humbler class, and the consequence was the ushering in of a memorable poetic era which it is customary to call the classical period of the Middle Ages. It extends from about 1170 to about 1230. Between those years there was a rich flowering of lyric song, and also of narrative poetry, both indigenous and exotic. It is all courtly, aristocratic. There is nothing that reflects the life of the common man, no prose worth mentioning, and no drama save the Latin drama of the church.

From first to last the new poetry is dominated by the knight and the knightly ideal of conduct. Great fighters there had always been, and from time immemorial the deeds of such had formed the favourite subject of the gleeman's song. But whereas the knight of an earlier period had been content with the character of a "swift thane," brave and strong and loyal, he now set himself up as an arbiter of manners and an exemplar of social graces. Knighthood meant the perfection of conduct toward God and man and woman, especially toward the one woman selected for more particular devotion. It comprehended the trifles of etiquette, as well as the larger matters of character, and laid much stress on form and show. And when the glamour of social leadership had thus been added to the prestige of a warrior caste, what wonder was it if the knight thought himself and made others think him the noblest of created beings? He became, with his fighting and tourneying and lovemaking, the central theme of all literary effort. Whatever hero was portrayed, no matter where or when the scene might be laid, was apt to be conceived as a mediæval knight.

To follow a strictly chronological order in dealing with the literature of the period would be quite impossible. It will be most convenient to treat of the genres one after the other, beginning, in this chapter, with the earliest extant specimens of the ancient gleeman's art as turned into literature for the reader, and then passing on to the great ballad epics, the *Nibelungenlied* and *Gudrun*. Those earliest specimens are *King Rother* and *Duke Ernst*. They have the form which had been brought into vogue by the clerical poets, that of the short couplet, with varying number of accents (mostly four) to the line, and with a rough assonance often taking the place of rhyme. Both are of unknown authorship and not precisely datable; but they belong to an earlier and cruder phase of art than that of the ballad epics.

KING ROTHER is a tale of bride-stealing and has the distinction of being the first German poem in which the passion of love plays any part whatever. Rother is a king of Italy who sends twelve good men and true to plead his suit for the hand of the emperor's daughter at Constantinople. The emperor shuts them up in a dungeon, whereat Rother assembles men and ships and sets sail, under the name of Dietrich, to liberate them. He ingratiates himself with the willing maid by fitting her with a pair of golden slippers, and she helps him to free the prisoners. Then he wins a battle for Constantine against the heathen invader Ymelot, and attains his end by means of an unchivalrous hoax: he hurries back from the battle-field and tells the empress that all is lost and that Ymelot is going to sack the city. The women flee for their lives, the princess takes refuge on one of Rother's ships, and he sails away with her. Afterward she is stolen from him by a disguised gleeman and taken back to Constantinople. Rother pursues her and rescues her just as she is about to be forced into a hateful marriage with Ymelot. Then Rother and his wife reign happily in Italy—not at Rome, but at Bari—and one of their descendants is Pippin the Great.

The main elements of the story—the far-famed and desirable beauty, the savage father, the brave lover and his band of doughty helpers, the capture of the prize by a trick—recur in the *Lay of Gudrun* and presumably hark back to an earlier time when the getting of a wife by force and fraud was nothing unusual. The workmanship of the poem is rough, and there are the stereotyped phrases and prolixities which stamp the gleeman's style. The author draws the long bow and delights in so doing. One of Rother's men is so fierce and strong that he has to be kept chained like a lion, and when he stamps upon

the ground his leg sinks into the earth up to his knee.
The love-story, if one may so call it, reflects the simple
and strenuous ways familiar in the viking tales of the
north. In the telling of it there is but little outlay of artistic finesse or of chivalrous sentiment. Rother wants a
wife. The knowing men of his entourage suggest the
emperor's daughter, and he resolves to have her. The
perils of the enterprise, the strength and prowess of Rother's men, the devices resorted to for outwitting her father
—these matters and not the softer emotions of the hero
and heroine are what interests the poet. Rother is made
a mighty musician, and his wild warriors are acutely
susceptible to the concord of sweet sounds. The princess
is vaguely drawn and we never hear her name. On her
first meeting with the distinguished-looking stranger
called Dietrich, and before she knows who he is, she
throws herself at him with a precipitancy which renders
wooing unnecessary.

In DUKE ERNST, on the other hand, love is not an
ingredient, any more than in the *Lay of Alexander* or the
Lay of Roland. Attention is focussed always on the hero
and his men. The saga, which is of Bavarian origin,
albeit the poem as known to us seems to have taken shape
in the Middle Rhine country, is of exceptional psychological interest. Ernst is a brave and upright Bavarian prince, whom a wicked calumny deprives of the
favour of the Emperor Otto. For a time he maintains
himself in a bitter and bloody feud with the empire,
but presently gives up the hopeless struggle, gathers
a band of followers and sets out for the East. Here
he has many wonderful adventures and carries himself

with such bravery and nobility that on his return
the emperor is constrained to take him back into
favour.

The interest of the poem, after the terrific fighting in
Germany is disposed of, turns upon the marvels of the
East. These are described with a matter-of-fact vividness which, in an age of boundless credulity, must have
produced a first-rate illusion of reality. One of the best
episodes is that of the magnetic rock in the Curdled Sea,
which Ernst and his men run into on the coast of Syria.
The rock has the power of drawing ships to it, if they
come within ten leagues, and holding them there for ever.
The gruesomeness of the scene—the forest of bleached
and rotting masts, the doomed ships full of dead men's
bones, the escape of Ernst and his men by sewing themselves up in skins and letting themselves be carried off by
griffins—has something of the weird effectiveness of the
Ancient Mariner. The saga of Duke Ernst enjoyed a
great and lasting popularity. In due time it was done
over into clumsy and sprawling prose, like many another mediæval poem, and formed thus a favourite
chap-book.

The irregular short couplet, characteristic of the *Lay
of Alexander,* the *Lay of Roland,* and the anonymous
poems just spoken of, was improved by the Low German
poet Heinrich von Veldeke, who introduced a stricter
practice in rhyming, and then became the accepted form
for the romances of chivalry. In South and West Germany it long remained the more usual metre for all narrative poetry whatsoever. In Austria, however, a new
form arose under the influence of the earliest minnesing-

ers. One of these, a certain Herr von Kürenberg, invented
a stanza like this: [1]

> *Now bring to me right quickly   my horse and fighting-gear,*
> *For I must ride away from   a certain lady here;*
> *She would e'en compel me   to love her whether or no,*
> *But she shall bide a-pining   for any love of mine, I trow.*

The few verses extant under the name of Kürenberg
show his measure in a crude inchoate form. But it was
readily perfectible, and when perfected it yielded a fairly
regular stanza consisting of four long lines, rhyming at
the end on a stressed syllable and divided in the middle
after an unstressed syllable. Of the half-lines the last
had four accents, the others three. Toward the end of
the twelfth century this perfected " Kürenberg measure "
was employed by a nameless Austrian poet in the composition of the long ballad epic known as the LAY OF
THE NIBELUNGS.

The poem is, on the whole, the most important poetic
production of mediæval Germany. When it was exhumed
in the eighteenth century, after ages of neglect during
which its very existence had been forgotten and the sense
for things mediæval had well-nigh vanished, the great
Frédéric, Roi de Prusse, declared that it was not worth
a charge of powder. A little later, in the ardour of the
romantic revival, it was extolled by enthusiasts as the

---

[1] In the original:

> Nu bring mir her vil balde   min ros, min isen gewant,
> Wan ich muos einer frouwen   rumen diu lant;
> Diu wil mich des betwingen   daz ich ir holt si:
> Si muos der miner minne   iemer darbende sin.

peer of the Iliad. The point of sanity will be found between these two opinions, but rather nearer to the latter. When the poem is put on trial the devil's advocate may justly urge that it is not a national epic at all in the sense of picturing great deeds performed by representatives of the nation, or of mirroring truly the national life at any period, or of embodying highly important elements of culture for the people at large. The core of it is a tale of foul murder and fiendish vengeance. It portrays an ethical code which is essentially revolting and was already happily obsolete when the poem was written. As a tale of the brave days of old it is no polychrome Homeric canvas, picturing a whole epoch and dominated by that admirable Greek temperance which would have nothing in excess—μηδὲν ἄγαν ; it is rather a black-and-white cartoon in which excess is the rule, and truth and proportion are subordinated to an intense setting forth of strong passion and ruthless conduct ending in a mighty disaster.

But with all its limitations the *Nibelung Lay* is a powerful poem and a human document of many-sided interest. It is really incommensurable—a thing of its own kind which it boots little to compare with anything else in literature. It is national in the sense of being thoroughly German. Its greatest merit is its strong delineation of certain characters, especially Hagen, Siegfried, and Kriemhild. These take the imagination captive and haunt it afterward as do only the creations of a great poet.

The theme is the murder of Siegfried and the vengeance wreaked therefor by his wife Kriemhild, who is the pivot of the whole story from first to last. The actual murderer is Hagen, but his deed is thought of as virtually that of the Burgundian royal house, whose total destruction is accordingly involved in Kriemhild's revenge. In an earlier phase of the saga Hagen was an independent king and his motive for the murder greed of wealth. But in the poem he and his motive are translated, so to speak, into the terms of mediæval chivalry. He appears as the vassal of the Burgundian king Gunter, and his motive is a desire to avenge the wrong done, as he thinks, to his liege mistress Brunhild. As Gunter's wife, Brunhild learns how she has been tricked by Siegfried in Gunter's interest on two critical occasions of her life—in the bride-winning games at Isenstein, her former home in the far North, and on her wedding-night at Worms. She must have the life of the overweening Netherlander, and Hagen makes himself the tool of her spiteful rage. After the cowardly assassination is done, Kriemhild continues for some time to live at Worms, giving generously to the poor. To prevent her from thus gaining a dangerous ascendancy the ruthless Hagen robs her of the treasure she has from Siegfried, and thus increases her dormant hatred. In due time she marries Etzel the Hun, invites her kin to visit her and brings on a fierce conflict in which they are all slain. In the end Kriemhild herself is put to death by the angry Hildebrand on account of the carnage she has caused, and Etzel is left to mourn with his court over the calamity.

As a first step toward a just appreciation of the poem one would like to know in what shape the author found his material. How far was he a true maker, how far merely a compiler or redactor? Did he follow a manuscript or an unwritten tradition? In either case, had his predecessors already combined the heterogeneous elements of the story into a semblance of artistic unity, or did he first make the combination himself? These questions cannot be answered in a manner to leave no room for doubt, and they are mixed up in the literature of scholarship with a manuscript question. Of the ten complete manuscripts of the poem which exist, there are three which are certainly nearer than the others to the lost original. They differ considerably in length and other respects, and each has had its eminent partisans. Basing his studies on the shortest of the three rival manuscripts, the distinguished scholar Lachmann concluded that the poem was an agglomeration of twenty old ballads— neither more nor less—pieced together with newer matter. On internal evidence of various kinds—incongruities, contradictions, confused chronology, strange lapses of memory, and so forth—he attempted a rigorous separation of the old matter from the new. For a long time after Lachmann's views were first fully set forth, in 1841, they held a prominent place in critical discussion, dividing scholarship into contending schools. Even now there is nothing like agreement over matters of detail, but two things have become tolerably clear. The first is that we really have to do, as Lachmann thought, with disparate elements of very different age, which were handed down for centuries by oral tradition in some sort of poetic form. The second is that the evidence relied on by Lachmann and his school is not sufficient to warrant his very rigorous and definite conclusions as to the number, character, and boundaries of these more ancient poetic elements. A keen and cautious Dutch scholar, R. C. Boer, sums up the results of a long investigation thus: "Neither episodic single songs nor a variform prose tradition formed the source, nor yet song-books in which certain groups of single songs were combined to represent a part of the tradition; but briefer versions of the entire story." [1] This means that the nameless poet of the twelfth century simply retold and expanded in his own way, under the influence of chivalry and with a veneer of Christianity, a story which was already old as a connected narrative. [2]

The probable genesis of the saga, or concatenation of sagas, was outlined in Chapter I. Very certainly the oldest stratum of it was a *Märchen* telling of Siegfried, the slayer of a dragon, the winner of a fabulous treasure, the unfaithful lover of a bewitched maid, whom he had found in an enchanted place, surrounded by flames or ice or difficult waters. By tasting the blood or anointing himself with the fat of the dragon, he had acquired some

---

[1] *Untersuchungen* (see above, p. 10), I, 179.

[2] In the *Lament*, a rather weak poem in short couplets which in certain manuscripts follows the *Nibelung Lay* as a sort of epilogue or appendix, and is concerned with the mourning at Etzel's court and the report of the disaster to surviving friends at Bechelaren, Passau, and Worms, it is stated that the author got his material from a book which Bishop Pilgrim of Passau (died in 991) had caused to be written by his scribe Konrad in accordance with information obtained from a gleeman named Swemmel, who claimed to have been an eye-witness of the Burgundian disaster. This statement has usually been regarded as a worthless *ex post facto* fabrication, but one must admit at least the possibility that there was a literary version of the saga dating from the end of the tenth century, and that this version was the basis of the poem written in stanzas two centuries later.

5

superhuman quality, such as an invulnerable horny skin
or the power to understand the voices of birds.   But
Hagen and a slayer of Hagen were already a part of the
story before the Burgundians and the historical Attila
ever came into it.   In the *Nibelung Lay* Siegfried has
become a Lowland prince, with home at Xanten, which
was once on the Rhine, though not so now.   In the main
he is a knight of the twelfth century, fitted out richly
with the swiftness of foot, bravery, strength, and beauty
which mediæval minstrelsy everywhere delighted to
exalt.   But on his way to becoming a pink of chivalry the
character of the ancient *Märchen* hero had passed, in the
hands of the gleemen, through an intermediate stage,
that of the *Recke,* or fighting adventurer who likes combat above all things, and is not over-compunctious in his
dealings with womankind.   Traces of this character cling
to him in the poem.   Thus he goes to Worms to woo the
famously fair Kriemhild, attracted by the supposed danger of the enterprise.   But on arriving at the Burgundian
court, instead of saying anything about his errand he
challenges Gunter to fight for his kingdom.   Further on
when he is vexed with Kriemhild for betraying a secret
that he has unwisely confided to her, he beats her black
and blue.   His whole relation to Brunhild is not that of a
chivalrous knight, but that of a gleeman's *Recke*, who
enjoys putting forth his strength for the conquest of a
she-devil.   Not much is made of his supernatural attri-
butes, though these, too, still cling to him.   The only one
of them that really counts in the story is the hiding-cloak
which he uses for tricking Brunhild—an unchivalrous
fraud such as the gleemen delighted in.   The idea of the

treasure-guarding dwarfs is translated into the terms of
feudalism. Alberich the dwarf-king is Siegfried's vassal,
having been conquered by him in single combat and put
in charge of his Burg, which seems to be located somewhere on the coast of the North Sea. When Siegfried
comes and demands men in order to make a show before
Brunhild, Alberich quickly furnishes a thousand richly
caparisoned knights.

The character of Brunhild was worked out very unfortunately by the German gleemen. In the *Edda* and
the Volsung saga she is a prophetic valkyr whom Odin
has pricked with the sleep-thorn for disobedience. There
is great poetry in her short-lived passion for Sigurd. But
it is not at all certain that she was from the first a valkyr.
She belonged rather, one may guess, to the general type
of *Märchen* heroine, the princess-hard-to-woo. She was
a maid bewitched by some superior power and left in
a lonely, forbidding place, approachable only by the one
predestined lover who, in addition to being fearless,
should have just the right equipment and know just
what to say and do. The gleemen were fond of providing
the maiden-hard-to-woo with a savage father who hung
all suitors to a tree or shut them up in prison. The more
perilous and difficult the game, the greater the successful
hero's glory. In the case of Brunhild some dim reminiscence of a former semi-divine character may have survived to the age of chivalry, when games of strength and
skill were only less important than fighting. So Brunhild
became an athletic maid, living in a remote isle of the
sea, mistress of her own fate, and resolved not to wed
unless it were some suitor who should first vanquish her

in certain games. Unsuccessful competitors were put
to death. She had the strength of many men combined,
but it depended on her virginity. In this conception there
was fun enough for the jolly gleemen and their none
too dainty audiences, but little of poetry for the after-
world. The Scandinavian Brynhild is majestic and terrible, the athletic vixen of the *Nibelung Lay* not much
better than horrible.

When did the Burgundians come into the story? As
Theoderic the Great died in 525, and as some time must
have passed before the facts of his life were so far forgotten as to make it possible to think of him as the guest-
friend of Attila, who died in 452, we may perhaps date
the incipient crystallisation back to about the year 600.
And then there are later historical incrustations. Thus
in the poem we find the Saxons and Danes invading Burgundian territory, where they are met and badly beaten
by Siegfried, fighting for King Gunter. So, too, in the
Latin *Waltharius* the Burgundians are identified with
the Franks. A curious fact is the appearance of Bishop
Pilgrim of Passau, a historical personage of the tenth
century, in the *Lay* as Kriemhild's uncle. She is hospitably received by him on her way from Worms to the
land of the Huns. It is as if a Tennysonian idyl should
represent Queen Guinevere as visiting her uncle, Bishop
Butler, of the *Analogy*!

In its fundamental character as an accretion of the
ages, rough-hewn little by little into a sort of artistic
whole, lies at once the strength and the weakness of the
Nibelung Lay. If one tries to regard it as an epic for
the reader and applies to it the criteria proper to that

species of composition, one can draw up a rather formidable list of shortcomings. In the first place, it is terribly prolix. A poet inventing outright and unhampered by tradition, if endowed with only a fair measure of architectonic talent, could have told the story in half the number of stanzas that the poem contains. It is full of irrelevancies and tedious repetitions, especially descriptions of clothes, equipage, and festal functions. The bard never tires of coming back to the splendours of court life, the costly trappings of his princely personages, the brilliance of their retinues, their wonderful hospitality, their lavish generosity toward their vassals, their studious observance of all the elegant formalities. And then the metrical form itself is responsible for much ineptitude. Very often the thought of a stanza is really complete at the end of the third line, and the fourth is quite vacuous—mere padding. Add to this the lavish use of stereotyped formulas and stock rhymes. The author, if one insists on literary criteria, was but a mediocre craftsman and did not really command the resources of the language.

From our modern point of view these are rather serious defects, and they are not exactly done away with by accounting for them historically. The maxim *tout comprendre c'est tout pardonner* has its limitations in the æsthetic as well as in the moral sphere. The critical reader will never get from the *Nibelung Lay* the degree of pleasure that epic poetry at its best is capable of affording. At the same time it is well enough to remember that our modern literary standards, which have evolved slowly through centuries of reading, were non-existent for the author of the *Lay* and his public. It is true that he wrote in a sense for the reader; but in so doing it was only natural that he should lean heavily on the tried and tested methods of the gleeman. And then he wrote for reading aloud; for even after the ability to read had become comparatively common among the aristocratic laity, the costliness of large manuscripts put them beyond the reach of the many. So the great majority of knights and dames continued to get their poetry by way of the ear. But he who listens is in a different position from him who reads. The listener has no time to reflect and compare and theorise, even if we suppose him capable thereof. What counts for him is the immediate thrill. If an episode is entertaining and he knows the story in a general way, he is satisfied and does not bother his head with any subtleties of literary criticism.

So it was with the mediæval gentry who listened to the *Nibelung Lay*. The groundwork of the story, with its exciting interplay of love, jealousy, hate, and vengeance, was familiar to them and sanctified, so to speak, by a long poetic tradition. We think of the poem as a product of their time, but they thought of it as a tale of long ago. And they were not troubled by anachronisms, for they knew no such thing as historical perspective. The scene was laid in a vague past in which strange things had happened and towering personalities had been swayed by towering passions. At the same time they looked into a mirror of present realities; for the dominant idea of the poem is loyalty, and that is precisely the idea that held the feudal system together. Hagen's crime, the cardinal fact of the whole story, and all his later insolence toward Kriemhild grow out of a perverted

Treue toward his liege mistress. It is his unswerving fidelity to her that saves him from being loathsome and makes him a hero. One can imagine the knights and ladies of the twelfth century following with an interest much more personal than it has for us that ancient tragic tale of a liegeman's *Treue*. Nor were they bored, we may be very sure, by the ever-recurring descriptions of raiment, equipage, and ceremony. These things bulked very large in their own lives, and to make much of them was a poet's surest passport to their favour.

The great vogue of the *Nibelung Lay* drew after it a train of imitations, of which the most important is GUDRUN. This, too, is an Austrian production. The only extant copy in manuscript is one made early in the sixteenth century by order of the Emperor Maximilian. The text conforms in spelling to the Vienna standards of that time—the name of the heroine, for example, appearing as Chautrun—and the lost original from which the copy was made may have been modernised in other respects. It is quite certain, however, that the poem originated in the thirteenth century, not so very long after the *Nibelung Lay*. The matter is an old North Sea tale of bride-stealings, followed by punitive expeditions and terrific fighting on land and water—the whole brought down to date, so to speak, under the influence of chivalry. The form is a stanza like this:

And when the night was ended and day came on apace,
'Gan Horand sing so sweetly that all about the place
The birds they ceased to twitter, forgetting their sweet song,
And folk that still lay sleeping, in sooth they kept their beds not
very long.

This is the Nibelung stanza with its characteristic peculiarity intensified by the addition of still another accent
in the last half-line. The dragging effect is not pleasant
to the modern ear.

Gudrun, the principal heroine, is the daughter of
Hetel and Hilde, king and queen of the Hegelings, a people who are to be thought of as living somewhere on the
southern shore of the North Sea. She is betrothed to
Herwig, King of Seeland, but is brutally abducted, in the
absence of her father and his fighting men, by Hartmut of
Normandy. The Hegelings pursue and a fierce fight
takes place on the Wülpensand (not far from the mouth
of the Scheldt). Hetel and the flower of his army are
killed and the Norman robbers escape with their prey.
For fourteen years, while a new generation of Hegelings
is growing up, Gudrun is detained in Normandy, where
she is cruelly treated by the wicked old queen because she
refuses to marry her abductor. Gudrun bears her trials
with fortitude and remains faithful to the far-away Herwig. In due time her rescuers appear, the Normans are
worsted in battle and true love gets its reward.

From an allusion in the *Lay of Alexander* to the far-
famed Battle of the Wülpensand, it is evident that the
story of the abduction of Gudrun was familiar in South
Germany early in the twelfth century. It was the ancient
nucleus of a kidnapping saga that originated in the viking
age among the sea-rovers of the North and found its
way, by means of a Low German intermediary now lost,
to Southern Germany. In the poem the Gudrun story is
preceded by an account of the abduction of her mother
Hilde by Hetel's men. Hilde is the daughter of " wild

Hagen," King of Ireland, whose early adventures—his being carried off in childhood by a griffin and growing up on a lonely and distant coast, whence he finally escapes with an " Indian " princess, Hilde, who becomes his queen and bears him a second Hilde of marvellous beauty—are narrated first of all. Thus the whole affair became a family saga running through three generations, with repetition of the favourite bride-stealing motive. The note of the gleeman's art is discernible in this repetition, also in a marked fondness for fantastic adventures, hair-breadth escapes, cunning tricks and disguises, and in general for the wildly fabulous. One might also note in this connection the extravagant homage paid to music. In the *Nibelung Lay* we have the great fiddler Volker, equally strong with the bow and the sword. In *Gudrun* the Dane Horand sings so sweetly that he not only bewitches Princess Hilde, but hushes the birds and halts the fishes and creeping things. But he is also a mighty warrior.

As poetry *Gudrun* is much less effective than the *Nibelung Lay*. It has no episode comparable in tragic pathos to the death of Siegfried, or to the struggle of Rüdiger between the duty of the liegeman and the duty of the guest-friend; no characters so impressive as Siegfried and Hagen and the wife of King Etzel. The thread of dark fatalism which runs through the *Nibelung Lay* is lacking in *Gudrun*, which is a more cheerful poem, with what may almost be called a happy ending. It is true that rigorous poetic justice is meted out to the old king and queen of Normandy for their brutal treatment of Gudrun—the king is killed in battle by Horand, and the

queen is decapitated by the ferocious Wate,—but Hartmut is pardoned and receives an acceptable wife, and the
whole story ends on a note of joy with four marriages.

The other poems that followed in the wake of the
Nibelung Lay relate mostly to Dietrich of Bern or to
men of his entourage. The actual Theoderic was characterised by a Roman writer as *justissimus unus et servan-
tissimus æqui.* He was also a great leader in battle.
" Alike when he smote the Gepidæ by the Danube, and
when he drove the *Fœderati* of Odoacer into the Adige,
the king had himself headed the final and decisive charge
which broke the shield-wall of the enemy." [1] These traits
are faithfully preserved in saga-lore. All through the
Middle Ages Dietrich was the favourite of the gleemen,
especially those of Austria and Bavaria, who ascribed to
him a temper slow to wrath, a deep-seated reluctance to
draw the sword, a high sense of kingly responsibility.
He needed some special provocation, such as a taunt, an
insult, the killing of a liegeman, to rouse in him the fighting spirit. But when it was roused fire would stream
from his mouth and he was invincible. Like an eastern
banyan-tree the saga of the mighty man of Bern spread
and grew and sent out branches that took root in the
ground and became new trunks with new branches, until
there resulted a jungle in which it is difficult to find one's
way and to make out the relation of things. In the course
of time the DIETRICH-SAGA furnished the matter of about
a dozen minor epics that have survived—some of them
in short couplets, some in stanzas. Only a few of them
can be touched on here, and those but briefly.

---

[1] Charles Oman, *The Dark Ages*, p. 20.

One of the best is the *Rose-garden,* a tale of fast and furious fighting, lighted up with touches of grim humour. It is written in the so-called Hildebrand stanza, which is like that of the *Nibelung Lay* except that the four accents of the last half line are reduced to three, making a more regular and symmetrical verse-form. The author was attracted by the great idea of bringing together the two invincibles, Siegfried of the Netherlands and Dietrich of Bern. His sympathies are clearly with Dietrich, and the story is managed accordingly. Kriemhild, after her marriage to Siegfried and before her calamity, has at Worms a wonderful garden of roses, which she has put in charge of twelve dauntless liegemen. In her overweening pride she challenges Dietrich the Amelung to fight with her wardens, promising a kiss and a wreath to any man who shall vanquish one of them. Dietrich is moved to undertake the enterprise, though it is not exactly to his liking. One after another, eleven Amelungs are matched against eleven Burgundians—with varying fortunes of war. When at last Dietrich faces Siegfried it goes hard with him at first on account of the Netherlander's magic sword and horny skin. Then old Hildebrand, Dietrich's inseparable friend and counsellor, sees that his master is not yet in fighting trim and causes a report to reach Dietrich that he, Hildebrand, has been killed. Then the man of Bern goes to work in earnest. His fiery breath softens Siegfried's horny skin, the mighty Dutchman is worsted and at last ingloriously saved from death only by the lively intervention of his too-confident wife. In his fury Dietrich is about to make an end of her, when he learns in the nick of time that Hildebrand is not dead, after all.   Then he is pacified and contents himself with the kiss and the wreath.

The central fact in the life of the legendary Dietrich is his " flight," to which nothing historical is known to correspond.   As King of Bern (Verona) he incurs the hate of his uncle Ermanric, who rules the Roman world from Rabe (Ravenna).   Through the machinations of two traitorous vassals, Heime and Witege, he is driven from his kingdom and takes refuge with the King of the Huns.   Etzel gives him an army with which he defeats Ermanric and recovers his kingdom.   Then he returns to Hunland and takes a wife, but presently hears that treachery has restored Ermanric to power.   Again Etzel furnishes an army and again Ermanric is beaten ; but two young sons of the noble-minded Etzel, who have been allowed to accompany the expedition, are killed.—These events form the general subject of a group of poems. *Alphart's Death* is concerned with the exploits of a brave youth who goes out to reconnoitre for Dietrich, and after incredible feats of fighting is killed by the dastardly Heime and Witege, who are so lost to honour as to attack him together before and behind.   *The Book of Bern* relates to the betrayal and flight of Dietrich, and the *Battle of Rabe* tells of the pathetic death of Etzel's sons and of the defeat of Ermanric.

Then there is a group of poems relating to that part of Dietrich's life which preceded his feud with Ermanric. These, while in the main faithful to the tradition of indigenous minstrelsy, begin to show here and there the influence of the courtly romances of chivalry.   This is the case, for example, with the *Lay of Ecke,* written in a

complicated stanza of twelve lines [1] whose cunning inter-
lacement suggests the metrical ingenuity of the minnesingers. Ecke is a young giant of twenty who is eager
to win glory by encountering the far-famed Dietrich.
Three queens of Jochgrimm in Tirol offer him the choice
among them if he bring in Dietrich a prisoner, so that
they may have a look at him. They provide him with
a highly romantic outfit of impenetrable armour and bell-
tinkling shield, and he rushes away through the woods,
while all the wild creatures gaze and listen in amazement.
At last he overtakes Dietrich in a forest by night, and
succeeds with the greatest difficulty in goading him into
a fight. The strenuous nocturnal duel results in the death
of the huge Ecke, whereat Dietrich mourns bitterly that
he has slain a man against whom he had no good cause of
war. He feels disgraced for life. Men will point him
out with aversion as the slayer of a king. " And even if
the world forgets it," he soliloquises, " I shall never forget it myself." Such remorseful introspection and delicacy of feeling over a slain foeman are quite foreign to
the earlier minstrelsy.

Several poems reflect the folk-lore of the Tirolese
mountains, picturing a romantic world of giants, dwarfs,
magic, and strange happenings in subterraneous palaces
of the hill-folk. The best of them is *Laurin*, written in
short couplets. Laurin, a king of the dwarfs, is the possessor of a magic girdle which gives him the strength
of twelve men, and also of a hiding-cloak which he takes
out of his pocket when need arises. He has decreed that

---

[1] Or thirteen, if one counts the last line, which is of double
length, as two. The scheme of rhymes is like this; *aabccbdefedd*.

any one who enters his wonderful rose-garden shall lose a hand and foot. Witege, at this stage of the saga a good vassal of Dietrich, wantonly commits the trespass and tramples down the roses. At the first tilt with the diminutive man, who fights on horseback like a true knight, Witege is unhorsed. Laurin is about to take the hand and foot when Dietrich interferes to save his man from shame. Then comes a long and hard battle between Laurin and Dietrich, at first on horse, then on foot. The doughty Berner is hard beset by his invisible little foeman, whose blows come from everywhere and nowhere, but finally gets the better of him by tearing off his girdle. Then the dwarf cries for quarter, agrees to be Dietrich's man, and invites him to his castle. The ensuing visit to the underground home of the dwarfs is described in an interesting manner. One gets the genuine savour of romantic saga-lore.

Finally, a word of WOLFDIETRICH, a popular mediæval poem of which there are several versions in different stages of completeness. The story has no connection with the Dietrich-saga, though its hero is represented as an ancestor of Dietrich, but sprang from the same soil that produced *King Rother*. It is an ancient blend of Gothic, Lombard, and Byzantine saga, retold in Nibelung stanzas by a poet, or rather by several poets, of the thirteenth century. Wolfdietrich is the son of Hugdietrich, the Byzantine emperor. Lending his ear to a wicked intriguer, the father disowns his little son and sends him to Duke Berchtung of Meran to be put to death. But the duke is moved to pity and love for the wonderful child, saves his life, and in time becomes his faithful liegeman.

When the story of the boy's rescue reaches Constantinople Hugdietrich pardons Berchtung, but as he has already divided his kingdom among his other sons there remains no portion for Wolfdietrich. The landless prince must conquer a kingdom for himself, and he proceeds to do so. In the battles with his brother and the other adventures that befall him in pursuit of his object, he is loyally aided by Duke Berchtung and his sixteen sons. Such of these as survive reap the reward of faithful service when Wolf-dietrich finally triumphs.

CHAPTER V

WHEN the dream-world of Arthurian romance was disclosed to Germany, toward the end of the twelfth century, the revelation came to a people well prepared for it. Thanks to the crusades and the Italian wars, the mounted knight with head full of sublime nonsense had become a familiar phenomenon. To see a man leave home for an indefinite time and cross the sea to face danger and death in fighting for an idea—something that was neither food nor raiment nor scrip—had become an every-day affair. Barbarossa himself was a romantic adventurer. Moreover, since the accession of the Swabian emperors, the minor courts had taken a greatly increased interest in the fine forms, the amenities and civilities of social existence. Education had become more general, there was a growing demand for literary entertainment and edification among the laity, and the old sources of supply no longer sufficed. The poetry of the gleemen took little account of the more delicate emotions, and harped unceasingly on two or three strings. It divided men into good and bad, that is faithful and false, and laid its stress on the adventures of the body rather than of the soul. Its ideals could be taken for granted at the beginning of the story; of development, through doubt and struggle and the inward digestion of experience, it had little to say. In the domain of religion it knew only of Christian *versus* heathen, and its Christianity was nothing but varnish—a matter of going to church, hearing mass, and swearing by Christ and the saints.

To say that Arthurian romance offered something in every way better would perhaps be saying too much; but it offered, at any rate, something new and complex and capable of endless variation. And notwithstanding all its absurd unreality and its frequent lubricity, the heart of it was sound and good. It enriched the lives of those who read and pondered, turned their thoughts to higher things, and fostered idealisms which were of inestimable value to mediæval life. And to-day those idealisms are the best part of our legacy from the Middle Ages. The gentle knight without fear and without reproach, pricking o'er the plain or through haunted woods at the will of his horse; free from all small anxieties and sordid cares; always ready to do instant battle with monsters dire or with human oppressors of Beauty; always victorious, and finding his sufficient reward in Beauty's favour—he never existed save in the dreams of poets, but how immensely poorer we should be without him!

The romances of chivalry came into Germany, as is well known, by way of Northern France. The main body of them is in a sense borrowed lore. Yet it is not literal translation. The German romancers were not in the least concerned to pose as original; they got their mat-

6

ter from the French, and they said so, sometimes naming the source or commenting on the merit of different sources. The French provenience was felt by them to be a recommendation of their work. Nevertheless, just in proportion to their own poetic talent—and three of them were richly endowed, each in his own way—they used a free hand on the borrowed matter, adding, rejecting, shading, and so transforming the whole in accordance with their own artistic insight. Thus the best works of the best romancers are to a great extent original productions, instinct with a German spirit, and each permeated with the poetic individuality of its author.

The pioneer among the adapters of the French romance of love and chivalry was HEINRICH VON VELDEKE, who Germanised a *roman d'Enéas* in short rhyming couplets. He was a Netherlander of knightly rank, and his native dialect was the Low Frankish of Maestricht, near which he was born about the middle of the twelfth century. After he had finished a large part of his *Eneid,* he lent the manuscript to a duchess of Cleves, who carried it away to Thuringia. The history of the affair is obscure; it is possible that a powerful churchman who disapproved of secular love poetry had a hand in the business. At any rate such poetry took no root in the Lowlands until long afterward. In Thuringia, on the other hand, it enjoyed the special favour of Landgrave Hermann, the great Mæcenas of the time, whose court became the gathering-place of the poets. To Thuringia Heinrich followed his lost manuscript, received it back after a long lapse of years, and then finished his work under the patronage of the art-loving landgrave. It was completed about 1190 and met with great favour among the High German poets, notwithstanding its unfamiliar dialect. They regarded the gifted Lowlander as one of themselves, and as the father of the rhyming romance of love. In a famous review of the poetic brotherhood of the day Gottfried von Strassburg speaks of Heinrich von Veldeke as the one who " grafted on the German tongue the first twig, from which came the later branches and blossoms."

The German *Eneid* is considerably longer than its anonymous French original, and it is clear that Heinrich drew on some other source, possibly Vergil himself. Of course the whole story is mediævalised. Eneas is a valiant knight invincible to all but beauty. His amour with Dido is portrayed at length, with much engaging realism in the setting of the scenes, and a close study of the havoc wrought by Minne in the hitherto happy state of the queen. The savour of his style will be got best from a literal prose rendering. After a sleepless night Dido wakes her sister and confides in her. " My honour is gone." " Sister Dido, how can that be? Tell me, what is your trouble." " Sister, I am almost dead." " You have been taken ill? When?" " Sister, my health is good, yet I can never get well." " Sister, how can that be? I judge, madam, it is Minne." " Yes, sister, to distraction." Further on, the conquest of Lavinia's heart gives another occasion for setting forth the nature and effects of Minne. Lavinia is fancy-free and her mother desires that she love Turnus. " For God's sake," the girl asks, " what *is* this Minne?" The mother explains as well as she can, and Lavinia declares herself proof against

the foolishness.   Not long afterward she catches a
glimpse of Eneas from her castle window, and then—
" She understood full soon her mother's words.   She
became very hot, and after that cold; she swooned and felt
miserable; she sweat and trembled and turned pale and
turned red; very great was her distress. . . . ' I sus-
pect,' she said, ' that this is that malady of which my
mother told.   Too early it has come to me.   Would that
I had been let alone by—Minne, if I recollect the name.
Yes, she called it Minne.' "

But it was not the epic of antiquity that was destined to flourish from the twig grafted on the German
stock by Heinrich von Veldeke.   The future was rather
with Celtic romance, as first Gallicised by Chrétien de
Troyes and his confreres, and then Germanised by Hartmann von Aue, Wolfram von Eschenbach, and Gottfried von Strassburg.   Under the hands of these men
the German language entered on a new stage as a vehicle
of artistic expression.   They created a graceful and
flexible poetic diction, whereby they were able to invest
knighthood with a charm and a glamour which are still,
after the lapse of seven centuries, very captivating.
HARTMANN VON AUE led the way.

Hartmann was a Swabian knight of scholarly proclivities, whose life seems to have been somewhat vexed
by the conflicting lures of pen and sword, the dilemma
sometimes presenting itself as God and the world.   In
his youth he followed the new fashion, chose a lady-love
and besought her favour in verses which have given him
a modest place among the minnesingers.   Then he would
appear to have tired of the business—sobered, perhaps,

by the death of his liege lord of Aue, whom he mourns in tender and deeply felt verses. Soon after this he renounced the world's vanities and joined a crusade— whether that of 1189 or that of 1197 is uncertain. He was still alive in 1210. This is about all that is known of his life. His important works are the two Arthurian romances *Erec* and *Iwein*, both based on Chrétien, and the two religious poems *Gregory* and *Poor Henry*.

In *Erec* Hartmann did not follow Chrétien closely, but interpolated and amplified with a free hand. He evidently meant to improve on his original, to see the characters with his own eyes and make his own comments. His verse has not that easy, graceful flow which was his later distinction, and there are some other signs of a style not yet settled and clarified. In substance the German *Erec* is the familiar story of a knight's intemperance rebuked by woman's devotion. Having won the lovely Enite, Erec finds life with her so blissful that he is recreant to the claims of knight-errantry. He becomes uxorious—*verliegt sich,* as the German pithily expresses it. His friends are shocked at the eclipse of his manly virtue. Enite herself is grieved and in a dream unwittingly reveals the state of her mind. Angered beyond reason, Erec calls for his horse and armour and commands Enite to accompany him, but to hold her tongue on pain of death. Whenever she breaks the command, to save his life or her own honour, he maltreats her. When he learns the full measure of her great devotion, he becomes contrite and asks her pardon for all his harshness.

It would appear that soon after the completion of

Erec Hartmann's serious mind revolted against the inanities of secular knighthood. The order of his works is a matter of some doubt, but it is probable that *Gregory, or the Good Sinner,* came next. In the opening lines he declares that his heart has often impelled his tongue to utter much that looked toward an earthly reward, but a precipitous end may overtake him who thinks to sin in his youth and postpone repentance. This seems to hint that Hartmann wished to atone for his youthful follies as minnesinger and author of *Erec* by telling a tale of sin, penance, and release. *Gregory* is based on a French poem of unknown authorship, first published by Luzarche in 1857 under the title of *Vie du pape Grégoire le Grand.* It may be described as a sort of mediævalised Œdipus legend. As militant knight Gregory rescues a woman from her oppressor, marries her, and then finds out that she is his mother. In anguish of soul he retires to a lonely rock in the sea, where he does hard and lonely penance for seventeen years. Then the burden is lifted, he returns to the world a sanctified man and is ultimately elected pope. In the telling of the story the stress is made to fall on the spiritual agonisings of the hero. Hartmann clearly wished to enforce the doctrine of the church that the worst sins may be blotted out and the soul relieved by penance.

Then came the admirable *Poor Henry,* a fascinating tale of the religious life. In the full splendour of worldly glory a proud knight is suddenly smitten with the most loathsome of diseases. The leper wanders far in search of a cure and comes to a wise physician at Salerno, who tells him that he can be saved only by the heart's blood

of a virgin willing to give her life for his.   In despair
he retires to the farm of a faithful tenant, whose little
daughter nurses him tenderly.   When she learns what the
physician has said, she insists upon offering herself for
the sacrifice.   Her parents and Poor Henry himself try
in vain to shake her purpose: what is a moment's pain
to the joy of saving her beloved master, and at the same
time winning heaven for herself?   Reluctantly the sick
man consents to accept the sacrifice, and they go together to Salerno.   The doctor forewarns the girl of
all that she must suffer, but she is resolute.   At the last
moment, as she is lying bound on the table and the doctor is sharpening his knife, the waiting Henry rushes in
and calls a halt.   He refuses to be healed at such cost.
God's will shall be done; he will bear his affliction.   He
sets out with the greatly disappointed girl for home, and
on the way is miraculously restored to health.   The maid
whom he had called in jest his little wife becomes his
real wife, and wealth and honours are his again.   He
has won back all by submitting to God's dispensation
instead of trying to escape from it.

What is most noteworthy in the poem is the fine
motivation of the girl's conduct.   If it is not great poetry,
it is at least subtle psychology, revealing a mind at home
in the whole mediæval logic of self-abnegation and other-
worldliness.   What Hartmann especially loved was the
problem of accounting plausibly for the incredible.   He
liked to build ingenious bridges over difficult intellectual
gaps.   In *Poor Henry* it is all done in sober travail of the
mind, but in *Iwein* the casuistry of feeling is often lighted
up with a mellow and delicious humour.   In this, his last

work, Hartmann followed Chrétien (the well-known *Chevalier au Lion*) more closely than in *Erec*; yet there are many independent touches, and the sunny charm of the style is the German poet's own. *Iwein* is a pendant to *Erec* in that the same fundamental conflict between love and knight-errantry is treated from another point of view and with a different distribution of emphasis. Iwein becomes so absorbed in the seductions of King Arthur's court that he forgets his promise to return within a year to his newly wedded wife Laudine. When she indignantly casts him adrift remorse drives him mad. After the recovery of his senses, by the aid of a fair lady with a magic ointment, he has many years of adventurous wandering and many a hard ordeal to pass through before he is happily reunited to his wife.

In that celebrated review of the poets which was cited above—it occurs in the eighth canto of *Tristan*—Gottfried von Strassburg says of Hartmann: " How admirably he bodies forth in speech the meaning of the adventure! How pure and clear is the flow of his little crystal words! They approach modestly, nestle close in one's heart, and endear themselves to the right-thinking mind." This tribute well describes the spell which Hartmann's art exercised over the poetic guild of his own day, and which made him a classic for those that came after. Very different is the estimate which Gottfried gives of another contemporary, whom modern scholars are pretty well agreed in ranking above Hartmann as a profound interpreter of mediæval life. Without mentioning a name he speaks sarcastically of some one who plays dice with words; who makes high and long leaps like the hare, and whose work is as a book of the black art, not to be understood without a key. There is hardly room for doubt that he means WOLFRAM VON ESCHENBACH.

There are not a few passages in Wolfram's works which refer to himself, but from all of them together it is not possible to extract much information concerning his life. He was a Bavarian knight who took pride in his fighting qualities. When he was at home he lived with his wife and daughter in very humble circumstances. He was a faithful husband, and extolled marital fidelity in an age when that virtue was not exactly fashionable. But he was addicted to roving. He spent some time at the court of Landgrave Hermann, where he completed two books of *Parzival* not long prior to the summer of 1202, and he visited other courts in South Germany. He was still living and poetising in 1217. In an oft-quoted couplet he declares himself ignorant of what is written in books, and his words are usually taken to mean that he could not read or write. There is, however, some ground for thinking that this profession of illiteracy is only a modest or humorous exaggeration. Perhaps it was his way of saying that he preferred to be regarded as a knight and man of the world, not as a bookworm. At any rate, he exhibits much out-of-the-way learning such as is difficult to account for if he was wholly illiterate. He was not a good French scholar, but had more than a smattering of the language. However it may have been with regard to his book-knowledge, he was a profound imaginative thinker, and a poet deeply versed, not only in all the ways of knighthood, but in the aspirations of the mediæval spirit after perfection. His great work, the only one that he completed, aside from a few lyric poems, is *Parzival*.

The nature and extent of Wolfram's indebtedness to his French sources is a difficult question. The middle portion of *Parzival,* amounting to about two-thirds of the whole, corresponds roughly to the finished part of Chrétien's unfinished *Perceval,* but even here the deviations are both numerous and important. Moreover, Wolfram has a long and significant introduction which is not found in Chrétien at all, and a long and still more significant conclusion of which the same is true. In the poem itself Wolfram professes to follow a certain Provençal poet whom he calls Kyot. As nothing is known to modern scholarship of any Provençal or French poet by the name of Guiot, who could have been his source, it has been conjectured that Wolfram's use of the name was nothing but a literary mystification. But the theory is not very plausible.

The original Celtic story of Peredur belongs to a type of folk-tale whose varieties might be roughly subsumed under the heading of the Brilliant Fool, or the Adventures of a Successful Simpleton. An ignoramus goes blundering through the world, but somehow always comes off well, learns by experience, and finally rises to something great. The French poets translated the idea into the terms of chivalry. Perceval becomes a knight of noble blood who is deprived of his birthright in childhood, and so grows up in ignorance of the world's ways. But he has great stuff in him. In due time he sets out to win his way, makes all sorts of absurd blunders as he goes, but learns wisdom, does great feats of arms, becomes a distinguished knight of the Table Round, a pattern of chivalry, and in the end a successful searcher for the Holy Grail. It was reserved for our German poet to convert all this into a symbolic narrative of man's upward struggle, through error, doubt, and darkness, to inward peace and light and the highest earthly happiness.

But while the soul of *Parzival* is a didactic idea, the visible body of it is a long succession of adventures and experiences, in the course of which the author lets his imagination stray into devious by-ways and linger over many a matter that has no very obvious connection with his general purpose. Beyond a doubt he wished to commend an ideal of perfection: one that included the ideals of secular knighthood, but also something more, namely, the idea of the purified soul at peace with God. His dream was of a spiritual knighthood not antagonistic to that of the Table Round, but transcending it. And he was a poet: he saw visions and thought in symbols, and his symbols are sometimes perplexing. Then, too, he was deeply interested in the objective world; in the fulness of life as he had known it, no less than in his visions of the marvellous. It was not in his nature to be constantly agonising over the mystery of life, when there were doughty deeds to be chronicled and fair women and brave men to be drawn in the flesh-tints of nature. So he was content, like the author of *Faust* in later times, to adumbrate his idea at the beginning and let it emerge at the end, without making a heavy burden of it all along the way.

Wolfram's art is at its best in his less ambitious passages of simple description and tender feeling. Such, for example, is the charming idyl of Parzival's boyhood in the woods, and the beautiful tribute to his heart-broken mother. The adventures of the young " fool " are related with winsome humour, and Gurnemanz's explication of the code of chivalry is excellent in its kind. Admirable, too, is the story of the winning of Kondwiramur and of Parzival's chaste vigil in the arms of his future wife, to whom he remains faithful through all his coming trials and triumphs. But when we come to the castle of the Grail there is a surfeit of wonders, a confusing splendour of details portrayed with mathematical accuracy. And just here, as it seems to the modern mind, is the weak point in the structure of the poem. Parzival's grand error, that which involves him in doubt and despair, leading him to abjure God and wander for years in spiritual doubt and darkness—is not a sin of the will at all; not even a sin of omission or carelessness. It is just an accident, such as might befall the most high-minded searcher after truth. He has been warned by his trusted teacher not to ask questions; and he has no means of knowing that the time of all times for making an exception is at hand. So he neglects to inquire into the malady of the mysterious sick man, and thus misses his great opportunity. However, the idea of momentous issues hanging upon the asking of a certain question, not in itself obviously important, is part of the legend in its incipient stages.

Wolfram's conclusion is an apotheosis of *Treue*. Even before his illumination Parzival is blameless in respect of all the lower loyalties. He is faithful to his knightly calling, to his mother, to his wife. But he

wavers in his allegiance to God, and the false liegeman
has to be set right by suffering. As purified King of
the Grail, approved of God and reunited to Kondwiramur, he is the perfect exemplar of a perfect fidelity that
has received its reward. In one form or another this
theme of *Treue* was always running in Wolfram's mind.
One of the many singular personages in *Parzival* is a
woman who clings year after year to the dead body of
her lover, who has lost his life in an adventure undertaken to gratify a whim of hers. From time to time
Parzival comes across Sigune and receives instruction
from her, but she never forsakes the corpse of Schionatu-
lander. Such astounding fidelity appealed strongly to
Wolfram's love of the bizarre, and he set out to tell the
story of the lovers in a separate poem. He chose a
stanza resembling that of the *Nibelung Lay*, and made
a beginning which is characterised by a certain sonorous
pathos and lyric intensity. The work was never completed. The existing fragment is called *Titurel* merely
because it happens to begin with a speech of Titurel, an
ancestor of Sigune.

Unfinished also is *Willehalm*, a poem undertaken by
Wolfram at the instigation of Landgrave Hermann. It
is based on the *Bataille d'Aliscans,* a *chanson de geste* of
the Charlemagne cycle. The wife of a Saracen king is
carried off by Guillaume (Willehalm) of Orange, becomes
a Christian and is baptised under the name of Gyburg.
A vast army of heathen come to recapture her, defeat the
Christians, and shut up Gyburg with a few knights in
the castle of Orange. Here she defends herself heroically,
until Willehalm comes with help from King Louis and

beats back the heathen with prodigious slaughter. The
part of the story completed by Wolfram shows the workings of an independent mind. He omits and adds according to his own poetic instinct, and his tendency is
different from that of the French poet in that he is more
tolerant of heathendom.

The last of the three more distinguished romancers
was frankly and at all times a poet of this world. If
he ever passed through spiritual crises or brooded painfully over the mysteries of sin and redemption, there
is no trace of it in his writings. Of the life of GOTTFRIED
VON STRASSBURG almost nothing can be made out with
certainty. He was a minnesinger of some repute, but his
fame rests on his love-intoxicated romance of *Tristan,*
in which he followed the French trouvère, Thomas of
Brittany. When he had written nearly 20,000 verses
and carried the story to the point of Tristan's entanglement with the second Isold, his work was interrupted
by death. He seems to have died about 1210.

Of the French *Tristan*, by Thomas the Trouvère, only
a few fragments have been preserved; but as we have
an English translation and a Norse translation, it is possible to judge with some confidence as to Gottfried's merit
in the way of originality. So far as the mere narrative
is concerned, he followed his original pretty faithfully.
His introduction shows that he felt the pride of an honest craftsman in telling the story as he had found it in
the best authority, without falsifying the tradition with
inventions of his own. He wished to reproduce its incidents and its characteristic savour, letting the whole
argument develop in a natural human way out of one all-

subduing passion. He had no fancy for the eccentric, and Wolfram's "wild tales" were an offence to him. On the other hand, within the limits of a tolerably faithful rendering, there was abundant room for comment and reflection, and here it is that Gottfried shows a distinct poetic individuality. He has not Wolfram's depth, but he is a more even artist than Wolfram, in whom there are long and dreary stretches of sheer rubbish. Gottfried never falls so far below the level of his own best.

The introduction to *Tristan* is mainly a warm eulogy of the love-romance as pabulum for noble souls. Gottfried avers that he does not write for hard worldlings, but for those who know what love is and gladly bear its pain for the sake of its joy. Such, he thinks, will have great satisfaction in reading of the immortal pair, Tristan and Isold. In the telling of the story the non-moral character of the original is faithfully preserved. From the first moment of their surrender to the delirium of passion, Tristan and Isold have no rule of conduct other than to avoid detection. A large part of the poem is taken up with the tricks and stratagems by which the adulterous queen evades or allays the suspicions of her simple-minded husband, and the stories are told without care for their moral aspect. Gottfried is not in the least anxious lest the depravity exhibited by his hero and heroine may forfeit the reader's sympathy. They wrap themselves in lies, plot to murder the all too faithful Brangäne, and make God himself the accomplice of their iniquity. But it is all told as if such things did not signify when set over against their great love and their monumental fidelity to one another.

The tone of *Tristan* is serious, yet nothing is taken seriously but carnal love. The famous episode of the ordeal of God is significant. King Marke, harassed by suspicion, demands that Isold prove her innocence by taking the hot iron in her hand. In her distress the guilty queen resolves to appeal to God, hoping that he will be " courteous " to a woman and help her out of her strait. After prayer a happy thought occurs to her. She writes to Tristan, asking him to present himself in disguise on the day of the trial. He does so, appearing as a shabby pilgrim. She selects the pious-looking stranger to carry her from the boat, and on the way she whispers to him that he is to stumble and fall with her in his arms. Then she goes to church and makes public oath that she has never lain in the arms of any man save the poor pilgrim in whose embrace all the world has just seen her. After this she handles the hot iron unscathed. " Thus," says Gottfried,

> *Thus was the truth made manifest*
> *To all the world by valid test*
> *That Christ in Heaven, the Worshipful,*
> *Is like a sleeve—adjustable,—*
> *Adapts himself with pliant ease,*
> *Takes any shape that one may please;*
> *Is ready at the heart's desire*
> *To help the saint or help the liar.*

This sounds rather blasphemous, but there is elsewhere no trace of free-thinking in Gottfried. Probably the shaft was aimed not at religion, but at the clerical humbug of the ordeal as a means of determining guilt and innocence.

But while Gottfried lacked high seriousness and was content to portray chivalry on its earthy side, he was an artist of rare quality. As a chooser of words and a fashioner of pleasing couplets he has no superior. Take him where one will, he is always graceful, lucid, readable. Sometimes, indeed, his fondness for the striking phrase and melodious jingle betrays him into mere poetic fooling.

Hartmann, Wolfram and Gottfried stand for what is best in the courtly romance of knighthood. They set the pattern for those who came after, and their influence is more or less discernible in a number of subsequent romancers. The most important of these is KONRAD VON WÜRZBURG, who is known to have died at a somewhat advanced age in 1287. His model was Gottfried, whom he styles a " cunning master-smith in golden works of poesy." He was himself an ingenious craftsman, a strict metrician and a pleasant narrator, who practised his art in the spirit of one mourning over faded glories. He is always lamenting the decay of knightly love, faith, and courtesy—an elegiac note which was destined to echo down through the centuries even to the present time. There is abundant evidence that he was highly popular. His works consist of songs and " sayings," allegories and romances. Toward the end of his life he Germanised the bulky *Partenopeus de Blois* in more than 20,000 verses, and the still more bulky *Roman de Troie* in somewhat less than 50,000. His other long poems— *Silvester, Pantaleon, Alexius*, and *Engelhart*—are based on Latin legends. The best of these is *Engelhart*, which goes back to a Latin prose tale, *Vita Amici et Amelii Carissimorum*, of two faithful friends living in the time

7

of Karl the Great. This Latin narrative is the ultimate
source of the French romance *Amys et Amyllyoun,* and
the English *Amis and Amiloun.* As retold by Konrad
from the Latin, in a poem of some 6,000 verses, the
story is a very readable romance of friendship. The
general drift of it is as follows:

Engelhart and his friend Dietrich, who resembles him
like a twin brother, make their way to the Danish court
as obscure gentlemen and flourish there. The king's
daughter can hardly choose between them, but finally
inclines to Engelhart for his name's sake, her own name
being Engeltrut. Dietrich is called away to become Duke
of Brabant. Engelhart distinguishes himself as a knight
and wins the love of Engeltrut. Their amour is reported
to the king by a rival, and Engelhart is constrained to
fight for his own and the lady's honour. But truth is
against him, and he cannot fight with a bad conscience.
So he goes to Brabant and states the case to his friend,
who promptly undertakes to fight in his place. Engelhart remains in Brabant, personating the absent duke and
sharing the bed of the duchess, but with a sword betwixt
him and her. Dietrich wins the fight and marries Engeltrut for his friend, the separating sword being again
called into play. Then Engelhart returns to Denmark as
the husband of Engeltrut, who bears him two children.
Presently the Duke of Brabant is smitten with a leprosy
which can only be cured by the heart's blood of Engelhart's children. Engelhart kills them for his friend's sake,
and Dietrich is made well again. Then the children are
restored to life by a miracle, Engelhart succeeds to the
Danish throne, and all is well. The introduction to

Engelhart, a warm encomium of *Treue*, is garnished with internal feminine rhymes in this fashion:

> *A hoary story in rhyme I dress*
> *Of real leal Steadfastness.*

The difficult form is so cleverly managed that there is little suggestion of forcing, the rhymes seeming to come of themselves.

Of Konrad's short tales the best are the *World's Reward* and the *Tale of a Heart*. The former is a religious apologue purporting to relate an experience of the knight Wirnt von Gravenberg, a contemporary of Konrad. It is related that Wirnt was once visited by a lady of surpassing beauty whom at first he did not recognise. She explains that she is that Dame World whom he and many other noble knights have served all their lives, and that she has presented herself in order that he may at last see her as she really is. Then she turns to leave him, and her body, so fair in the front view, is seen to be a mass of corruption and loathsomeness. The *Tale of a Heart* tells of a love-lorn crusader who pines away and dies after enjoining on his squire to cut out his heart, enclose it in a precious casket and carry it to his distant lady in Europe. As the squire approaches the lady's castle it happens that her husband encounters him, takes the casket away from him, and gives the heart to his cook with orders to prepare it as a morsel for his lady's table. When she learns that she has eaten her lover's heart she refuses all other food and dies. The tale, essentially revolting as it is, is told with charming art, though perhaps with a little too much insistence on the superiority of the old standards of *Treue*. Like Gottfried, Konrad idealises the adulterous lovers as patterns of a fidelity that once was but is no more.

Of other epigonal and minor romancers who imitated or continued the work of their more eminent predecessors there were many. Shortly before the end of the twelfth century a Swiss cleric named Ulrich von Zatzikhoven, who had felt the impulse of Hartmann's *Erec,* Germanised the romance of *Lancelot*. About 1205 Wirnt von Gravenberg, the Bavarian knight who was lately referred to as the hero of a tale by Konrad, wrote his *Wigalois,* which enjoyed a considerable and lasting popularity. It is an Arthurian romance (Wigalois is the son of Gawan of the Table Round), based on Renauld de Beaujeu's *Li bel inconnu*. A little later Heinrich von Türlin, a Carinthian, worked out, from Chrétien and other sources, an Arthurian romance which he called the *Crown*. The Swiss Konrad Fleck adapted the French romance of *Flore and Blanchefleur* (about 1220). Rudolf von Ems, a Swiss knight whose life coincided nearly with the first half of the thirteenth century, Germanised *Barlaam and Josaphat,* and left an unfinished *Alexander*, as well as an unfinished *Chronicle of the World*. Rudolf patterned after Gottfried and was widely read, albeit his work now seems rather frosty and mechanical. Gottfried's unfinished *Tristan* was completed first by Ulrich von Türheim, later and more effectively (about 1300) by Heinrich von Freiberg. A poet who is known only under the name of Der Stricker wrote an Arthurian romance, *Daniel of the Blooming Vale,* which is less concerned with love than with giants, dwarfs, and magic, and also a romance of Charlemagne. A Bavarian whose name is not known composed the long romance in stanzas called the *Younger Titurel*—an imitation and continuation of Wolfram's *Titurel*. Of Bavarian origin, too, is the very mediocre *Lohengrin*, which was written toward the end of the thirteenth century.

The genre continued to flourish in the fourteenth century, but the style which had been brought to such perfection by the earlier poets was no longer a matter of concern. When the sense for rhythm and poetic beauty had well-nigh atrophied, the old metrical romances were turned into prose, in Germany as elsewhere; and these paraphrases, devoid for the most part of all stylistic charm, continued for ages to be favourite reading.

CHAPTER VI

THE MINNÉSINGERS

THE German lyrists of the twelfth and thirteenth centuries were men of knightly rank who sang the praise of women, the joy and pain of love, the happiness of springtime, the beauty of flowers, the sweet music of birds. Sometimes they gave expression in more serious strains to religious feeling or commented on the burning questions of the day. But the most and the best of their production was in the erotic vein, for which reason it is customary to call them "minnesingers." *Minne* was at first the nobler word for love, *Liebe* the coarser. In time the two words changed places, and in the fifteenth century the former dropped out of use.

The general type of erotic poetry which we associate with the name "minnesinger" had its origin, as is well known, in Southern France, where it grew naturally out of social conditions. Young women of the Provençal nobility were apt to be given in marriage at an early age and for reasons of convenience. Thus the young mistress of the castle would find herself surrounded by a band of her husband's retainers, to whom the mere sight of a high-born lady, emerging now and then from the seclusion of the women's apartments, was an event. It was worth while to win her favour, apart from the romance of it; and the lady herself, even if virtuously minded, would often find the game an agreeable diversion in her monotonous life. The spice of danger, the necessity of being very cautious lest she be compromised, added zest to the wooing. A small token of her favour, a smile, a nod, might become the occasion of inward rapture and jubilation. And if the lady was not virtuous the clandestine relation was full of perilous excitement. There were watchers to be evaded and secret messages to be conveyed. Gossip was to be feared, and a false step might bring disaster. Little by little the knight's actual relation to his feudal lord was made the norm for an ideal relation to the liege lady whom he chose to be the mistress of his heart. It was his duty to " serve " her faithfully by singing her praises, executing her commands, and maintaining with his lance her superiority to the rest of her sex. Her favour was his supreme reward, her coldness his greatest grief.

Thus arose a kind of erotic poetry characterised on the one hand by secrecy and circumspection, and on the other by the expenditure of much rapturous emotion over trivial things; things, that is, that seem trivial from the point of view of a society in which love-making is normally thought of as a preliminary to marriage. The troubadour's verses were usually addressed to a married woman.

Similar conditions in Germany, aided to some extent by direct imitation, gave rise to the poetry of the minnesingers. Its history may be conveniently divided into three periods. In the first period of crude beginnings, say roughly from 1150 to 1190, the singers were Austrian and Bavarian knights who lived remote from the French border, knew little or nothing of French and Provençal, and got their impulse from the love-messages and invitations to the May-dance, which were already current among the people.[1] The more important names are Herr von Kürenberg and Dietmar von Aist. In their songs assonance has not yet been fully replaced by regular rhyme, and the idea of the service of love is not discernible. The second period, say from 1190 to 1230, is that in which the new lyric art reached its greatest perfection. A brilliant festival given by the emperor at Mainz in 1184 had greatly increased the prestige of the knights in Western Germany, a fresh impulse had been given to the poetic art by the patronage of Landgrave Hermann, and Barbarossa's crusade of 1189 had quickened the spirit of adventure for an idea, while at the same time bringing the German nobility into closer relations with France. The tone and style of the troubadours began to be copied. Romanic forms such as the day-song were imitated, and the all-dominating idea of the service of love was taken over. The making of verses to a liege lady, real or

---

[1] It is a moot question of scholarship whether the earliest minne-singers, even in Austria, did not get their art from the Provençal poets. Anton E. Schönbach, *Die Anfänge des deutschen Minne-sanges*, 1898, shows that knowledge of the Provence poets *may* have come into Austria by way of Northern Italy and Tirol. But the evidence of such influence is virtually nil. On the other hand, it must be admitted that the evidence for the folksongs is very tenuous, since none of them exist. In the text I take the view which seems on the whole the most plausible. The little book of Schönbach gives the literature of the controversy.

imaginary, became a fashion of the gentry from emperor and king and duke down to the poor landless knight who sang for food and shelter. The mania spread eastward to Austria and there exerted a galvanic influence on the earlier indigenous art, which now quickly culminated in the exquisite songs of Walter von der Vogelweide. The more important of Walter's immediate predecessors were Heinrich von Veldeke, Reinmar von Hagenau, Friedrich von Hausen, and Heinrich von Morungen.

Then came a third period, from 1230 on, in which the now familiar notes were repeated endlessly by an ever-increasing number of nightingales, as the minnesingers liked to call themselves. None of them is comparable to Walter in perfection of artistry or in weight of personality. The more noteworthy developments of this epoch may best be observed in Ulrich von Lichtenstein, a gifted but ill-balanced poet who converted the service of love into fantastic and sickly extravagance; in Tannhäuser, who made his lady's exorbitant demands a subject of satirical raillery, and in Neidhart von Reuental, who turned his back on the refinements of *courtoisie* and pictured his noble self as the irresistible dance-partner of the buxom country girl. In due time the knights as a class lost their interest in verse-making, and their art was taken up by peripatetic " masters," who were not of gentle birth, and who practised for pay like any other journeyman. The next stage was the formation of local societies for the training of mastersingers and the public exhibition of their wares.

We return to the Austrian pioneers, who, as was remarked, got their impulse from the love-message and the invitation to the May-dance. In the dearth of literary records it is not possible to say much about this early indigenous lyric poetry, but its existence in a crude form is hardly open to question. Back in the ninth century we hear of lawless nuns who sent out amorous effusions in defiance of propriety and discipline. Such an effusion was called a *winileod*, that is, a love-ditty, and the currency of such things was a scandal to the churchmen. This accounts for the paucity of manuscript records, but we may be very sure that human nature continued to assert itself. From Lapland to Madagascar love makes poets; and the lover who cannot himself frame a message in words more choice than those of every-day speech will have recourse to the inventions of those who are more expert. It is probable that the gleeman, always a convenient go-between in affairs of the heart, often made himself useful as a conveyor, or on occasion a composer, of love-messages. There is a well-known and very pretty love-ditty which is possibly older than the knightly minnesong, and has come down to us embedded in a girl's Latin letter to her teacher. It runs:

> *Du bist mîn, ich bin dîn,*
> *Des sollt du gewis sîn.*
> *Du bist beslozzen*
> *In minem herzen,*
> *Verlorn ist das slüzzelîn,*
> *Du muost iemer drinne sîn.*[1]

---

[1] In English: Thou art mine, I am thine; of that thou art to feel assured. Thou art locked up in my heart, the little key is lost; thou must stay there alway.

One surmises that the writer drew on a stock of current love-rhymes available for quotation. Who knows how many such wildflowers had sprung up in times that precede the hothouse productions of the minnesinger?

And then the invitation to the merry May-dance was a poetic occasion of much greater import than one might at first suppose. The German winter is apt to be a dreary affair of darkened skies, depressing fog, and cold rain. One may live for weeks without seeing the sun. Six or seven hundred years ago winter meant imprisonment and manifold discomfort. Good roads were lacking, it was not easy to move from place to place, the houses were cold and cheerless, the resources of amusement few and slender. No wonder that the coming of spring, associated from time immemorial with happy festivals, was for high and low a season of heartfelt gladness. When the lover, in nature's pairing-time, summoned his sweetheart to go with him to the fields, to gather flowers, wreathe garlands, hear the music of the birds, and join in the dance, he was inviting her to the very keenest pleasure that the year afforded. The song-motive, " Come, love, let us go a-Maying," has been worked so hard by many generations of poets and musicians, that it has become like some of the faded metaphors of our daily speech: one must make an effort of the imagination to realise the poetry that it held for our forebears of long ago.

Simple as it was, the love-message proved capable of no little variation when the suggestion it offered was taken up by men of courtly mind and some little artistic talent. The message might be thought of as coming from

the man or from the woman. It might be an assurance
of love and fidelity or express misgivings. It might tell
of loneliness and longing, allude to the cause of separation, give utterance to the hope of reunion. It might
crowd much meaning into a word or a comparison such
as would remind the recipient of past intimacies. It
might picture the situation or illustrate it with a symbolic
narrative. On the other hand, the invitation to the May-
dance pointed the way to the direct lyrical expression of
the vernal mood; of the sense of relief and exultation;
of joy in the witcheries of field and forest. Such are the
poetic resources of DER VON KÜRENBERG and DIETMAR
VON AIST, both of whom are fond of picturing the de-
serted woman pining for her lost lover. The man is not
the pursuer, but an escaped captive, or a renegade who
has been driven away by gossip. Kürenberg makes a
woman lament:

> *The heart is sad within me, the hot tears start,*
> *For I and my Beloved must e'en dwell apart.*
> *'Tis all the work of liars—God send them misery!*
> *Were we two reunited, 'twere sooth a happy day for me.*

In another stanza a woman tells how she stood alone
in her chamber at bedtime, blushed and thought sadly of
her lover. Another tells how she had trained a falcon
to obey her will, and how one day he flew away—to reap-
pear later wearing the golden fetters of a new captor.
A song of Dietmar pictures a woman standing alone at
her window and gazing out on the heath. She sees a
falcon fly past. " Happy falcon," she says, " that fliest

wheresoever thou wilt and seekest in the wood a tree that pleaseth thee. So did I, too. I chose a man who was pleasing in my eyes. For that fair ladies envy me. Why can they not leave me my love? I never wished to deprive them of theirs."

All the extant poems of Kürenberg are in the stanza which bears his name (page 51). Dietmar has different verse-forms, all of which are simple and make free use of assonance. Like Kürenberg he usually exhausts his theme in a single stanza; that is, his songs are mono-strophic. This is the case also with the poems that have come down under the name of Spervogel, who was a con-temporary of the other two. Their author, however—or authors, for it appears that the Spervogel poems are the work of two different men—was not a minnesinger, but a pioneer cultivator of the poetic *Spruch,* or saying. The German name is something of a misnomer, since the thing in question was originally intended to be sung rather than spoken. It means simply a metrical " deliverance," usually of a didactic or gnomic character, but capable, in the hands of a genius like Walter, of taking on the glow of true poetry. The more serious poems of Spervogel set forth the infinitude of God, the darkness of hell, the merit of the Redeemer, and other such transcendental matters; while the lighter ones give expression to shrewd common sense and home-baked philosophy.

The second period saw the rapid dissemination of the lyric art in all parts of Germany. It was marked by the development of amazing technical virtuosity and the growth of an *esprit de corps* which imposed something like professional ethics. Of course the minnesinger was a musician as well as a poet. He sang his verses to the accompaniment of a fiddle, rebec, or small harp, with music of his own composing. His stanza with its tune was called a *Ton*, and professional honour required that a man's *Ton* be respected as his property. In general the better minnesingers were not given to using the same form repeatedly, but took pride in inventing a new one for each new poem. But there are exceptions; some of them have favourite forms which they use again and again, especially in religious and gnomic verse. In the *Lied*, or song proper, the stanza was generally a tripartite affair, consisting of two identical movements called *Stollen*, or pillars, these constituting together the *Aufgesang*, or ascending node; and then of a third movement of different character, called the *Abgesang*, or descending node. The following stanza from a well-known poem of Walter will illustrate a simple form of the tripartite arrangement:

> "*Take, damsel, take this wreath,*"
> *Quoth I to a maiden sweet and fair;*
> "*Our dance upon the heath*
> *Wants not bravery if my flowers you wear.*
> *A happy man were I in sooth,*
> *Would flowers come at my call*
> *To deck your head withal;*
> *Believe me for I speak the truth.*"

It is difficult to characterise the minnesingers separately on account of their strong family resemblance. The fashion restricted them to a narrow range, and the conditions imposed a certain vagueness of treatment. The consequence is that in reading them one does not often get the savour of a distinct poetic individuality. Their art consists in expatiating on the feelings aroused by a situation into which one sees as through a glass darkly. Very many of their songs seem operose and brain-spun. To only a few, aside from Walter, and to them not often, was it given to achieve a lyric expression of the kind that makes one forget the artificer. A few pretty songs were composed by the Lowlander HEINRICH VON VELDEKE, who was one of the first to come under the influence of the French poets. In his songs, as in his *Eneid*, his charm consists in a certain naïve directness and simplicity. In those of FRIEDRICH VON HAUSEN, on the other hand, the characteristic note is a pensive toying with bitter-sweet thoughts of a lady who has responded somewhat icily to her lover's ardours. He was a knight of the Middle Rhine country who fought in the East and met his death in Asia Minor on May 6, 1190. His verses evince the temper of the noble sufferer. His faithful devotion has not been rewarded or even appreciated, yet the pain is dear to him and he has remained faithful; no one has heard him utter a hard word of his lady or of other women. His most famous song, *Heart and Body,* expresses the conflicting emotions with which he joined the crusade in which he lost his life. His body and his heart are at variance: the one would fain be fighting the heathen, while the other is bound to a love that will neither reward him nor let him go in peace to fight the battles of God.

More passionate is the cry of the Thuringian HEIN-RICH VON MORUNGEN, the most gifted of Walter's immediate predecessors. The object of his devoirs would seem to have been a queen or a princess who gave him some token of favour that called forth lyric raptures of joy and praise. But his hopes were excessive; the virtuous lady had meant less than he dreamed. So he is left to mourn her aloofness and sigh for the return of a vanished joy. Were he only as dear to her as the pet bird that she has taught to speak, he would sing for her better than any nightingale. Yet his misfortune is precious. He would have his epitaph some day tell the world how he loved her and how she grieved him without cause.

But it was not in Thuringia, nor along the Rhine, that the courtly minnesong flourished most splendidly; it was rather in Austria, where the exotic scions were grafted on a vigorous native stock by REINMAR VON HAGENAU. Reinmar seems to have attached himself to the Austrian court as early as 1185. At any rate, he accompanied Duke Leopold on the crusade of 1189, and the untimely death of the prince a few years later drew from him a tender poetic tribute, purporting to express the grief of the widowed Helen. It begins:

> *The spring has come once more, they say,*
> *The joy is here again,*
> *And therefore it were meet that I be glad:*
> *But how may that be, tell me, pray,*
> *When cruel death has lately slain*
> *My joy and left my heart forever sad?*

As a minnesinger Reinmar is characterised by nobility of sentiment and dignified temperance of expression. There is no rapture in him, and very little of sensual suggestion. He praises his lady for her beauty and goodness and for the joy that he has had in seeing her and thinking of her. For her sake he reveres the name of woman. "Hail," he sings in a stanza that was particularly admired by Walter,

> *Hail woman! What a blessed name!*
> *How sweet to speak, how grateful to the heart!*
> *There is naught else such eulogy may claim,*
> *When she is prone to goodness, as thou art.*

The fame of Reinmar flew far and wide. "Who shall be the leader of the nightingales, now that Reinmar is dead?" queried Gottfried von Strassburg in his *Tristan;* and the far-away Alsatian, himself one of the tuneful band, proceeded to answer his own question in an enthusiastic tribute to WALTER VON DER VOGELWEIDE. It is a judgment in which all the world has since concurred.

It has proved impossible for modern scholarship to settle positively the question of Walter's birthplace. The name Vogelweide means nothing more than a clearing or settlement where birds were fed, and a number of places that once bore the name have been identified in Austria and Bavaria. All that Walter himself tells us is that he learned to sing in Austria. Latterly there is a preponderance of opinion that he was born in southern Austria, perhaps in Styria. There is nothing to connect him with Bozen, in Tirol, which a few years ago erected a fine monument to his memory. He grew up in the country and learned to love country things, but

8

there is no mysticism in his feeling for nature. It is just
the ordinary love of birds, flowers, running brooks, and
spring sunshine. He must have been poor, for he inherited nothing and was compelled to shift for himself at an
early age. Yet the conditions were evidently more than
tolerable. A happy boyhood is inferable from a passage of
the noble elegy which he wrote late in life—it dates from
the autumn of the year 1227—on returning to the home
of his childhood and finding all things sadly changed:

Alas, what ails the young folk? What means their sober air?
Of yore their hearts were merry and never knew a care;
But now they groan in spirit—ah me, why do they so?
Turn where I may my footstep, no joy they seem to know.
　No dancing, laughing, singing: instead, a solemn mien;
I trow, a time so dismal no Christian e'er hath seen.
Look at the women's headgear! No more the posey crown,
And proud knights, oh the pity, go drest like any clown.

As a young man Walter went to Vienna, attached
himself to the court of Duke Friedrich and learned from
Reinmar to sing. The death of Duke Friedrich in 1198
left him an "orphan at the gate of Fortune." The new
Duke Leopold, a lavish giver, was promptly reminded
of his needs, but with little effect. An early song tells, in
mildly cynical humour, of his efforts to attract Fortune's
attention: she always happened to be looking the other
way, and he wished that she had eyes in the back of her
head. He became a wandering singer and journeyed far
and wide. His position was better than that of the ordinary gleeman because of his gentle birth, which gave him
access to courtly society everywhere. But he was like

the gleeman in his begging and his unabashed acceptance of material favours from any prince who was willing to provide for him. His travels took him from Hungary to the Seine, from Northern Italy to the Baltic. In particular it is known that he spent some time at the court of Landgrave Hermann, albeit the story of the singing-match at the Wartburg in 1208 is mythical. During the bitter political feuds which followed the death of Hein-rich VI in 1197, he was successively a partisan of Philip of Swabia, Otto IV, and Friedrich II, but always a stanch anti-papist. In the year 1217 the emperor gave him a small estate—near Würzburg, it would seem—and the hitherto homeless knight expressed his emotions in a jubilant poem beginning, " I have a fief! I have a fief! " At the end of the elegy cited above Walter declares that his heavy heart would be made light if he might go to the Holy Land as a warrior of God. Whether this wish was realised is uncertain. There is a song of his which purports to have been composed in Jerusalem, but its extreme tameness—it is hardly more than a pensive review of Christ's life—is suspicious. It is probably an attempt to imagine the emotions of an ardent crusader on reaching the holy city. Walter died about 1230 and was buried at Würzburg.

As a minnesinger Walter is characterised, before all things, by chivalrous delicacy of feeling. The knightly law of moderation is the law of his muse, which is never tame and never coarse. His verse gives the impression of a fine and jocund nature wearing the fetters of art like a graceful garment. He strikes all the notes of the courtly minnesong, as it had been developed by Reinmar, at the same time making it richer and more spiritual. But he is a poet of sentiment rather than of passion, the sensual vehemence of many of the troubadours being foreign to his nature. He is a lover of women and never tires of complimenting them, but his greatest joy is in simply looking at them. " When on a May morning," so runs one of his well-known songs, " the flowers are peeping out from the grass, as if they were laughing at the bright sun, and the little birds are singing their sweetest tunes, what joy can be compared with that? I will tell you. When a lovely maid of high degree, well robed and with bejewelled hair, goes a-walking with other lighthearted women, and in modest gayety glances about her now and then, sun-like outshining the stars—then we pay no heed to the flowers, and have eyes only for the beautiful woman." Another song has the thought that joy comes only from women; wherefore we should honour them all, but especially the best. It would be too much to say that Walter's verse is always chaste, but it is always modest and careful of the limits. If there is a carnal suggestion, it is only a roguish hint of forbidden paths whereon the innocent imagination may turn back when it will.

More than one of Walter's songs conveys the thought that the lover's best reward is the ennoblement of his own character. The love of a good woman, he insists, uplifts a man and guards him from ignoble conduct; wherefore, it is worth while even if she withhold her favour. Yet his love of womanhood is not so abstract and ethereal as to prevail over national prejudice. Of all the women he has seen in his travels those of Germany are the best.

In conformity with the fashion Walter at first chose an aristocratic lady to be the object of his devotions, but her service seems to have brought him little satisfaction. One of his songs pictures her as surrounded by elegant flatterers, while he waits afar and waits all too long for a token of her favour. His best minnesongs, so far as they have any personal tinge at all, were inspired by a maid of low degree, whom he praises for her goodness and for charms that owe nothing to wealth or station. Thus he prepared the way for later singers, like Neidhart von Reuental, who found the village maid more to their liking than the capricious and inaccessible court dame. But all coarseness displeased him. He bewails the decadence of courtly refinement even in his own time.

A different and more austere side of Walter's nature is disclosed in his " sayings." While in his songs he appears as a graceful artist and an amiable exponent of mediæval woman-worship, these tell of a profoundly serious nature watching the course of events with keen anxiety. One of them pictures him as sitting in a pensive attitude and pondering sadly over the incompatibility of honour, riches, and God's grace. This is evidently the posture that was thought to characterise him best, for thus he is represented in the great Heidelberg manuscript of the minnesingers. The man of ardent temperament who sees the world going on its way without regard to his private opinions is always prone to conclude that it is going wrong and getting worse. Walter suffered much from this very common illusion. In particular he was pained by what seemed to him the growing tendency to put riches before honour. In a number of poems he mourns over the degeneracy of the times, the decay of chivalrous virtues, the rudeness of the young, and so forth. He shared the widespread belief that the world would soon come to an end for its sins. His religious nature seems to have been completely satisfied with the ordinary symbols and cult of the mediæval church. One can see that the dogma of the virgin birth was especially dear to him. " Lord Christ," he says in a morning prayer, " make manifest in me the great power of thy goodness, and guard me well for the honour of thy mother." Nowhere in his writings is there any trace of a critical temper toward the mysteries of the faith or the traditional teaching of the church, albeit he confesses ruefully his hopeless inability to love his enemies. But he was a sharp critic of Pope and clergy. He accused Pope Innocent III of avarice, trickery, and falsehood. The excommunication of Otto IV, two years after he had been accepted and proclaimed by the pontiff as the god-given emperor of Germany, drew from Walter the bitter comment that on the one occasion or the other the priest must have lied. The effort of the same prelate to raise money in Germany for a crusade provoked a satirical outbreak in which the Pope is made to soliloquise gleefully: " Their German silver is flowing into my Italian coffers; ye priests, eat fowl and drink wine, and let the silly German starve."

Walter von der Vogelweide is the most interesting literary personage of his time, as he is the greatest of mediæval lyrists anywhere. But it is particularly difficult to do justice to him in an English book, because the appeal he makes to the reader is so largely dependent on his artistry, which is seldom reproducible in English without disastrous sacrifices.

For about one-half his years Walter was a contemporary of the amazing ULRICH VON LICHTENSTEIN, whose bulky *Service of Women*, completed in 1255, might be regarded as an early precursor of *Don Quixote*, if it showed any trace of a satiric purpose or a sense of humour. As it is, the book is something of a psychological puzzle. It is a seemingly matter-of-fact autobiography, containing a prosy record of incredible follies, but containing also a multitude of interspersed songs, some of which are gems of lyric art. The author was a Styrian knight, born about 1200. He relates that it was borne in upon him in early boyhood that he ought in his own interest to devote himself to the service of some highborn lady. He chose such a person to be the object of his adoration, became her page, and signalised his devotion by drinking the water in which she had washed her hands. This was when he was twelve years old. His father then took him away and had him put through a course of schooling. When he was old enough to be dubbed a knight, he renewed his service to the lady, broke many a lance in her honour, and began to send her his verses by the hand of a kinswoman. But the lady was cold; she declined to accept as her knight one who had been her servant, and besides she did not like Ulrich's hare-lip. So he submitted to an excruciating surgical operation and took pains to have this new proof of his devotion reported to her. She was still obdurate but admitted that his verses were good. Presently she observed that he was still in possession of a finger which he had

reported as lost in jousting for her, whereupon he
hacked it off and sent it to her. Later he dressed himself
as Dame Venus and, with twelve squires clad likewise in
woman's attire, travelled from place to place, challeng-
ing all comers to battle for the honour of his lady. And
so on in a crescendo of lunacy.

It has been clearly made out that the actual Ulrich
von Lichtenstein was not at all the moony cavalier that he
himself depicts. He was a reputable gentleman, of much
shrewdness and energy, who did good service in the practical sphere of knighthood. He had a wife and children.
The lady whom he besieged was a sensible and virtuous
woman. All this, as was said above, makes a puzzle; for
when due allowance has been made for an ingredient of
tasteless fiction, one must still wonder why such a man
should have proceeded to imagine such follies and to set
them down in cold blood, as if he had been a praiseworthy
hero. It is clear that the woman-cult was here coming
perilously near to insanity. In reading the story of this
cracked gentleman, one comes to a better appreciation of
that temperance—*diu Mâze*—which Walter was so fond
of extolling.

Many of the songs of Ulrich are very good in their
way, but their way was already becoming an old story,
and they are without the saving grace of humour, which
makes Walter perennially delightful. The beauty and
the duty of woman-worship constitute for him a very
solemn doctrine, which he enunciates in a great variety
of verse-forms without ever a smile. " I think God has
created nothing so good as a good woman," he says in
his introductory stanza, and a little farther on :

Women are pure, women are fair,
Women are lovely and debonair,
Women are good for the heart's distress,
Women they bring all worthiness,
Women the man to honour call:
Oh, well for him that deserves it all!

This is the whole message of Ulrich, who stood manfully by " high love," declaring it better, even if never satisfied, than the " low love " which was the death of joy.

Of a different mind were his contemporaries TANN-HÄUSER and NEIDHART VON REUENTAL, who seem to have preferred an easy conquest in the lower social stratum to an infinite longing in the upper. Not much is known of the actual minnesinger Tannhäuser, nor is it possible to identify the particular hook by which the far-famed legend of the Venusberg attached itself to his name. The ballad which tells of his long sojourn at the subterraneous court of the Love-goddess, of his repentance and remorseful pilgrimage to Rome to procure absolution at the hands of Pope Urban IV, of his failure to obtain it, of his return to perdition, and of the damnation of the Pope—is of the fifteenth century. The few songs that have come down under the name of Tannhäuser are of no great interest. In one of them he makes merry, in a rather solemn way, over the exorbitant demands of his lady : she will hear him if he turn back the Rhine at Koblenz, or bring her sand from the sea where the sun sets, and so forth. The songs of Neidhart are frankly sensual, without being exactly gross, and seem to have been influenced by the French *pastourelle*. His specialty is to depict the emotions of the village maid as she thinks of the lusty May-dance, and of his own irresistible self as partner. He makes her argue the case with her vigilant mother, sometimes pleadingly, sometimes defiantly—with a beating as consequence. Again it is the mother herself who takes the infection, begins to hop about like a kid, calls for her good clothes, and rushes away to the arms of the bewitching Reuental.

Thus the very extravagance of the chivalrous woman-cult led at last, by an inevitable reaction, to parody and crass realism. By the end of the thirteenth century the great era of the courtly minnesong was already becoming a romantic memory to which idealists of sentiment harked back as to a golden age. It was then that collections began to be made. The most important of these is that contained in a bulky and splendidly illuminated manuscript dating from the first half of the fourteenth century, and now preserved at Heidelberg. No less than 140 minnesingers are there represented.

CHAPTER VII

THE AGE OF EXPIRING CHIVALRY

THE two centuries that immediately preceded the invention of printing were for Germany a period of literary decadence. During that long stretch of time nothing of any great literary importance was written in the German language. There was indeed no sudden dearth of production: the minnesong and the *Spruch*, the ballad epic and the romance of knighthood continued to be produced or worked over on the old lines, but these forms had seen their best days. There is also quite a body of satirical, humorous, and didactic verse, some of which is interesting for the light it sheds on the temper of the times and on the momentous changes that were taking place in the social order; but it lacks artistic distinction, and is for the most part clumsy in method and parochial in its point of view. The lyric poetry of the period is at its best neither in the belated minnesong, which tended more and more to mere ingenuity of rhyme and metre, nor in the mechanical mastersong which would fain have succeeded to its honours, but in the folksongs which sprang up abundantly in the fifteenth century. In Germany, as in other parts of Western Europe, a species of drama flourished, but it was a great open-air show rather than a literary phenomenon. Prose is represented by local chronicles, sermons, and the writings of the four-teenth century mystics, who, however, belong to the annals of religion rather than of literature.

In its relation to the general history of European civilisation the age of expiring chivalry is profoundly interesting. During this period the monocracy of the Roman Church was undermined, and the way gradually prepared for the great Lutheran revolt. Commerce and trade developed wonderfully, and walled cities arose that were able to defend themselves against marauding knight or oppressive prince, as the case might be. The citizen class came to the fore everywhere, took the fine arts into its hands and gradually prevailed in strength and im-portance over its competitors. The artistic sense of the burghers found expression in the building of fine cathe-drals, guild-halls, town-halls, and, as wealth increased, of private dwellings. There arose that patrician or intel-lectual *bourgeoisie* which was to be the hope of literature and to furnish the literary public in ages to come. The invention of fire-arms gradually reduced the heavy-armed knight to an impotent anachronism.—All this is reflected to some extent in the writings of the time, but it is reflected in a fragmentary and sporadic way. No writer appeared who had the genius, the insight, and the breadth of view which would have been needed for a classic expression of what was going on. Indeed, so het-erogeneous are the literary phenomena of the time that it is difficult to find in them anything like a common char-acter and tendency. Perhaps the best formula would be to say that literature, which had first been clerical and then courtly, now became more and more plebeian. It is true that the ideals of chivalry continued, even down to Luther's time, to find occasional champions who pleaded for them and tried to turn them to account in a literary way. So, too, there were here and there art-loving princes and godly priests. But in general, from the middle of the thirteenth century on, the drift was against courtly refinement and its artistic expression, and against all supermundane idealisms. As the knights took more and more to roistering and plundering, and the clergy to the mammon of unrighteousness, the voice of reproof and instruction was raised here and there by men of a didactic bent. A taste developed for coarse humour, satire, and the realistic portraiture of life on its seamy side. Even in the time of Walter and the great romancers there had been moralists, preachers, and ethical legislators. Such, to begin with one of the earliest, was THOMASIN VON ZERCLAERE.

Thomasin was an Italian cleric who served the Patriarch of Aquileja and learned German in the neighbouring Alpine regions. He knew French, was something of a man of the world and otherwise well qualified to write a treatise on conduct. He wrote first in French (or Italian, it is not quite certain which), and then treated the same matters in a German book which he called *Der welsche Gast*, that is, the *French Guest*, because he hoped that his work would be hospitably received by the Germans notwithstanding its admitted linguistic shortcomings. And it was; there is evidence that the *Guest* was much read for some two centuries. The book was written rapidly in the year 1215 and is a long-winded affair in ten books, which cover pretty nearly the whole range of human conduct from a caution to ladies against sitting with crossed legs, up to the weighty matters of the moral law. The metre is the ordinary short couplet. The first book is devoted to the training of the young, general etiquette, table manners, the proprieties of horseback riding, and other such things. Others expound particular virtues—*Stæte*, or steadfastness, is regarded as the greatest of them, and *Mâze*, or moderation, as coming next—or expatiate on virtue and vice, wisdom and folly, riches and poverty, and so forth. The author had hardly a spark of poetry in him, but he had observed widely and had much good sense, which peeps out quaintly from among the traditionary pedantries and prepossessions of the moralist.

Thomasin is diffuse and wordy, but his contemporary FREIDANK understood the virtue of conciseness. His so-called *Bescheidenheit,* which means the insight or wisdom that comes of experience, is a miscellaneous collection of short sayings in rhyme. It enjoyed great popularity, and is often quoted by later writers. Not much is known of its author's life, except that he accompanied Friedrich II to Palestine in 1228 and witnessed the terrible mortality among the crusaders at Acre. "The graveyard," he observes, " is the most prosperous landlord at Acre, and gets all the guests. A hundred thousand might die there and be mourned less than one donkey elsewhere." The pseudonym Freidank means free-thinker, and indeed it is a keen and independent mind that is revealed in the sayings, though not that of a free-thinker in the modern sense.

> *Fetters to hold the mind*
> *No man will ever find,*

he says, and again:

> *Be the Kaiser e'er so great,*
> *By thought I climb to his estate.*

The clergy are scourged for their gross appetites:

> *The highest teach us to aspire,*
> *The many lead us through the mire.*

A cycle of the sayings is devoted to the Papacy. Rome is characterised as a " wretched hole " into which all the streams of treasure flow and stick fast. The papal ban has become a joke; the Pope's honour is sick; the shepherd of the sheep thinks only of shearing. Such are some of the early premonitions of the storm that was to burst in Wittenberg three centuries later.

One of the most interesting products of the thirteenth century is the story of *Farmer Helmbrecht,* a metrical novelette of the realistic order. It was written about 1250 by a man calling himself WERNHER THE GARDNER, and professing to relate what his own eyes had seen. His hero is a young peasant who tires of hard work on his father's farm—the *locus* is a few miles north of Salzburg —and becomes enamoured of the life of the knights. So he dresses himself up like a gentleman—several pages are devoted to his egregious outfit—and rides away, against his father's pleadings, to " court," that is, to the castle of a neighbouring robber-knight, whose band he joins.

For a number of years he robs, burns, and outrages the peasantry in the height of the fashion; then he falls into the hands of a justice, who puts out his eyes and turns him loose, to be hung finally by a bevy of his victims. In the course of his career the young reprobate visits the home of his parents, astonishes the household by speaking in unintelligible foreign languages, and sets forth, in conversation with his old-fashioned father, the ways of the new knighthood. " Their minnesong runs," so he avers, " in this wise: ' Come, sweet maid, fill the wine-cup.' There are some fools who, instead of drinking, torment themselves about women. But the liar is now the hero, deception is what pleases at court, and back-biting is the true courtesy. The best man is he who can curse in the vilest words."

The style of *Farmer Helmbrecht* is ruggedly realistic. The author has an ugly story to tell, knows it and does not mince matters. He meant, so he says at the end, to give a warning to self-willed and disobedient sons; but in general he is content to let his story speak for itself without the aid of preaching. This inspires confidence in his trustworthiness. His literary cunning is not great, but his pictures of mediæval life, on the side of its depravity, cruelty, and wanton outrage, constitute a human document of considerable interest.

Another sort of comment on the depravity of the age is seen in the humorous poem *Parson Ameis*, written about the middle of the thirteenth century. Its author was that STRICKER who was mentioned, at the close of Chapter V, among the minor romancers of knighthood. But while his romances *Karl* and *Daniel of the Blooming*

Vale belong to a fashion already on the wane, his *Parson Ameis* strikes a new note. There was a time, so the introduction runs, when truth and honour and virtue prevailed; it was Parson Ameis who first practised lying and deception, and thus started the world on its downward course. The poem is an account of the tricks perpetrated by this prototype of wandering swindlers. Ameis is represented as an English priest who excites the animosity of his bishop by a too lavish hospitality. The bishop threatens to take away his living unless he can tell how far it is from earth to heaven, how much water there is in the sea, and so forth. These questions having been cunningly answered, the bishop requires him to give a crucial proof of his powers by teaching an ass to read. This problem is also solved in a way to put the joke on the bishop. Thus the priest becomes locally famous, the demands on his benevolence increase, and he sees that he must put money in his purse. So he enters on a wandering life and roams about Europe many years, hoaxing people in all sorts of ways, and acquiring great wealth. At last he repents, retires with his spoil to a monastery, leads an exemplary life, and in time is made abbot.

Parson Ameis belongs to the light literature of amusement. It is not directly satirical, there is no bitterness in it; but the general scheme of the poem, with its pervasive levity of mind in presence of ecclesiastical solemnities, is significant of an important trend in public opinion. A fair sample of its humour is the story of the offerings. Ameis appears in a town and announces that he has a very holy relic, for which God has commissioned him to

9

build a church. He desires offerings, but they must be
pure; in particular he is under divine injunction to receive nothing from unchaste women. Some of the women
are alarmed at first, but as they see that no one's gift is
really refused, the erring ones dare not hold back. Every
one gives liberally. The comment is: Thus Ameis got
much treasure and became a great favourite with the
ladies.

A similar disposition to find matter of mirth in the
abuses of the church and the vices of the clergy is discernible here and there in the Low German *Reynard the
Fox*, though the poem did not originally spring from a
satiric impulse. The genesis of this late-mediæval favourite is a rather complicated subject. There is a literary tradition, having an ancient Esopian fable for its nucleus, which can be traced back in mediæval Latin for
some centuries prior to the first appearance of the Reynard stories in any modern language. The main points
are the lion holding court in human fashion as king of
beasts, and the pranks played by the cunning fox on the
other animals, more especially on the dull-witted wolf.
The material furnished by this tradition was augmented
by new inventions and by folk-tales such as spring up
everywhere, and the whole was finally elaborated—first
by a Frenchman—into a connected story. But long
before the bulky *Roman de Rénard* came into being, separate incidents under the name of *branches* were current,
and certain of these formed the basis of the earliest German poem of the Reynard cycle. It was the work of an
Alsatian, Heinrich der Glichezare, who wrote about 1180.
His production was called *Isengrin's Trouble*, Isengrin

being the name of the wolf. Only a fragment of it has been preserved, but it was worked over half a century later by an unknown author whose work has come down in High German under the name of *Reinhart Fuchs*.

The humour of this High German *Reinhart*, which is comparatively free from pungent satire, is well enough illustrated by the incident of the fish-catching. Isengrin appears one day before the cell of Reinhart, who has turned monk, and having had his appetite whetted with some fragments of Reinhart's fish dinner, wishes to be initiated into the brotherhood that he may become its cook. Reinhart approves, saying: " Just thrust in your nose." Isengrin does so, whereupon Reinhart douses him with hot water. " But this hurts," says Isengrin. " Do you expect to win heaven without pains?" Reinhart queries. Isengrin is satisfied, but wants more fish; so Reinhart takes him to a frozen pond, ties a bucket to his tail and bids him sink it through a hole in the ice. " Just wait till I drive them this way," says Reinhart. Isengrin waits until he is frozen fast, whereupon Reinhart runs away. A hunter comes along and rushes on the wolf with his sword, but slips on the ice and succeeds only in cutting off the prisoner's tail and thus releasing him.

Much more important is the Low German *Reinke de Vos*, which passed through several stages of evolution before it got into print at the end of the fifteenth century. This version, divided into books and chapters and published at Lübeck in 1498 with many illustrative woodcuts, is directly or indirectly the parent of all the later ones, including that of Goethe. It is easy to understand Goethe's fondness for it, not so easy to understand his turning it into hexameters. The easy-going doggerel of the original short couplets seems to chime perfectly with the peculiar quality of Low German humour, with its close study of details, and its love of incongruity. Everything is localised, so that the whole is like an indigenous product of the German lowlands. For the most part the author recounts the deviltries of the rascally but ever plausible Reinke with an eye single to the fun of the thing, but occasionally the fun has a sting to it. Thus at the end of the second book Reinke confides to his nephew, Martin the Ape, that he would gladly go to court and defend himself against the charges of his enemies, but cannot, as he is under the Pope's ban. Martin replies at length in the tone of an influential politician. He himself is on the way to Rome and will have the ban raised. He knows all the ins and outs of the papal court. Dr. Getquick and Lord Turncoat are his powerful friends. It is only necessary to have a plenty of money at hand. And so on.

One should not infer too much, however, from such incidental gibes at the clergy and the papacy. They are common enough from the beginning of the thirteenth century on; and while they undoubtedly show which way the wind was blowing, they indicate no very deep-seated unfriendliness to the mother church : the *sæva indignatio* was yet to come. It lay in the temper of the time to take the church very seriously as the teacher and custodian of divine truth, and at the same time to criticise her human organs with the utmost frankness, and on occasion to extract uproarious fun from her most solemn traditions and observances. This is evidenced on a large scale by the evolution of the Easter plays presently to be considered.   Even the mystics of the fourteenth century, while an agency of some importance in the gradual undermining of papal authority, were in no sense enemies of the church.   There was no objection to the claim of divine authority on the part of pope or priest, so long as he could be regarded as a good pope or priest.

As was remarked above, the mystics and preachers who, along with the local chroniclers, are the earliest writers of Middle German prose, belong to the history of religion rather than of literature.   It was they who kept spiritual religion alive, in an age which was in the main unfavourable to it, by insisting on the possibility of an immediate relation of the soul to God.   But this meant, in the long run, that priest and sacrament were after all but accessories of religion; the heart of the matter being the ecstatic communion—the feeling, rather than the form or symbol.   The Franciscan and Dominican friars had brought preaching into vogue and made it a new power in the religious life.   An intense other-worldliness, combined with an extraordinary gift for apt and homely illustration, characterises the sermons of the great Franciscan preacher BERTHOLD VON REGENSBURG, who spoke to enormous audiences in all parts of South Germany and brought multitudes of sinners to repentance. He died in 1272.   Seventy-one of his discourses, taken down probably by an auditor, have been preserved and exhibit mediæval prose at its best.   The writings of the later mystics, MASTER ECKHART and HEINRICH SEUSE (or SUSO), are for the most part unpalatable on account of their obscurity and clumsy diction, the sermons of

JOHANNES TAULER somewhat less so; but in all of them
there are sporadic passages in which the mystic attitude
of the soul is expressed in vivid sensuous language that
anticipates the pantheistic poetry of a later time. The
earliest attempt at imaginative prose is the so-called *Bo-
hemian Farmer*, dating from 1399. It is a passionate dialogue between Death and a widower who bewails the loss
of his wife. The form is not that of conversation, but
that of alternating attack and defence in speeches of considerable length. The whole ends with a devout prayer
for the repose of the dead wife's soul.

It will be next in order to consider the late-mediæval
drama—those singular performances which by the end
of the fifteenth century had developed into great popular
spectacles lasting several days and employing an army
of actors. The nucleus of the EASTER PLAY was a brief
and solemn church function that followed a Latin ritual.
Semi-choruses, singing in Latin, were made to person-
ate the mourning women who go to the Saviour's tomb
at daybreak, also the angels who tell them that Christ has
arisen. Here was a dramatic motive which was capable
of indefinite expansion. As the sole object of the function was to bring the events of the Resurrection vividly
before the minds of unlettered folk, it soon became customary to repeat in German verses, with more or less
of amplification, the substance of the Latin parts. Once
admitted, this German element rapidly prevailed over the
Latin, while at the same time the action was expanded
on realistic lines. Thus the women who were going to
anoint the body of the buried Lord had to be provided
with ointment. The natural way to get ointment is to

buy it. So a swindling quacksalver was introduced, along with a scapegrace boy assistant and a contumacious wife. In one at least of the extant texts the rough comedy of these people runs through some nine hundred lines, and must have occupied a long time in the acting. The descent into hell was similarly elaborated by the introduction of various devils and of Old Testament personages waiting to be set free. Comedy was also made of the efforts of Peter and John to reach the tomb in haste after hearing of their Lord's resurrection. The two disciples run a race: John makes good time, but Peter stumbles, falls headlong and gets up, cursing his luck and sputtering over his infirmities.

The Easter plays, as known from the texts that have survived, are anything but literary masterpieces. They were not written to be read by any one but those connected with the performances, and the object in view was to impress and amuse an open-air crowd on which literary refinements would have been wasted. As horseplay and clowneries abounded in the action, so the verse is generally crude, the language commonplace, the humour coarse and often indecent. On the other hand, there are serious passages, especially such as preserve the tenor of the original Latin chants, which appeal to the modern reader by their tender pathos and simple dignity of expression. So it was that the spectacle ranged from the heights of religious emotion to the level of everyday banality and the depths of pointless coarseness—and all without intentional disrespect to religion. Easter was the time of joy, and the people who, in their imaginations, lived on very good terms with biblical personages, had no reason to suppose that a free expression of the festive mood could possibly be displeasing to the heavenly powers. These powers were conceived much less austerely than they are by the modern world—else the Landgrave of Thuringia would not have been so appalled by the representation of Christ as relentless judge in the *Play of the Ten Virgins*.

There is a tradition that, after witnessing this play at Eisenach in the year 1322, Landgrave Friedrich fell into a moody despair, which lasted five days and ended in an apoplectic stroke from which he afterwards died. The play is an ascetic churchman's rendering of the New Testament parable. Bidden by an angel to prepare for the heavenly wedding feast, the wise virgins at once bestir themselves and get oil for their lamps; but the foolish ones think they have time enough and can count on the efficacy of a late repentance. So they play and dance and feast until the great day is at hand, and then they find that there is no oil to be had. One after another they plead for admission, and the Holy Virgin intercedes for them on her knees. But Lucifer claims them, and Christ, as righteous judge, remains inexorable. " What then is the Christian faith," exclaimed the terrified Landgrave, " if the intercession of the saints and even of the mother of God cannot avail to procure pardon for the sinner? "

Such austere views of human destiny found expression also in other simple dramatisations of scripture, but the trend of the time was against them. The people preferred divinities and saints whom they could conceive in the terms of ordinary human nature, and they demanded realism—the realism of their own outlook on life—in their dramatic performances. In the passion plays—unlike the resurrection plays—a serious tone prevailed; generally also in the Christmas plays, though in these room for comedy was sometimes found in the treatment of the character of Joseph. The shrovetide plays, on the other hand, went to the utmost limits of vulgarity and indecency. These were at first mere carnival frolics, having no literary character whatever, and no character of any kind worth preserving by means of ink and paper. But they gave rise to the earliest type of German comedy; a type that flourished abundantly in the fifteenth and sixteenth centuries, and was brought by Hans Sachs to a certain degree of artistic and literary perfection. This is reason enough for giving some attention to the earlier stages in the evolution of the SHROVETIDE PLAY.

The mediæval carnival was very much the same in Germany as in the other parts of Western Europe. On the eve of the long Lenten fast the people laid aside, from Sunday to Wednesday, the ordinary social restraints and went in for fun and folly. A favourite kind of diversion was the mummery. A bevy of masked merry-makers would present themselves in a public house, in the taproom of a guild-hall, or wherever it might be, and do a dramatic scene for the reward of food and drink. At first, probably, the mummers relied chiefly on make-up and mimicry; but soon the spoken word began to acquire importance, and when a hit had been made it was natural that the representation should be repeated in other places. This led to the necessity of memorizing the parts from a written text. A multitude of plays have been preserved —the most of them beneath contempt as literature—and

their number and variety, taken together with the great
spring festivals, testify to the popularity of dramatic
performances at a time when theatres and professional
actors were still far in the future. Some of them deal
in a serious tone with matters of church and state. Thus
there is a shrovetide play, written not long after the fall
of Constantinople, which introduces the Grand Turk in
the rôle of a reformer of abuses in Germany. A far
greater number present incidents and characters of every-
day life—the bad mother-in-law, the scolding wife, the
unfaithful husband, the farcical trial of a case, the quack
doctor, and so on. There are generally but three or four
characters, and the incident is such as might be acted
in half an hour. The humour is of the rough, plebeian
sort, and sometimes sinks to abysmal vulgarity.

At last the time came for raising the query: Is there
in truth more of folly at carnival time, when all men try
to be fools, than on other days of the year, when no such
conscious effort is made? Are not all men fools all the
time, each in his own way? What is folly and what is
wisdom? Such questionings grew naturally out of the
general relaxation of traditional standards that characterises the fifteenth century. The classical answer to
them was given in Brant's *Ship of Fools,* wherein the
entire motley spectacle of life is conceived as a voyage of
fools to Fool-land. It is Germany's first real contribution
to world-literature. The book was put into Latin by the
Humanists, and was translated three times into French,
and twice into English. SEBASTIAN BRANT (1457–1521),
a native of Strassburg, devoted himself to the study of
Latin writers in the spirit of the new humanism that

was now invading Germany, took his degree in law and began his literary career as a maker of Latin verses. He published his *Ship of Fools* at Basel in 1494 in his own Alsatian dialect. It consists of disconnected chapters—over a hundred in all—which describe the various types of fool that have taken ship for Narragonia. There is no story whatever; nothing is made of the voyage-idea, and the passengers do not arrive. Sometimes the ship-fiction drops out of sight altogether, and the author thinks of his work as a " mirror of fools," in which every reader can see himself reflected if he looks. The procession opens good-humouredly with Brant himself in the rôle of book-fool; only the foolishness is not that of " poring over miserable books," but that of collecting and treasuring learned tomes that one cannot understand. Then come the fool of avarice, the fool of fashion, the old fool, the fool who neglects the training of his children, the fool of profligacy, the fool of gluttony, the fool who tries to serve two masters, the babbling fool, the fool of too little care, the fool of too much care, the fool of procrastination, and many more.

Of humour, as we moderns understand it, Brant has hardly a trace, nor is there any poetry in his jolting verse. He had none in his soul. There was no tenderness in him for any of his fools, and he lavished no artistic sympathy on them. His tone is not exactly bitter, but severe, militant, objurgatory. It was his serious conviction that the world was in a bad way, and could be set right only by accepting the ideas and obeying the commands of the mediæval church. He was a reactionist, not a reformer of the forward-looking type. In Chapter 66 he

classes with the fools those who try to find out the size
and shape of the earth, and whether there be antipodes.
His pages are largely made up of saws and maxims
culled from the Bible and from classical and mediæval
writers.　There is little originality in his book, which
savours more of the library than of life.　What strikes
the modern reader most strangely is the fact that trivial
weaknesses and foibles of human nature are grouped together, under the head of folly, with grave transgressions
of the moral law and the extreme of reprobate conduct.
But this loose conception of folly, which brought every
one into the ship, no doubt contributed to the popularity
of the book as a universal mirror of fools.　It fell in with
the censorious, satiric temper of the age.　The old ideals
of religion and chivalry had lost their hold to a great extent, and no new ones of equal power had come to take
their place.　There was thus a lack of sound criteria for
judging human conduct.　One of Brant's chapters has
the alluring caption, " The Lesson of Wisdom."　One
turns to it hoping to find the true antidote for the ubiqui-
tous folly of mankind.　But it turns out a mere conventional encomium of wisdom, the exact nature of the
priceless possession not being explained.

One of the wood-cuts in the *Ship of Fools* represents
a pilgrim standing in front of a lawyer's desk and holding out a document.　About the pilgrim's neck is a rope,
and the end of the rope is held by a knight in the panoply
of the time.　A part of the comment is to the effect that
the knight fleeces the people openly, the lawyer secretly.
" It is a great shame," says the accompanying text, " that
our rulers do not clear the highways, so that pilgrims

and merchants may be safe. But they say that would be bad for the safe-conduct business." One sees that " knight," which had once connoted gentle birth and the perfection of manners, had come to mean " knight of the road." Those who bore the name had become a social pest. It signified little that, even as late as the fifteenth century, men of knightly rank and poetic bent had tried to revive the moribund style and methods of the courtly minnesinger. Such, for example, was the Tirolese OSWALD VON WOLKENSTEIN, who made a pilgrimage to Jerusalem at the behest of his lady, in an age when such love-lorn idealism was becoming unfashionable. Oswald spent some years fighting the Prussian heathen, visited Italy and Spain, and in general led a wandering and adventurous life, which is reflected to some extent in his poems. These have accordingly a greater variety and freshness than are usual in the later minnesingers, but the verse is mechanical, though often cunningly elaborate, and the thought turns about the familiar old pivots. And then there had been commoners like MICHAEL BEHEIM and PETER SUCHENWIRT, who left a trade to become soldiers of fortune, and then, as hangers-on of a princely court, devoted their literary talent to describing the military exploits in which they had taken part, praising the prowess of their patrons, and writing heraldic disquisitions or allegorical and didactic tales and shrovetide skits in the degenerate taste of the time. The voluminous Beheim was a mere rhyme-smith, without a spark of poetry in his soul, though some of his work is of historical interest. Suchenwirt, who died about 1400, had more of poetic talent. His allegorical *Discourse of Love,* wherein he overhears the outraged Minne telling over her grievances to her sisters Justice and Steadfastness, and gets from her a commission to right her wrongs, is still readable, even if the invention is rather puerile.

Such men as Beheim and Suchenwirt, plebeian soldiers of fortune who cultivated poetry and song in connection with the profession of arms, form a sort of connecting link between the courtly minnesong of the knight and the mechanical mastersong of the artisan. Even in the time of Walter von der Vogelweide the minnesingers had been addicted, some more and some less, to didactic, erudite, and moralising verse, which usually took the form of the *Spruch*. The mastersong is the continuation of this current. There came a time when a boy, on being apprenticed, say to a weaver or a shoemaker, would take lessons in singing and verse-making from an approved " master " of the art, whom professional honour required to teach gratuitously. Gradually the business passed into the hands of local singing-schools, which were organised on the pattern of the artisan guilds. The earliest of these societies of which we have knowledge, that of Augsburg, dates back to the year 1450. In the sixteenth century their name is legion, the Nürnberg school being the most important. Each society had its code of rules and its official critics. When the candidate could sing acceptably a certain number of approved " tunes," he was received as a " singer." When he could compose a text to a familiar tune he became a " poet." When he could make a new song, with both words and music original, he was a " master." The mastersingers took great pride in devising elaborate metrical schemes, to which they gave curiously fantastic names. The subject-matter of their songs was generally religious, scholastic, metaphysical, after the beginning of the Reformation, biblical. As poetic literature, the prosy and mechanical mastersong has no standing in the court of history. Nevertheless, the mastersingers stood for the historic connection of music and poetry; and the mere fact that ordinary German artisans should thus have devoted themselves, on a large scale and with great ardour, to the "noble and pleasant art of the mastersong," is of considerable sociological import in the general history of the period.

Meanwhile, the spirit of fresh and spontaneous song, untrammelled by literary tradition or conventional guild-rules, had never died out among the unlettered folk. The fifteenth century was emphatically a singing epoch. The fairly large number of FOLKSONGS that have chanced to be preserved are of course but a small fraction of those that were composed and sung. Hardly a common occasion of joy or sorrow, hardly an employment or vocation that did not find some characteristic expression in tuneful words. There were love songs, happy and sad; drinking songs and dancing songs; songs of the seasons, of games, and of work; songs of the care-free vagabond student, the dare-devil soldier, the reckless and brutal highwayman; ballads of strange adventure, of crime, vengeance, and remorse; historical ballads of battle and siege; legendary ballads, like those of Tannhäuser and the *Noble Moringer*, both relating to historical minnesingers who had become mythical; or like the *Younger Lay of Hildebrand*, in which the ancient tragic tale was given a humorous and happy ending. Quite frequently a song tells at the end that it is the work of a peasant lad, a scholar, a jovial student, a hunter, a soldier good, or a mendicant singer. But they were all impersonal in the sense of denoting collective or communal feelings, and many of them were actually the work of several persons, since any one was free to add, subtract, or modify a stanza, if he thought he could improve the song. The metrical structure is simple, the expression of feeling direct and hearty, and there is the·ancient gleeman's fondness for the stereotyped formula, the refrain, the repetition. The story, when there is one, is apt to be told in vivid dramatic pictures, which leave much to the imagination. The language is realistically careless, the artistry often very crude. Not every old German folksong is a pearl, but among them are pearls enough to justify the pride and enthusiasm with which they were rediscovered in the nineteenth century after having been long forgotten.

The "last of the knights" was Emperor MAXIMILIAN (1459–1519), who deserved the appellation for more reasons than one. By his abolition of neighbourhood warfare, and his employment of hired and drilled soldiers to do his fighting, he helped greatly to end the mediæval military system. At the same time he was very fond of the old chivalry, spent immense sums on tournaments, had much of the temper of a romantic adventurer, and took such interest in what are now called the mediæval classics that he caused a number of them to be copied in a large embellished manuscript—the so-called Ambrasian —which is now one of the literary treasures of Vienna. He sympathised with the humanistic movement, and occasionally bestowed a laurel crown on some promising maker of Latin verses. That such a prince should wish to provide for his own immortalisation by means of the written word was but natural. For the poetic herald of his deeds he chose his confidential counsellor, Melchior Pfinzing, who had the assistance of his majesty himself. By such collaboration the famous poem *Teuerdank* was concocted, an allegorically veiled account of the wooing of Mary of Burgundy by Maximilian. In his knightly quest of the Princess Ehrenreich (Mary) the hero Teuerdank (Maximilian) meets successively and overcomes three redoubtable enemies, namely, Unfallo (Accident), Furwittig (Insolence), and Neidelhart (Malignity). When he has triumphed over these and reached the coveted presence, Ehrenreich requires him, as a condition of accepting him for a husband, to undertake a campaign against the infidels. The wooden style of the book accords well with the insipidity of the invention, and the puerility of the incidents. It is a shining testimony to the degeneracy of literary taste in court circles at the beginning of the sixteenth century.

Teuerdank was printed in 1517—that memorable year in which mediæval sacerdotalism, as it had come to be, was held up to merciless ridicule in the *Epistolæ Obscurorum Virorum,* and in which Martin Luther nailed his ninety-five theses to the church door at Wittenberg.

10

CHAPTER VIII

THE LUTHERAN REVOLT IN ITS LITERARY ASPECT

To the literary historian Luther is less important for the books he wrote than for what he set going in the intellectual life of his countrymen. The pen was indeed the great instrument of his labour, and he was almost incredibly productive; yet he wrote little that is now readable by any one for purely literary edification. He was a mighty pamphleteer; but when his pamphlets had done their immediate work and the religious controversy that begot them had subsided, they ceased to interest the public at large, even the Protestant public. His translation of the Bible, which was destined to feed the young imaginations of Goethe and Schiller and Lessing, was the only classic that came from his hands. The great mass of his writings belongs to the history of German Protestantism and the history of theology, but not, in the narrower sense, to the history of German literature.

On the other hand, Luther's part in shaping the conditions out of which a new national literature was to evolve was extremely important. This epoch-making influence of his can be traced in many by-ways, but especially along four main lines. In the first place, although himself a good Latinist, he stood valiantly by the German language against both humanists and Catholic clergy. Secondly, he enormously stimulated the production and reading of printed books. Thirdly, he fixed the literary centre of gravity in the Midland country—in Saxon Leipzig. Finally, the Upper Saxon dialect in which he wrote, developed, after a long struggle which lasted into the eighteenth century, into the accepted literary language of all Germany. It is to be noted that all this has nothing to do with the merits of his religious controversy with the mother church. Whether the abuses which he sought to remedy were exaggerated by him, as Catholic writers have always contended; whether the evils complained of might have proved remediable by a patient and temperate effort within the church, as Erasmus and his friends believed; whether Luther's substitution of bibliolatry for ecclesiolatry really made matters fundamentally better for the religious progress of mankind—all these are questions on which the modern mind can hardly fail to have an opinion, but they need not concern the literary historian.

The great intellectual awakening that began with the revival of learning in Italy soon made itself felt in Germany, but its immediate effect on German letters was surprisingly small and not altogether favourable. The new ideas stimulated philological scholarship and educational reform, and they laid the foundation of a new science of antiquity which the church could no longer control or regulate. They also bore fruit in numerous translations. The earliest of the translators was NIKLAS VON WYL, a Würtemberg chancellor whose *Translazionen*, first printed, probably, in 1478, included the lu-

bricious tale of *Euryolus and Lucretia*, which had been
composed in Latin by Enea Silvio (Pope Pius II),
some novels of Boccaccio from the Latinised versions
of Petrarch and Aretino, some writings of Poggio, and
the *Golden Ass* of Apuleius, then ascribed to Lucian.
The work of Niklas von Wyl teems with Latinisms; indeed, he thought it a merit to conform his version as
closely as possible to the Latin mode of expression.
More independence, in the matter of idiom, was shown
by ALBRECHT VON EYB, a dean of the Bamberg cathedral
who translated two plays of Plautus and wrote a *Mirror of Morals*. From this time on translations from
the Latin, Greek, and Italian came copiously from the
new printing-presses and served to disseminate at least a
knowledge of the matters treated. To be sure it was a
spurious antiquity that was thus disclosed—on account
of the persistent mediæval habit of seeing the past in the
colours of the present.

Of humanistic influence on artistic production in the
vernacular there are, for a long time, but meagre traces.
The seed fell on unprepared ground. The entire fifteenth century brought forth nothing that savours in
any notable degree of the humanistic spirit. The study
of the ancient historians begot an interest in German history, but the numerous treatises were all written in Latin,
with the exception of Wimpfeling's *Germania*, which appeared in both Latin and German. In general, the patriotism of the humanists exhausted itself in proclaiming
the glories of their country's history, and demonstrating
that they at least were not the barbarians that all Germans were reputed to be. It was far as yet from in-

cluding any such sentiment as pride in the vernacular. The grandest of literary achievements for them was to make a good imitation of Cicero, Vergil, or Terence. They translated their German names into Latin, wrote in Latin, lectured in Latin, and regarded that language, to quote a phrase of Lowell's, as the " only infallible pickle." In the course of time they formed a sort of close corporation of scholars who wrote for one another, or for an international public, and looked down on their mother tongue as barbarous and unfit for elegant literary expression.

But this contempt of the vernacular on the part of the German humanists is not difficult to understand— much less so than the same phenomenon in England, France, and Italy. The German language was really in a deplorable condition. The great mediæval poets had been virtually forgotten, and the old feeling for the beauty of their art was lost. The tales they had told in delightful verse were now read, if read at all, in a crude and sprawling prose which had no other aim than to convey a knowledge of the story. There was no longer a poetic diction understood in all parts of Germany, as there had been in the thirteenth century. The garden brought to such perfection by Walter von der Vogelweide and his contemporaries had run to weeds. In the absence of any strong unifying influence, the local dialects had resumed their sway, and these had developed variously: there were now sharp and far-reaching differences between those of the Southeast and those of the Southwest, and both these were now farther than ever before from those of the extreme North. Each region clung tenaciously to its own speech-form, spelling was utterly chaotic, and every scribe a law unto himself. The sense for rhythm and melody, that is, the old feeling based on accent, cadence, and the regular recurrence of heavy and light syllables, had almost ceased to exist. Verse had become doggerel.

All this being so, it is not very surprising if a German humanist, say of the year 1500, upon reading any German production that would have been likely to fall into his hands and comparing it with his idolised Greeks and Romans, came to the conclusion that the vulgar tongue was never intended for a vehicle of literary expression, and was hardly worth bothering one's head about. So far as the " intellectuals " were concerned, the literary tradition had been ruptured in the fourteenth and fifteenth centuries; so that the Renascence came to a Germany that had forgotten its own past and had no accepted literary language in which to express the new life. This rupture is the most momentous fact in the history of German letters; for it divides the subject into two parts of which the second does not grow out of the first. England, Spain, and France emerged from mediævalism, each under a centralised monarchy, and each in possession of an accepted literary language, well established by the prestige of a venerated author or group of authors. In Italy, if the centralised monarchy was lacking, there was at least the triumphant language of Dante, Petrarch, and Boccaccio. It was very different in Germany, where political decentralisation went hand in hand with separatism in language, where no one city prevailed as an intellectual capital, and where the most gifted contemporary of Chaucer was, peradventure, Peter Suchenwirt.

MARTIN LUTHER (1483–1546) was a man whose temper had little affinity for the humanistic pursuits that flourished at the University of Erfurt, where he studied in his youth. Erfurt was just then the German centre of the new humanism, unless one choose to say that its centre was wherever Erasmus happened to be sojourning. But what are a few dead pagans to a man who is agonising over the safety of his immortal soul? Luther came into friendly relations with several eminent scholars and caught something of their spirit; but the only book that he greatly cared for was the Bible, the only learning biblical learning. There was that in his nature, indeed, which responded to the mystic Tauler's doctrine of a personal communion with God, independent of priest and book and cult. But this could not fully satisfy Luther, whose nature demanded an external authority and sanction. These he found in the Bible. Having passed through terrible anxieties in which he could get no comfort from scholastic philosophy or ecclesiastical practices, and having at last found peace in the reading of the Bible, he came to the conclusion that Scripture was the only infallible source of truth for all men; that it was the foundation of the church, and the only foundation; and that a scripture text was the highest possible sanction for any human arrangement whatsoever. With such thoughts in his head, the Augustinian monk, at first timid and hesitant, became a teacher and preacher at Wittenberg. As he taught he gained confidence, and his inward assurance grew into a militant conviction that he was right, and that God was on his side. In Rome, which he visited in 1511, he had no pleasure in the secular glories of the Italian Renascence: he saw only the depravity of a corrupt clergy that was engaged in exploiting Germany for revenue. The fighting mood was now upon him, and it needed only an occasion to bring on the inevitable conflict. The theses of 1517 were but the manifesto of an indignant theologian who was still within his rights as a son of the church and did not foresee how great a flame he was kindling. The burning of the papal bull meant open defiance of the hierarchy, and the *Address to the Nobility* (1520) sounded the bugle-blast of revolution.

From this time forth Luther was the centre of a terrific logomachy which absorbed the best intellectual energies of his countrymen for a century to come, and ultimately changed the course of history for the entire Germanic world. He fought with the indomitable courage of an old saga-hero, and his one weapon was the word of the Lord, as he found it in the Bible. Withal, however, he had some of the qualities of a far-sighted practical statesman. Had he been only a theologian, called by his own conviction to a championship of God against Antichrist, he might have written in Latin. And this indeed he did, whenever it was his chief concern to influence the learned mind. But from the first he took strong ground in favour of the supremacy of the temporal power in temporal matters, identifying his cause with the cause of the German people, oppressed and deceived by a corrupt foreign priesthood who used Latin in the service of the church. Thus from the outset he

intrenched himself behind that ethnic feeling, based on
language, which was destined more and more to sway the
politics of Europe, and in time to regenerate the political
life of the Germans.

When, therefore, Martin Luther set about making a
Bible for the people, he saw the importance of going
back to the Greek and Hebrew. The work of Erasmus
and Reuchlin had not gone for naught. There were
already some fourteen High German versions of the
Bible, but they were all based on the Vulgate; and who
could tell how far this official version of the church had
sophisticated the original word? On the scholarly side
of his undertaking, Luther had the priceless aid of
Melanchthon, and the two worked together with unweary-
ing diligence to make a version that should be at once
faithful and idiomatic. Pedantries were to be avoided.
" One must not, as these asses do," says Luther, " ask the
letters of the Latin language how to speak German, but
one must ask the mother in the house, the children in
the street, the common man in the market-place; one
must ask *them* about it, and watch their mouths to see
how *they* talk, and then translate accordingly. Then they
will understand you and note that you are talking to them
in German." The New Testament was published in 1522,
the complete Bible in 1534. The influence of Luther's
Bible on subsequent German literature has been similar in kind, and perhaps even greater in degree, to that
of the King James Bible in English literature. It has
furnished countless writers with imagery and phrases that
could be used with the assurance that they would find the
heart as well as the mind of readers. In the Psalms and

Job it has provided a noble standard of lofty poetic expression, while the parables of Jesus have stood as a perpetual object-lesson—too often, alas, unheeded—on the literary value of simplicity.

Luther's most important writings in the vernacular, aside from his Bible, are the various appeals, tractates, and contentious pamphlets whereby he provoked and organised the Protestant revolt. Besides these there are his letters, sermons, fables, and a small body of verse. The distinguishing marks of Luther's prose are hard hitting and plain speaking. He spoke from his heart in the language of the common man, wrote as he spoke and printed as he wrote; albeit with increasing years he gave more attention to the little matters of form. German prose was so new, it had been so little employed by men of great intellectual force, that it had not yet learned to run in conventional grooves. The many artifices of diction that develop little by little in a nation's literary language; that separate the spoken from the written idiom and come to be associated with ideas of beauty, dignity, and rhythm—all these were virtually non-existent for Luther. There was no great regulative tradition. He was a pioneer in the field of prose style, no less than in that of religious reform. To the reader of to-day his page is apt to seem chaotic, straggling, ill articulated. It is a rushing torrent of speech, which overflows its banks, bears along whatever comes in its way, dashes itself against obstacles, and surges back on itself in vehement eddies. Like an impetuous popular orator, he begins a sentence without thinking how it is to end, pours out what is on his mind with little care for a lucid syn-

tactic subordination of parts, illustrates, amplifies, quali-
fies, repeats, and brings up perhaps with an anacoluthon.
This seeming incoherence makes him difficult to read, but
the incoherence is only apparent and grows out of the
fact that he wrote as he spoke. As one of his editors
remarks, his sentences need to be uttered aloud rather
than read in silence. Studying him closely one finds that
the logic is there; only it is the logic of a passionate
orator rather than that of a cunning stylist. And amid
the jungle of intricate and careless syntax one can always
feel the heart-beat of the man whom the Catholic Father
Döllinger called " the mightiest *Volksmann*, the most
popular character, that Germany has ever possessed."

As for the dialect in which he wrote, Luther's own
oft-quoted words—they occur in his *Table Talk*—are as
follows : " I have no distinct and peculiar language of
my own, but use the common German language, so that
both Uplanders and Lowlanders may understand me. I
talk according to the Saxon chancelry, which all the
princes and kings in Germany follow." This is true only
in a somewhat restricted sense. The imperial chancelry,
having to deal with many lands in which different dialects
were spoken, had already made some progress toward
what might be called a standard official German ; and
this form of the language agreed in the most important
particulars with that used by the Saxon chancelry, which
Luther took for a model. But while this language of the
chancelries existed before Luther's time and formed the
foundation of a standard literary language, it had little
vogue outside the Austro-Bavarian and Upper Saxon
territories. Moreover, any official diction—something

always and everywhere tending toward stiff and wooden
verbosity—could not have gone far in furnishing a man
like Luther with the needed resources of expression.
What he really did was to use the language of the people
as he had learned it, not in his early childhood at Eisle-
ben, which was then in Low German territory, but in the
course of his long sojourn at Eisenach and Erfurt. By
so doing he was able to address the people of the Mid-
lands and the Southeast in a language which was readily
intelligible. As the momentum of the Reformation
increased, and the number of printed books multiplied
rapidly,[1] the partisans of Luther naturally followed him
in the matter of language. Clergymen from the North,
after studying at Wittenberg, went home to teach and
preach and write in the language of the master. The
Low German dialects sank into the status of a provincial
patois. Before the end of the sixteenth century the victory of Luther's German was virtually complete in all the
northern regions. In the South progress was much
slower : Catholic writers fought Luther's German, even
as they fought his religious doctrines.[2] Switzerland was

---

[1] In his interesting little book, *Von Luther bis Lessing*, page 10,
Friedrich Kluge gives statistics showing the number of books known
to have been printed in Germany just before and just after the outbreak of the Lutheran revolt. For the eight years 1510–1517 the
average annual output of the German printing presses had been
110 books. Then the figures mount rapidly, as follows: 1518, 150;
1519, 260; 1520, 570; 1521, 620; 1522, 680; 1523, 935; 1524, 990.

[2] A liberal Catholic contributor to a Jesuit magazine published
at Freiburg, Baden, toward the end of the 18th century says (I
quote again from Kluge, p. 141): "Wenigstens waren die Schriften
eines Gellerts, eines Rabeners und noch viel mehr eines Gessners
selbst Schullehrern verbotene Bücher. Ja sogar Gottscheds Sprach-
lehre—wie uns ein Ex-Jesuit versicherte—muste man von den

last to fall into line. It was not until the third quarter of
the seventeenth century that the Swiss towns and chancelries began to surrender their local dialect in favour
of the standard Upper Saxon.

Patriotic feeling, which in Luther's nature was after
all subordinate to a holy zeal for evangelical truth as he
saw it, was the dominant incentive of ULRICH VON HUT-
TEN (1488-1523). He was a Franconian of knightly
rank. Schooled in a monastery, like Erasmus, he early
came under the spell of the humanistic spirit, and his revolt against the intellectual pretensions of the church was
vehement and uncompromising. Before the agitation at
Wittenberg began he had attacked the papal methods in
mordant Latin epigrams, denounced the traffic in indul-
gences, published a forbidden book with approving comment, and contributed largely to the second collection of
Epistolæ Obscurorum Virorum, which came out in 1517.
For Luther's theological hair-splitting and proofs from
scripture he cared very little; but when the schism began
to take on the political character of a fight for German
independence, he went over heart and soul to the Reformation. With true insight into the situation, he now
laid aside his humanistic Latin and began, in 1520, to
sound the revolutionary note in stirring German verses,
which were really a call to arms:

Obern verborgen halten. Freilich haben die Katholiken aus diesen
Werken viel Gift gesogen. Wenn nichts wäre als das lutherische *e*,
das sie sich durch Lesung derselben allmählich angewöhnten—
immer schade genug! Es klang doch ehemals so genuinkatho-
lisch: die Seel, die Cron, die Sonn, die Blum u. s. w.—und nun
schreiben die unsrigen fast durchgängig: die Seele, die Krone, die
Sonne, die Blume—wie die leibhaften Ketzer auch schreiben."

Proud noblemen, on you I call,
Arise, ye goodly cities all !
Stand fast together for the right,
Let me not wage alone the fight!
Have pity on the fatherland !
Ye doughty Germans, stir your hand !
The time is come, God points the way,
To strike for freedom.   Now's the day.[1]

Such was Hutten's message—war to the knife with
the Roman hierarchy and reliance on the arm of flesh.
Other poems express a determination so stern that, had
his cause failed, men would have called it fanaticism. " I
will not desert the truth," he said, " not for armed
resistance, nor ban, nor banishment, nor for the tears of
my mother—God comfort her ! " He quickly became
a leader of the southern reformers, whom he stirred by
his rugged and vehement verse, and by the vigorous prose
into which he now began to translate some of his earlier
Latin writings. Had he lived out the ordinary span of
life he might have become a literary figure of the first
importance ; for he united in himself, as did no other
German of his day, the best humanistic enlightenment,
the fine traditions of the knightly class, an ardent love
of country, and a good command of the resources of expression. But he was fated to die in his prime. The
defeat and death of Franz von Sickingen drove Hutten
into exile. By the help of Zwingli he found an asylum
on the Island of Ufnau in the Lake of Zürich, and there

[1] From the poem *Clag und Vormanung gegen dem übermässigen,
unchristlichen Gewalt des Bapsts zu Rom, und der ungeistlichen
Geistliehen,* dating from the year 1520.

he died in 1523. His brave, sad song, *Ich hab's gewagt mit Sinnen*, is perhaps the best lyric poem begotten directly of the Reformation.

As for the Catholic side of the great controversy, it was perfectly natural, and yet a strategic error of the greatest moment, that its ablest champions wrote in Latin. One looks in vain among them for any writer who can compare with Luther and Hutten in dignity of leadership and virile literary power. The most noted of the men who had recourse to the vernacular, in a vain effort to beat back the resistless tide of the new era, was THOMAS MURNER (1475–1536), the Franciscan friar who translated the Latin disquisition of Henry VIII on the seven sacraments, visited the English court in the mistaken belief that he was wanted there as an ally of the king against Luther, and was courteously sent home with a gift of a hundred pounds sterling. Murner was an Alsatian by birth, and his German writings are in the Alsatian dialect. He joined the Franciscan order very early in life, later became a priest, a doctor of law and theology, and a wanderer, according to the scholastic fashion of the time, from one centre of learning to another. He lived mostly in Strassburg, but we hear of sojourns in Freiburg, Bern, Lucerne, Vienna, Rostock, Prague, Cracow, Cologne, Frankfort, Paris, Bologna, Venice, and London. He was a restless, energetic, contumacious man, with a biting wit and a turn for satire; but there was too much of the buffoon in him for the most effective literary service. Even when he was most in earnest, which was nearly always, his lack of dignity and high seriousness came to the fore and set on what he wrote a certain stamp of vulgarity. On the other hand, there is nothing in his writings to justify the savage attacks of his enemies. As a youth he became involved in a bitter feud with Wimpfeling, the leader of the Strassburg humanists, over the Alsatian question; Wimpfeling claiming the province on historic and linguistic grounds for Germany, Murner taking the side of France. A little later he was involved in the wordy war between the Franciscans and the Dominicans over the dogma of the immaculate conception, which he warmly defended. In the frenzy of battle his adversaries called him *jurisconstultus, asinus plumbeus, cucullatus diabolus.* One of them provided him with an epitaph beginning *Requiescat in pice,* and many accused him of lechery and all intemperance. They glossed his name as Murr-narr, the snarling fool. The student of Murner will do well to remember that he belongs to the ill-fated class of men whose reputation was made for the after-world mainly by his enemies.

As a preacher Murner gained notoriety by his wit and his turn for satiric invective. Having a very censorious temper he naturally found in the *Ship of Fools* a book after his own heart. Following in the track of an earlier Alsatian preacher, Geiler von Kaisersberg, who had turned Brant's satire to account in the pulpit, Murner also delivered homilies on fools and then worked the matter into verse and published, in 1512, the *Guild of Rogues* and the *Muster of Fools* (*Narrenbeschwörung*). Seven years later came the *Geuchmat*, or *Meadow of Fools*. In these satires Murner is a continuator of Brant, from whom he borrowed freely, but his verse is more fluent and dramatic. He takes a shot at vice, folly, and error of every sort, and is particularly scathing in his pictures of female and clerical sensuality. In the *Guild of Rogues* (*Schelmenzunft*) he represents himself as the chosen scribe of the guild, whose duty it is to describe the membership faithfully. In the *Exorcism of Fools* he is a conjuror who has learned the art of driving out the multifarious fools that lurk in the bodies of men. In the *Meadow of Fools* he apologises for his jocosity, on the general ground that jest is good in the intervals of serious striving. Dame Chastity appears and complains that there is no longer a place for her on earth: she has returned to Mary in heaven, and Dame Venus has the world to herself. Then follows a muster of the fools who have been beguiled by woman's frivolity and sensuality.

In all these early satires the underlying spirit is a demand for reform within the church itself. Murner is no less vehement than is Luther in denouncing ecclesiastical evils and abuses and the vices of the clergy. But at heart he was a conservative. Necessary as reform might be, he could not brook the thought of a reform that attacked the divine authority of the church, or proposed to sever Germany from all allegiance to the Roman See. Very soon, accordingly, he turned against Luther, calling him "a savage bloodhound, a senseless, foolish, blasphemous, renegade, rascally monk," and other such names, which now sound a little scurrilous, but are no worse than those which Luther applied to other adversaries, though he took very little notice of Murner. In 1522 came Murner's most celebrated satire *Of the Great Lutheran Fool*, with the motto *Sicut fecerunt mihi, sic*

11

feci eis. In this, while playing his old rôle of fool and fool-exorciser, he lashed his enemies as with a whip of scorpions. In the wood-cuts he appears as a monk with the head of a cat (Murr-narr, Kater Murr). The " great Lutheran fool " is not Luther himself, but a swollen personification of all those who had been misled by Luther's teachings. Out of this giant Murner conjures forth a number of little fools, who unite under the captaincy of Luther for an assault, first on a secular fortress, where the only booty they capture is a hog, then on the ancient stronghold where Murner is defending the faith. A sort of capitulation is made on the condition that Murner receive Luther's daughter in marriage. He woos her properly in the good old way, but on the wedding night she confesses to a loathsome disease. Murner drives her away with insults and blows. Presently Luther dies without taking the sacraments, and Murner casts his body on a refuse-heap and makes cat-music over it. Meanwhile the " great Lutheran fool " has been so weakened by the extraction from his body of the many little fools that he too pines away and dies. There is a great contention over his property, and Murner secures the fool's-cap for himself.

By such means did a learned and loyal Catholic doctor, four centuries ago, imagine that he could serve the cause of the mother church in the evil days upon which she had fallen.

CHAPTER IX

DRAMA, FICTION, AND SATIRE IN THE SIXTEENTH CENTURY

DURING the entire sixteenth century the German mind was very much preoccupied with religion, especially with the questions growing out of the Lutheran revolt. A new morality based directly on the Bible was fighting for acceptance, and the didactic note is everywhere dominant. Literary production flourished, and the printing-press became a more and more important factor in the national life. At the same time, no masterpieces were achieved, and no independent profession of letters came into being, though we find an approach to it in the case of Fischart. Notwithstanding the example of Erasmus, the time had not yet come for the roving eye and the liberal mind. The business of writing was always ancillary to that of preaching or that of teaching. Latin was the preferred language not only of scholarship but of all would-be elegant literary effort. A favourite diversion of the erudite was the writing of Latin plays, on the general model of Terence. These plays, called " school comedies " because they were extensively acted by school-boys for practice in Latin, exercised some influence on dramatic production in the vernacular. The ablest of the

Latinists, Nicodemus Frischlin, wrote some relatively
unimportant things in German, but such condescension to
the plebs was viewed with disfavour by his learned confreres, the most of whom went on their way with
increasing contempt for their mother tongue. Thus the
bourgeoisie was left either to produce its own literary
pabulum, or else to feed on that which was furnished by
clergymen and schoolmasters. The greatest writer of the
century, Luther excepted, was a Nürnberg shoemaker.

Poetry flourished in the form of the Protestant church
hymn and the folksong. Luther himself delighted in
music, and understood full well the importance of enlisting the ancient art in the Protestant cause. His own
noble hymn, *Ein feste Burg*, based on the forty-sixth
psalm, was a tower of strength to the Reformation. And
he wrote or adapted other sacred songs which found the
hearts of his followers and gave a powerful impulse to
German psalmody. But Luther was not born for a great
singer. In *Frau Musica*, the best of his independent
poems, there is something, it is true, of the pure lyric
quality, but still more of the militant logic which is bent
on proving its case from the Bible. Nor did the century produce any other eminent lyrist. On the other hand,
the people sang as they had never sung before. A large
part of the great modern collections originated in that
wonderfully tuneful century. All the older varieties,
some of which were enumerated above (page 133), continued to be produced in great numbers, partly by the
process of variation and working over, partly by new
invention after old models. Every phase of life, every
employment and diversion, every emotional experience,

found expression in song for its joy or its sorrow, its pathos or its humour.[1]

A species of drama developed, notably in Switzerland, as a phase of the general revolt against the papacy. Among the earliest productions in this vein were two plays which were acted in the streets of Bern in 1522, printed with additions two years later, and eagerly read by the Swiss people. Their principal author was NIK-LAUS MANUEL (1484–1536), a man of repute in Swiss history both as a writer and as a painter. The longer of the two plays, called the *Pope and his Priesthood*, represented the Pope in his temporal glory, attended by a rout of cardinals, priests, and soldiers, while Peter and Paul walked humbly behind, wondering who the great man might be. The text is a long series of rhymed speeches, in which the papists are made to divulge their own infamy. One learns that their great concern is to get money, and that now their revenues are endangered by the spread of the new fashion of Bible-reading. Every peasant can quote Scripture, and all are refusing to be duped any longer by non-scriptural exactions. " But what do I care," says Deacon Skinboor, " for what Christ may have said? Were I to rest satisfied with that, I should never have a fat roast." A lewd woman who cohabits with a priest tells of the grievous taxes she must pay the bishop as hush-money. A knight comes from Rhodes and prays

---

[1] See in particular Erk und Böhme's *Deutscher Liederhort*, 3 vols. quarto, Leipzig 1893-94, which contains a multitude of songs in variant versions, together with the original music wherever it has proved recoverable. A good smaller collection is Tittmann's *Liederbuch aus dem 16. Jahrhundert*, Leipzig, 1881.

for aid against the terrible Turk. But the Pope refuses: he needs all his soldiers to fight Christians and put money in his purse. The shorter play represented the Pope riding in state on one side of the street, while on the other was Christ, mounted on an ass and followed by a troop of the halt and blind. The text is a dialogue between two countrymen who comment in strong disgust on the great difference between Christ and his vicegerent.

While the sensation produced by these bold plays was still fresh in the far Southwest, another dramatic attack on the mother church was made in the far Northeast. The play was the *Prodigal Son,* by BURKARD WALDIS, a Hessian who drifted to Riga in his youth, went over to Lutheranism, suffered torture and imprisonment, and then, after studying at Wittenberg, ended his days as a Protestant pastor in his native province. His play of the Prodigal was written in Low German and acted at Riga in 1527. It is a vigorous production in its kind. While it conforms to the type of the shrovetide play in being without dramatic entanglement, it shows some influence of the Latin school comedy. The prologue alludes to Terence, the text is divided into two *actus,* and the chorus is represented by psalms designed to be sung by five voices. The conduct of the Prodigal, his father, and his elder brother is motivated as in the parable, but the characters are German to the core, and there is much added realism of detail. The thieves and harlots are drawn to the life and made to sing a dissolute folksong, in which the Prodigal joins. The whole production enforces with much iteration the Lutheran doctrine that salvation comes by faith and not by works. Even the

bawdy landlord, in whose house the Prodigal wastes his
substance, and who complains at first that his business
is being ruined by Dr. Luther's advocacy of chaste wedlock, is made to turn from the error of his ways and
find grace.

Twenty-five other *Prodigal Sons* followed that of
Waldis in the course of time, and other biblical dramas
multiplied until their name was legion. In Switzerland
every town seems to have had its playwright or adapter,
and the new scriptural drama became a highly popular
mode of diversion. The plays were sometimes given with
great splendour, and on occasion author and actors might
receive a guerdon from the public funds. While the Old
Testament furnished the most of the subjects, profane
history was sometimes drawn upon, as in Bullinger's
Lucretia and Brutus (1533), or local saga, as in the plays
of William Tell. A sombre *memento mori*, akin in spirit
to the English *Everyman*, is met with in the *Five Considerations* (the five, namely, that lead men to repentance), wherein a giddy youth sets at naught the words
of his pastor, goes out to spend his Easter holiday in
jollity, and is brought to penitence by a wound from the
dart of Death. The most meritorious playwright, on
the whole, was SIXT BIRCK (1500–54), a schoolmaster
who followed his calling several years in Zürich. He
wrote a number of plays, the best of which is *Susanna*.
In this ancient tale there were two elements that Protestant Germany particularly liked: its divine vindication
of a chaste wife, and its condign punishment of wicked
judges. Besides, it involved a trial at law—always a
favourite scheme with the early playwrights. Birck wrote

two plays on the subject, one in German, one in Latin; and after him came a procession of *Susannas*.

By far the most interesting of them is that of PAUL REBHUN (died in 1546), a clergyman who explained to a friend that he wished to provide " something agreeable, and at the same time useful "; something that would " strengthen faith, teach people to bear the cross in patience, and show how every wife should cherish her honour, how magistrates should conduct themselves in matters of law, and what is proper for gentlemen, ladies, children, girls, and serving-men." Rebhun's *Susanna* was first acted in 1535, and was published the following year. It is the earliest German play that shows a conscious striving for artistic effects of poetic form and dramatic construction. It is divided into five acts, and has a prologue, an epilogue, and a chorus. The author evidently felt, however, that it was his solemn duty to give the Bible story without adding anything of his own. After he has introduced the wanton elders and made them confide their lust to each other, as in the story, he sees that the exposition is not complete: they must be shown up as corruptible magistrates. So he makes a rich citizen appear before them with a scheme to rob a poor widow, and apologises for the invention thus: *Hæc scena cum sequenti extra argumentum admixta est, ad depinguendam judicum iniquitatem*. What is most noteworthy in the play, however, is the very careful attention given to the verse. There are regular iambic and trochaic cadences, and the length of the lines in different scenes is varied to avoid monotony. The rhyming is almost perfect. But for an occa-

sional harsh contraction, and the rather frequent adding
of a final *e* where it does not belong, Rebhun's lines would
read as smoothly as those of an eighteenth century poet.
The metrical reform for which Opitz was to get such
great credit a century hence was really introduced by
Rebhun, but unfortunately no one followed his example.
The so-called *Knittelvers*, which paid little heed to word-
accent, and may best be described in English as a jolting
tetrameter doggerel, was too firmly intrenched in popular
favour to be ousted by any reformer of this period.

In the dramatic productions thus far discussed the
didactic tendency is specifically religious, if not always
aggressively Protestant; in the numerous plays and poems
of HANS SACHS (1494–1576) it took a wider range,
albeit he, too, was an ardent Lutheran and drew much of
his wisdom from Luther's Bible. Sachs was born at
Nürnberg, and after some schooling in Latin was apprenticed to a shoemaker. At the age of nineteen he commenced taking lessons in singing and verse-making,
became a " master " in due time, and henceforth to the
end of his long life divided his energies between the art
poetic and the art sutorial. As a journeyman he travelled
extensively, wandering as far north as Aachen and
Lübeck, and becoming very familiar with the life of
the people in all its phases. From 1515 to his death he
lived at Nürnberg, an exemplary and highly honoured
citizen. He was a keen observer, and had an extraordinary knack of vigorous, homely word-painting. His
spirit was compounded of honest evangelical piety that
knew no misgiving, and a genial, roguish humour that
knew no bitterness. In his writings he stood valiantly

for the decencies of life and for temperance in all things. He was a philosopher in the original sense of the word. His blood had a decidedly moral flow, but he described things as he saw them, and was content to let the lesson emerge in a natural way from the facts. Good sense— a goddess not usually included in the sacred nine—was the muse of all his poetic efforts. Withal he had an insatiable appetite for reading and caught through translations much of the humanistic spirit. He was at home in Greek and Roman mythology, and his writings teem with allusions to ancient poets and philosophers. Mediæval romance, Italian novels, the folk-lore of his own people, all furnished him with material. Everything human interested him, and he wrote with unprecedented facility. His vocabulary is enormous.

It was the habit of Sachs to copy his writings in a large folio or quarto volume. On taking an inventory at the age of seventy-three, he found that he had filled thirty-three volumes, and had to his credit more than six thousand separate productions. His total of verses has been computed at half a million. He himself classified his manuscript volumes as *Gesangbücher* and *Spruchbücher,* using the latter as a general name for all productions not intended to be sung. Among these are more than two hundred works in the dramatic form—tragedies, comedies, shrovetide plays, and simple dialogues. (A tragedy was a play in which there was fighting; a comedy one in which there was no fighting). In the longer plays the method of Sachs is to convert a narrative into dialogue, letting the separate scenes or pictures follow one another until the story has all been told. There is nothing of what we moderns call plot. Nor is there any profound psychologising. The character of each personage is a fixed datum from the start; and no matter what the historical setting may be, the characters are all Nürnbergers of the sixteenth century. In the delightfully naïve comedy the *Unlike Children of Eve*, God makes a call in Adam's house and talks like a benevolent parson from across the street.

The dramatic gift of Sachs is at its best in his shrove-tide plays, of which he wrote eighty-five. They average about four hundred lines in length, and the most of them have three, four, or five characters. The plays are acted anecdotes, mostly of a humorous drift. In the *Hot Iron*, for example, a jealous wife confides to a gossip her suspicions of her husband. The gossip suggests that he be required to prove his innocence by the ancient ordeal of the hot iron. The husband consents good-humouredly, hides a chip in his sleeve, and by its aid carries the iron unscathed. Then he insists that his wife prove her virtue in the same way. She is thrown into a flutter, begs and entreats, confesses several indiscretions, but is finally constrained to take the iron in her hands. It burns her badly. In the end her husband reads her a lecture and forgives her. By-gones are to be by-gones. Of the shrovetide plays in general it may be said that Sachs brought the type to perfection. He discarded the pointless indecency of his predecessors and aimed to treat the subject in such a way as to enforce some wholesome moral. He lived in a plain-spoken age that delighted in coarse fun, but his own humour is essentially clean. His personages are social types whose character was evident from their

names, or could be indicated by a few bold strokes of
portraiture. His favourite comic figure is the stupid and
gullible peasant. Sometimes the characters explain themselves, like the pictures in an old woodcut. They come
and go as Hans Sachs needs them, doing *his* errands
rather than their own. But the conventions of the type
being once for all accepted, the most of the plays will
be found genuinely entertaining. Some of them, for
example, the *Vagabond Student in Paradise*, the *Stolen
Shrovetide Cock*, the *Peasant in Purgatory, Dame Truth
and the Peasants*, are little masterpieces of farcical comedy. Taken as a whole the shrovetide plays of Hans
Sachs are a priceless mirror of German life in the sixteenth century.

The inventory above referred to includes 4,275 mas-
tersongs, written to 275 different tunes, of which thirteen
were original. Hans Sachs is thus entitled, by the sheer
bulk of his output, to his renown as a mastersinger. But
it is here that he is least interesting to the modern reader.
The conditions of the " lovely art," as it was affection-
ately called by its votaries, were not favourable to free
lyric expression. And even if they had been, Sachs had
but a mediocre gift for pure song. He could portray
a biblical instance, and argue, and show how one ought
to feel, but the lyric wing was denied him. On the
other hand, as a narrator, especially of humorous stories
(*Schwänke*), he is admirable. He was a born story-
teller and lived in his creations with the naïve delight of
a child fashioning artistic figures out of some crude
material. He could take a coarse or lubricious anecdote,
and by his manner of retelling it in verse—by recasting

the details, changing the emphasis, and infusing his own
wholesome humour—convert it into a work of literary
art. In his best work one finds something of the characteristic charm of the *Canterbury Tales.*

After a lapse of years, when poetry of any kind save
the folksong had ceased to be a vital concern of the plain
people and had passed altogether into the hands of
scholars, it became the fashion to sneer at the Nürnberg
shoemaker, and to imply that he had cobbled in verse
as well as in leather. This fashion came to an end when
Goethe discovered in him a kindred spirit, worthy of
admiration as a "masterly poet, not like those knights
and courtiers, but a plain burgher." In the early prints
the verses of Sachs were badly botched. Now that a large
part of them have been published from his own manuscript, we can see that he had a fairly good ear for rhythm
and essayed a certain regularity. Still, read them as one
will, his lines often jolt. He deserves the immortality
that is now securely his, not for the fine chiselling of his
verses, but because he envisaged a larger part of life
and expressed it more fully than did any other German
of his century.

The plays of Hans Sachs drew on the same exhaust-
less fund of ancient history, mediæval legend, and Renascence novels that was presently to furnish the raw
materials of the English Elizabethan drama. If that had
happened which did not happen, namely, if private wealth
or civic pride in Nürnberg had turned its attention to
the building of theatres and the nursing of the histrionic
art, there might possibly have been a brilliant flowering
of the German drama in the sixteenth century. But no

great dramatic literature has ever come into being without theatres and professional actors. In Germany these were lacking. It was thus a revelation when, toward the end of the century, English players began to visit Germany and to exhibit there the art of acting as it had developed in England under the patronage of king, court, and gentry. The earliest record of this English invasion dates from 1587. From that time on for more than half a century the notices are numerous. The English " comedians " penetrated to all parts of the country, playing sometimes under princely patronage, more often in the cities by special licence of the town council. In this way the people became familiar with the plots of a large number of plays by Marlowe, Kyd, Greene, Shakespeare, Dekker, Beaumont and Fletcher, Massinger, and others. The poetry and the artistic structure of the originals, which would not have been comprehended in a foreign language, were remorselessly sacrificed. The visitors were not bent on holding up the banner of the ideal, to use Ibsen's phrase, but on making money. They had to amuse or thrill their audiences as best they could. So they substituted a prose digest for the English verse, and relied for their effects on histrionic vehemence, songs, dances, acrobatic feats, and especially on the antics of the clown, whose part was usually taken by the leading man of the company. In the course of time the popularity of the visitors and their pecuniary profits led to the formation of German companies which strolled about the land, imitating the style and methods of the aliens, and even calling themselves " English comedians " by way of captivating advertisement. They used a rough translation or paraphrase of the English prose digests, or else an original German concoction of the same general character. The clown, under various names, was always the central attraction.

While the great mass of these plays were never printed and had no influence on literary developments, there are two writers in whom the effects of the English invasion are discernible—Duke HEINRICH JULIUS, of Brunswick (1564–1613), and JAKOB AYRER (died in 1605). Duke Heinrich, who is known to have had English players at his court, wrote a number of prose dramas, of which ten were published in 1593 and 1594. In all of them but one there is a fun-maker who speaks Low German and bears the name of Johan Clant (clown) or Johan Bouset (Posset). They are plays of adulterous intrigue coming to grief, or of horrible deeds horribly avenged. The obvious aim is to show that the way of the transgressor is very hard. In some of the plays the bad person is carried off by devils. There are long expository soliloquies, exclamatory tirades, with frequent juxtaposition of the grave and the frivolous, in genuine Elizabethan style. Thus, in *Susanna*, the main drift of which is, of course, eminently serious, we find not only the clownish servant with his privileged fooleries and banalities, but also a number of peasant folk from different parts of Germany. These speak in their local dialects and otherwise act out their boorish natures. In the end they join with gusto in the stoning of the wicked judges, because they have each a private grievance.

Jakob Ayrer is a lesser Hans Sachs. He was a

lawyer by profession and spent the last twelve years of his life at Nürnberg, where English players were just then operating. He wrote a large number of plays, of which sixty-nine have been printed. His form is generally the old *Knittelvers*, which he handles with the facility of Sachs but with less of poetic warmth. Nor has he the pleasant humour of the immortal shoemaker. In his tragedies and comedies he is more diffuse than Sachs, and equally unconcerned about what is now called plot. He has a series of five plays on early Roman history as recorded by Livy, and there are other sequences of three or four plays. Most often he has six acts, sometimes seven or eight, in one case nine. In his shrovetide plays he is more gross than Sachs, and has not his predecessor's knack of evolving a wholesome lesson out of his unsavoury materials. He is most original and most pleasing in his *Singspiele*, a literary type which he first made popular. They differ from the other shrovetide plays, with which he classed them, in that song takes the place of dialogue, all the parts being sung to a familiar tune. The influence of the English players on Ayrer has probably been overestimated. It is discernible, however, in his partiality for a clownish servant or messenger, and in his bent for histrionic horrors. His tragedy of the fall of Constantinople rivals *Titus Andronicus* in its exploitation of ferocious bloodshed.

We turn now from the drama to the narrative literature of entertainment and reproof. It is customary to regard Wickram's *Galmy*, published anonymously in 1539, as the starting-point of the German novel. But there was no lack of prose fiction before Wickram. The

chap-books, which had been and long continued to be
the favourite reading of the people at large, may be
divided into three classes: (1) collections of anecdotes;
(2) prose paraphrases of German metrical romances,
such as *Duke Ernst, Tristan, Wigalois;* (3) translations
from the French, Latin, or Italian of romances and short
tales, such as the *Seven Sages,* the *Knight of the Tower,
Fortunatus, Melusine,* the *Decameron.* Of these three
types of popular fiction, the first—the *Schwank*—enjoyed,
it would seem, the greatest favour. There were collections in verse like *Parson Kalenberg,* a rather degenerate
and untidy scion of *Parson Ameis,* and then there was
the delectable *Eulenspiegel,* which may have been originally written in verse, though the earliest version now
known, that of 1515, is in prose. There seems to have
lived in the fourteenth century a real Dill Ulenspiegel,
who may have done some of the pranks attributed to him
in the book. But the name soon became, like that of Doctor Faust, a mere peg on which to hang stories of a certain kind. Eulenspiegel is a simple-seeming rustic who
wanders about the land playing practical jokes which
usually evince his own shrewdness and turn the laugh
on the people with whom he has to do. Another highly
popular collection of stories, mostly culled from mediæval
literature, was the *Jest and Earnest* of J. Pauli, published
in 1522.

These stories, which are rather clumsily told, and
sometimes touch the extreme limit of vulgarity, did not
win their way into general favour in virtue of any literary qualities. And the same is true of the exotic
romances: it was not their form but their subject-matter

12

—the hard facts and naked lubricities of the story—that made them interesting. Naturally, therefore, the quickened moral sense of the Reformers found them offensive and dangerous. Always more or less vulnerable on moral grounds, the romances of chivalry were doubly so when turned into quotidian prose. Serious minds began to regard them as pestiferous.[1] From this feeling as fountain-head proceed two literary currents, which, however, do not flow separately, but with more or less of interfusion : a current of didactic and satiric production, and a current of creative efforts to feed the appetite for fiction with more wholesome food.

JÖRG WICKRAM, the pioneer novelist, was a native of Colmar, in Alsatia. He seems to have learned a trade, but early became a mastersinger, an adapter of biblical dramas, and a writer of shrovetide plays. *Galmy*, his first attempt at prose fiction, is a semi-independent romance of knighthood—morally unimpeachable, but otherwise quite in the traditional vein. This was followed by other chaste romances of adventure in far-away lands, the best being the *Goldthread*, wherein a poor shepherd boy rises by virtue, thrift, and studiousness and marries the daughter of a count. The scene is laid in Portugal. More important, as marking a first step toward the realistic treatment of German life, is the *Mirror for Boys*. It is frankly didactic, and the scheme

---

[1] A Latin treatise of 1523, quoted by Goedeke, *Grundriss*, I, 340, says, after mentioning a large number of the popular favourites: Quos omnes libros conscripserunt ociosi, male feriati, imperiti, viciis ac spurcitiis dediti; in queis miror quid delectat, nisi tam nobis flagitia blandirentur.

of the Prodigal Son is apparent throughout; but it was based partly on observation, and the scene is laid in Prussia. The general temper of Wickram is that of an evangelical moralist with a sense of decency somewhat in advance of his time. His most popular work was the *Rollwagenbüchlein*, or *Coaching Booklet*, a collection of short stories intended to while away the tedium of travelling. Here, as the dedication states, he aimed at good entertainment rather than instruction or reproof. The tales were to be such as virtuous wives and modest maids might listen to. If some of them now seem to fall a little short of that ideal, it is because standards have changed.

Notwithstanding the beginning made by Wickram, the time proved not yet ripe for realistic prose fiction of an ambitious kind. A hundred years elapsed before Grimmelshausen wrote the first German novel that is now readable by any one save the student of origins. In the sixteenth century the portraiture of life is always subordinate to a didactic or satiric purpose, or is mixed up with an extravagant humour that amounts to caricature. So it is, for example, with RINGWALT (born in 1532), a Brandenburg clergyman who found many readers, especially for his poem *Faithful Eckhart*. In this he employs the old mediæval device of a visit to hell; the various classes of society being made to describe the sinful life that has brought them to perdition, His *Speculum Mundi* contains interesting glimpses of the seamy side of life among the minor nobility, the dominant idea being a castigation of drunkenness.

· But the satiric humour in which the age delighted

found its strongest, if not exactly a classical, expression in the writings of the Alsatian JOHANN FISCHART (born about 1550). In his boyhood Fischart was a pupil of Caspar Scheit, the translator of the Latin *Grobianus*, about which a brief digression will be in order at this point. The idea of the perfect gentleman, as inculcated by the mediæval codes of behaviour, gave rise in time to the antithetic conception of the perfect boor. In the *Ship of Fools* Brant speaks of a new saint, Grobian, who has his votaries everywhere. Grobian was conceived as the perfect exemplar of all things abominable in human intercourse. The name found favour, and in 1549 a scholar named Dedekind published a Latin satire, *Grobianus*, which described the ideal boor in revoltingly plain words, and gave explicit directions for the attainment of perfection in bad manners. The book, which gives glimpses into an abysmal depth of coarseness and boobyism in social intercourse, was a great literary success. It was at once translated into German verse by Scheit, a schoolmaster living at Worms. Several new editions followed, both of the Latin original and of the German translation, and the book continued in high favour for more than a century. As late as 1739, although the satire had been done into English more than a century before, an Englishman by the name of Roger Bull thought it worth while to retranslate it and dedicate his *Compleat Booby, an Ironical Poem*, to Dr. Jonathan Swift, " who first introduced into these Kingdoms of Great Britain and Ireland an Ironical Manner of Writing, to the Discouragement of Vice, Ill-manners and Folly."

As a native of Alsatia, the land of Brant and Murner,

Fischart was, so to speak, born into an atmosphere of satire and censoriousness. In his boyhood he studied under Scheit at Worms, and got from him, it would seem, the idea of turning *Eulenspiegel* into rhyme. His schooling finished, he visited Holland, England, France, and Italy, and took his degree in law at Basel. But instead of following the jurist's profession, he became an assistant to his brother-in-law Jobin, a Strassburg printer, and drifted thence into miscellaneous pamphleteering, poetising and translating. He began in 1570 with a rhymed lampoon directed against a Jesuit named Rabe, a renegade from Protestantism. It is a long-winded and rather futile invective, designed to show up the secret intrigues and diabolical wickedness of the Jesuits. This was followed in 1572 by the *Grandmother of all Almanacs*, a humorous and effective prose satire on the popular prognosticators. In the same year appeared the *New Eulenspiegel in Rhyme*, in which the stories of the chap-book were versified with much discursive comment, and with wearisome amplification of unsavoury details, but without any pervading satiric purpose. The next year there came from Jobin's press a burlesque poem, the *Flea Hunt*, in which the domestic flea was made to complain to Jupiter of the persecutions it had to undergo at the hands of the women in its innocent pursuit of a livelihood. The amusing skit was not the work of Fischart, but he took up the idea, added a second part, giving the reply and defence of the women, and published the whole under his own pseudonym, Hultrich Elloposcleron.

One sees from all this that Fischart was no creator. He needed an impulse from another mind; but the impulse once received, he went his own way, commenting, amplifying, giving free play to his humour, and so, in a sense, making the thing in hand his own. And so it is also in his later productions. The most famous of them, *Gargantua* (1575), is nominally a translation of the first book of Rabelais, but the additions swell the matter to thrice the dimensions of the original. Not only the language but the whole setting is Germanised. The cachinnatory satyr of France is transferred to a German environment and gains nothing thereby in cleanness or intelligibility. There is an obvious effort to outdo Rabelais in his own specialties. The book is hard to read on account of its allusiveness, its chaotic erudition, its pedantic divagations, its profusion of outlandish words and recondite puns; but hidden away in the repellent jungle of the diction there are some excellent pictures of contemporary German life. After *Gargantua* Fischart published several other prose works, of which the best is a booklet on marriage (*Ehzuchtbüchlin*), compiled from Plutarch and other sources. He also renewed his warfare on the Jesuits in a satiric poem, *Jesuiterhütlin*, in which the four-cornered Jesuit hat was described as the devil's latest masterpiece—a climax of fiendish malignity following the one-horned cowl of the monk, the two-horned mitre of the bishop, and the three-horned tiara of the Pope.

Notwithstanding his immense erudition, wide experience of life, ardent temperament, and sturdy personal character, Fischart can hardly be classed with the great or epoch-making writers. He lacked originality, lacked the artistic sense of form and proportion; and hence it was that, while deeply versed in all the literature of humanism, he was not the man to interpret it effectively for the Germans. Besides, he wrote in the Alsatian dialect. His popularity waned with his own century, and he exerted no great influence on subsequent writers. For the reader of to-day he is most enjoyable in his poem of the *Lucky Boat of Zürich*, in which he describes, with much warmth of feeling, the memorable feat of a band of Swiss oarsmen in rowing from Zürich to Strassburg in a single day.

It remains to say a few words about the unique chapbook of DOCTOR FAUST, which belongs to none of the three types enumerated above (page 167). The earliest known Faust-book dates from the year 1587—about half a century after the death of the actual charlatan whose operations furnished the groundwork of the saga. The anonymous author, seemingly a Lutheran pastor, states in a dedicatory epistle that he got the materials for his work from a good friend in Speyer. The book itself is a curious patchwork of genuine folk-tales that were really current about Doctor Faust—some of them old stories retold with a new setting—and learned demonological rubbish taken from pre-existent treatises. Of literary talent the author had hardly the faintest glimmer : a more addled and slovenly composition were hard to find in any language. But its purpose, enforced as it is with endless iteration and much quotation from Scripture, is not left in doubt. The author wished to warn all Christians against magic by giving the story of Faust's wicked life and awful death as a terrible example. He is credulous, superstitious, and benighted to the last degree: not a ray of the new secular science had pierced the dark recesses of his mind. In the Faust that he pictures there is very little that savours of aspiration or of intellectual titanism, though in one passage he is represented as "taking eagle's wings to himself and proposing to fathom all the depths of earth and heaven." In the main, Faust is simply a wicked sensualist who sells his soul to the devil for a mess of pottage, gets the pottage and goes to perdition as per contract. The Mephostophiles of the Faust-book is perhaps the dullest devil in all literature.

But while the chap-book can lay no claim to literary or intellectual merit, its story of a presumptuous and lordly sinner, jumping the life to come for twenty-four years of earthly power and pleasure, bit itself deep into the imagination of the age. Marlowe wrote his *Faustus,* which was brought back to Germany and there gave rise to a German drama, no copy of which has been preserved. All through the seventeenth century and to the middle of the eighteenth, it maintained itself as a popular show, with devils in abundance, startling mechanical effects, and the clown as prominent attraction. When at last it was dropped by actors of flesh and blood, it became a puppet-show; and in that form—after Lessing had insisted on the dramatic possibilities of the story—it struck immortal fire in the imagination of the young Goethe.

CHAPTER X

In the early years of the seventeenth century educated Germans began to feel with a degree of shame that their country's vernacular literature was in a backward state as compared with that of Holland, France and Italy. It seemed to be lacking in good taste, artistic finish, nobility of expression. The increasing recognition of this unpleasant fact led presently to a new literary movement which is characterised, first and foremost, by the extensive importation of foreign ideas and forms. At the same time there was a reformatory agitation which had for its object to improve the language and encourage its use by the cultivated classes, to regulate poetry, and to create a poetic diction. In all this laudable effort Martin Opitz was the acknowledged leader and revered authority. He and his followers ushered in a new epoch, in which the ideas of the Renascence found at last a dignified literary expression. It is, however, a rather arid epoch of scholars poetising for scholars. The idea fixed itself in the minds of the new generation that poetry was a branch of polite learning—a matter of forms and rules and clever imitation of good models. Unlike the earlier humanists, they loved and honoured the German language; but their work is not rooted in the life of the

nation. It stands apart as a refined diversion of the
scholar class. Their cultivation of the formal side of
poetry was praiseworthy; the pity is that when they had
duly improved the means of expression it turned out that
they had nothing very momentous to express. On the
whole, the Opitzians leave an impression of vacuous
artificiality. Yet there is lyric warmth in Fleming and
manly sincerity in Logau.

The first harbinger of the coming renascence of form
was the Swabian GEORG RODOLF WECKHERLIN (1584–
1653), whose *Odes and Songs*, published in 1616, were
in a way an anticipation of Opitz. After completing
his university studies at Tübingen, Weckherlin found
employment in the diplomatic service of the Duke of
Würtemberg. He resided some time in France, and still
longer in England, where he was sometime assistant
to Milton in the government secretaryship for foreign
languages. He was a good linguist and familiar with
the various types of Renascence poetry current in English, French, Dutch, Italian, and Latin. Withal he was
a sincere lover of his native German, and wished to do
it honour by proving its capacity for elegant poetic
expression. He wrote sonnets, alexandrines, odes, epodes,
anacreontics, occasional poems, and songs in a variety
of stanzas. He had the soul of a courtier, and court life
was his Castalian spring. Extravagant praise of the
" gods and goddesses " of this earth, either in direct odes,
or in effusions commemorating their goings and com-
ings, their joys and their sorrows; conventional toying
with mythological names and conceits—such is Weckherlin's element. There are a few poems that charm by

their simplicity and evident genuineness of feeling, but the great majority are little more than a froth of words. The "songs" are purely literary productions and mark the beginning of the modern dissociation of music and lyric poetry. In his versification Weckherlin used a certain freedom in respect of accent and the regular alternation of stressed and unstressed syllables. He declined to follow the strict rule of Opitz; wherefore he was coolly ignored, much to his annoyance, by the Silesian reformer, who regarded himself, and succeeded in making his countrymen regard him, as the first German poet.

MARTIN OPITZ (1597–1639) was born at Bunzlau, Silesia, a land then famous for its excellent schools. As a student at Breslau and Beuthen he came into contact with a number of wide-awake scholars who knew what was going on in the world and were ready to hear discussion (in Latin, of course) of the question whether Germany's literary backwardness was an irremediable condition. Opitz was patriotic, capable, ambitious; and when the Dutch poems of Heinsius appeared, in 1616, he began to dream of becoming the German Heinsius, the German Ronsard. At the age of twenty he wrote his *Aristarchus, sive de Contemptu Linguæ Teutonicæ*, in which, after glorifying the ancient Germans and their language, he animadverted forcibly on the recent depravation of the noble German tongue. It was becoming, he wrote, a sewer into which flowed all sorts of filth from other languages. Monstrous words and cancerous growths were creeping in, at sight of which an honest German could hardly restrain his indignation and disgust. The tractate closed with a modest contention that it was, after all, possible to do in

German what Petrarch and Ronsard and Heinsius had done in their several languages, and to do it in the same metres and with equal dignity. To prove this he submitted some alexandrines, a sonnet, and some other specimens of exotic verse that he had composed.

Full of his ambition Opitz went, in the summer of 1618, to Heidelberg, which was just then the foremost German university, and the temporary abiding-place of a number of young men of poetic bent. The young Silesian found himself in his element; he took to poetising in German, the verses came copiously, and he began to think, in conjunction with his friend Zincgref, of publication. The outbreak of the Thirty Years' War, which was to be so disastrous to German civilisation, drove him from Heidelberg. He went to Leiden and spent two months with Heinsius, who now became his guiding star. On a visit to Jutland he wrote the best of his longer poems, *Consolation in the Adversities of War*. By this time he had arrived at certain views of correctness which made his earlier verses seem crude. He would have been glad to delay their publication till he could revise them, but Zincgref chose to proceed. So, in order that the true theory of poetry might go to the world along with the poems which were to usher in the new era, he dashed off in five days his *Book of German Poetry*. It was published at Breslau in 1624, the same year in which his *Teutsche Poemata* were put through the press at Strassburg. In after time the Germans fell into the habit of regarding the year 1624 as the Year One in their literary history.

The subsequent career of Opitz to his death in 1639 is of minor importance. He had done his work, reached his full stature, and delivered his message. The *Book of German Poetry* is anything but a masterly treatise on poetics. It consists of eight short chapters based, almost sentence for sentence, on Scaliger, Ronsard, Heinsius, and other Renascence scholars. The most significant chapters are the sixth, which treats of poetic diction, and the seventh, which is devoted to rhyme, metre, and the genres. Opitz urged that poetic diction should be elegant and dignified. Foreign words and provincialisms were to be avoided. Epithets might be advantageously borrowed from the Greeks and Romans, but should always be significant—not mere padding. Verse should consist either of iambs or trochees, but these ancient terms were to be taken in a new sense independent of syllabic quantity. An iamb was to be understood as a foot of two syllables, of which the second should bear the natural word-accent, the first being unaccented. In the trochee this order would be reversed. Opitz did not expressly assert the indispensableness of rhyme, but that thought is implied in his work. As the iamb and the trochee were to be the only allowable feet, there was no place in the scheme for the ancient hexameter or for the distich: for these the French alexandrine was to be substituted. This meant in effect that the alexandrine was to be the accepted form for nearly all the genres, except the song and the ode.

To have imposed this scheme on German letters for a century and a half, to have created a standard of correctness and regularity in verse-making, and to have aided in the movement for purging the language of useless and incongruous alienisms—such are the achievements on which the renown of Opitz rests. By his con-

temporaries, who had no literary criteria but those he
gave them, and who knew nothing whatever of the
minnesingers, the *Nibelung Lay*, or the romances of
chivalry, he was extolled as a very great man.   Said
Logau in a laudatory couplet :

> *Im Latein sind viel Poeten, immer aber ein Virgil;*
> *Deutsche haben einen Opitz, Tichter sonsten eben viel.*

To his contemporaries Opitz seemed to have invented
German poetry.   He had given proof that the German
language could do all that any language could do, and
he had thereby put his country all at once on a par with
its neighbours.   But in truth he was only a scholar, with
a strong bent and a considerable talent for adaptation
and imitation.   His songs and odes are unimpeachably
regular, but lukewarm and conventional.   In the best of
them, such as *Sey wohlgemuth, lass Trauren sein,* and
Ich empfinde fast ein Grauen, we get not so much the
lyric expression of the feeling—in the one case hope, in
the other the attraction of outdoor things for the bookworm—as a demonstration that the feeling is reasonable.
The sonnets of Opitz are extremely prosaic.   Speaking
generally of his *Poemata,* his lavish and serious use of
Greek and Roman mythology gives to his work an air
of unreality, as of an erudite virtuoso disporting among
outworn conventionalities.   What had the Germans, in
the terrible throes of the Thirty Years' War, to do with
Venus and Diana and Bacchus and Pan and Favonius
and Galatea?   What use could they make of metrical
babble about the love-lorn Corydon, and the coy Phyllis?
And yet Opitz was an earnest patriot and on occasion

could deal vigorously with realities. His *Consolation in the Adversities of War*, a long poem in four books, has passages of telling description and virile feeling. To be sure they are impaired for the reader of to-day by the droning sing-song of the alexandrine verse. This measure, admirable in French because the character of French accent permits subtle variations of cadence, tends in German, with its strong syllabic stress, its invariable iambs, its regular bisection of every line, and its unfailing alternation of masculine and feminine couplets, to a deadly monotony. The following lines will show Opitz at his best, and illustrate his handling of a verse-form that was to dominate the more serious poetry of Germany for a century and a half, until it was thrown off as an intolerable fetter by Klopstock, Lessing, Goethe, and Schiller.

Der Alten graues Haar, der jungen Leute Weinen,
Das Klagen, Ach und Weh der Grossen und der Kleinen,
Das Schreien in gemein von Reich und Arm geführt,
Hat diese Bestien im minsten nicht gerührt.
Hier half kein Adel nicht, hier ward kein Stand geachtet,
Sie mussten alle fort, sie wurden hingeschlachtet,
Wie wenn ein grimmer Wolf, der in den Schafstall reisst,
Ohn' allen Unterschied die Lämmer niederbeisst.[1]

---

[1] The gray hair of the old, the young folks' tribulation,
  The mourning and the groans of every age and station,
  The outcries of the rich, the poor man's misery,
  Have touched these savage brutes not in the least degree.
  No merit now avails; all ranks, conditions, classes,
  Are driven from their homes and done to death in masses;
  As when a ravening wolf breaks in among the fold,
  And falls upon the sheep, nor recks of young or old.

Of the writers who followed in the track of Opitz
and formed what is known as the first Silesian school,
the most gifted was PAUL FLEMING (1609–40). He
was a Saxon by birth, and received his scholastic training
at Leipzig, where he heard lectures on medicine, at the
same time writing much verse in Latin and in German.
Silesian fellow-students called his attention to Opitz and
put him in the way of seeing the great man, whom he
afterward pronounced, in the extravagance of obituary
eulogy, the peer of Pindar, Vergil, and Homer, the
" duke of German harp-strings," and the " wonder of our
age." On leaving the university, in 1633, Fleming
joined an embassy which the Duke of Holstein was just
then sending to Persia. The preparations for this
famous expedition, the journey itself by way of the
Volga, the sojourn in Asia Minor, and the return, occupied five years—for Fleming years of rugged and fruit-
ful experience. Shortly after his return his fine pros-
pects and ambitions were suddenly brought to naught by
a premature death. A sonnet written during his last ill-
ness contains a touchingly brave expression of resignation, coupled with the proud assurance that he has surpassed all his countrymen in song, and will live for ever
in their memory.

While Fleming accepted the forms prescribed by
Opitz and never quite outgrew the scholar's fondness
for ancient mythology and other conventional trappings,
his verse is in the main more convincing than that of
Opitz. It came from an honest need of self-expression:
it has substance and warmth. His work was mostly of
the lyric order, and the best of it is found in the occa-

sional poems, especially the sonnets, written by him during his long absence from the fatherland. As a sonneteer he has certainly not the Petrarcan or the Shakespearian glow; but, on the other hand, he is seldom trivial or coolly ratiocinative, like Opitz. He had a poet's feeling for the inner form of the sonnet, and was the first German to make anything more of it than a metrical curiosity. In the great majority of his sonnets he uses the alexandrine line, but he experimented with the iambic pentameter and even with tetrameter.

Both Opitz and Fleming essayed the epigram, but with small success, for lack of a trenchant wit. It was reserved for FRIEDRICH VON LOGAU (1604–55) to take the type for his specialty and to win lasting fame as a virtuoso of the epigram. The scion of a noble but impoverished Silesian family, Logau studied law in his youth and became a counsellor of the Duke of Liegnitz-Brieg. His life was cramped by poverty and saddened by the terrible war whose ravages he witnessed from beginning to end. Under all the depressing influences of that most gloomy period in German history he kept a clear head and a fresh sense of spiritual values, though not a stranger to the moods of the cynic. His works consist entirely of so-called *Sinngedichte*—a good name, which he was one of the first to employ for short poems of a pensive, gnomic, or epigrammatic character. A collection of more than 3,000 numbers, containing the garnered wit and wisdom of a lifetime, was published in 1654. They seem to have been rather indifferently received by the contemporary public; at any rate, half a century elapsed before they were reprinted, and then another half

13

century before they were rescued from undeserved neglect by the critical edition of Lessing and Ramler (1759).
Logau is, on the whole, the most interesting writer of
the Opitzian era. He had not the lyric faculty of Fleming, but that very lack perhaps saved him from the dif-
fuseness and rhetorical verbosity from which Fleming
is by no means free. He has a pleasing variety of forms,
his diction is pure, his thought noble and worth attending
to. He was interested in the realities of the living present,
also in the eternal verities; but not in the tuneful repro-
duction of conventional conceits or of other men's ideas.
Alike in his grave expressions of religious and patriotic
feeling; in his satiric thrusts at the demoralisation of
the age; in his love of the simple life and his hatred of
shams and hypocrisies; in his terse maxims of practical
wisdom, and his scintillations of caustic wit—everywhere
one gets the impression of a sturdy, virile personality.
In an age of artificial sentiment and conventional verbi-
age Logau's terseness is very refreshing. The key-note
of his thinking is contained in the couplet which avers,
apropos of the agitation for a pure and elegant German,
that he will be the best German who speaks the language
from his heart:

Deutsche mühen sich jetzt hoch, deutsch zu reden fein und rein;
Wer von Herzen redet deutsch, wird der beste Deutsche sein.

Neither Logau nor Fleming attempted play-writing
in any form. Opitz translated an Italian musical drama,
with a chorus of shepherds and an Arcadian setting,
but did not turn his hand to original dramatic author-

OPITZ AND HIS TRAIN185

ship. For a vital drama the conditions were unpro-
pitious in the highest degree. The internecine war,
with its wholesale destruction of cities and villages, and
its continual atrocities of pillage and murder, produced
everywhere a feeling of depression and insecurity. The
impoverishment of the nobility and the towns checked
the rising interest in dramatic performances. Companies
of English players continued to visit Germany from time
to time, but their business, like that of the German troupes
that followed in their wake, became less and less profit-
able. There was no encouragement for the histrionic
art or for the artistic drama. All this is to be taken into
consideration in judging the plays of ANDREAS GRY-
PHIUS (1616–64), whose talent lacked the indispensable schooling of the stage. While yet a school-boy
Gryphius won distinction for his scholarship and his
Latin verses. At the age of twenty he found in Pals-
grave Georg Schönborner a patron who bestowed on him
the poet's laurel crown, the title of doctor of philosophy,
and a patent of nobility. Aside from these prematurely
won honours the story of his early life is a record of
misfortunes that made the world look very dark to him.
His odes and sonnets reveal a mind brooding habitually
on the ugly aspects of the time, or on the misery of man's
estate. Life had presented itself to him as all vanity and
bitterness, redeemed only by the hope of heaven. In 1638
came a change. Having acquired the means to travel he
went to Holland, where he spent several years in study
and teaching. At Leiden he lectured on an almost
incredible variety of subjects—logic, metaphysic, astron-
omy, optics, chiromancy, anatomy, geography, theory of

tragedy, Roman antiquities, and what not. After a year
and a half in France and a year in Italy, he returned in
1647 to his native Glogau, where he was made town syn-
dic and spent the rest of his days as a respected official,
writing plays by way of avocation.

He began with a series of tragedies in alexandrine
verse, the general purpose of which, " seeing that our
whole fatherland is now buried in its own ashes and converted into a theatre of vanity," was to " represent the
mutability of human affairs." In *Leo Armenius* we have
a mighty emperor deposed and put to death by conspira-
tors. In *Katharine of Georgia,* the tragic idea is the
heroism of a Christian queen who chooses a horrible
death in preference to apostasy. A similar idea—that the
essence of tragedy consists not in action of any kind, but
in the steadfast endurance of a terrible fate—underlies
Carolus Stuardus, or Murdered Majesty, which was written directly after the execution of Charles I. It is in
effect an arraignment of the English regicides by an
ardent royalist. There is no action—nothing but talk
and argumentation and woful jeremiads. In the first
act the ghosts of Strafford and Laud and Queen Mary
appear and make portentously long speeches. There is
an ever-changing chorus at the end of each act : in the
first, it consists of the ghosts of murdered English kings;
in the second, of sirens; in the third, of English women;
in the fourth, of Religion arguing from the clouds with
a bevy of heretics; while the whole ends with a monody
of Vengeance. It is all very solemn, very unreal, very
undramatic. *Cardenio and Celinde* is a chamber of horrors, based on a story heard by Gryphius in Italy. Car-

denio, a hot-blooded Spanish student living at Bologna, falls in love with the chaste Olympia, but loses her to a base rival, Lysander, and is caught on the rebound by the wanton Celinde. He sets out to kill Lysander, but is beguiled away by a phantom in the form of Olympia. Having thwarted the murder, the lovely spook turns into a hideous monster. At the same time Celinde receives a similar lesson. In a desperate effort to retain the wandering love of Cardenio she decides, on advice of a witch, to use a charm for which she needs the heart of her dead lover Marcellus. She repairs to his grave and begins her gruesome surgery, whereat the loathsome corpse comes to life and reproaches her. Then Cardenio and Celinde renounce their wicked love—frightened into virtue by the sight of death and corruption. Here again the play is nearly all talk, the horrors being, for the most part, merely reported.

Judged by his tragedies alone, Gryphius would appear to have had hardly an inkling of the dramatic. In his comedies there is more of life and movement, though they show little originality, and are concerned with well-worn types of character. The best of them is *Horribilicribrifax*, wherein the ancient *miles gloriosus* is re-embodied in two braggart captains, Horribilicribrifax and Daradiridatumtarides, who swagger in French and Italian, and turn out to be cowards. Then there is a scholar Sempronius, who talks to an old procuress in Latin and Greek, which she does not understand and interprets comically in her own way. The humour consists mainly in the would-be imposing use of foreign languages by pompous wind-bags and a brainless pedant.

In a general way, it may be said of the First Silesian School that they created a pure and dignified poetic diction and a fairly definite standard of correctness in prosody and High German grammar. So far as elevated poetry was concerned, the battle was quickly won, and its results remained as a permanent acquisition. Not so, however, in prose, where the evil of language-mixture proved much more tenacious of life, and a certain pedantic ungainliness of style continued in vogue down to the time of Wieland. To promote the use of pure German, the famous Fruit-bearing Society was founded at Weimar in 1617, in imitation of the Florentine Accademia della Crusca. The members were noblemen and scholars who were actuated by a laudable purpose, but they occupied their minds very largely with symbolic names, emblems, mottoes, and other fooleries which were ill calculated to further a serious object. Other similar societies sprang up in different parts of Germany, but their total literary influence was small, and in part bad, because of the encouragement they gave here and there to fantastic aberrations of pedantry and puerility. Next to the Weimar Society, the most important one was that of the Pegnitz Shepherds at Nürnberg. Here the leading spirit was Harsdörffer, who emitted the far-famed *Nürnberg Funnel*—a manual which promised to make a poet in six lessons by the pouring in of its rules. Harsdörffer and his group took pleasure in framing verses into the shape of a cross, a pyramid, or a heart.

What is known as the Second Silesian School consisted of a group of writers who undertook to exploit the sensual and the brutal man, and invented for the purpose a peculiar style, of which the main ingredients were pedantry and artificiality. They took their cue from the Italian decadents of the sixteenth century, that is, from Marini and his satellites, who had lately perfected their wonderful art of hiding a mustard-seed of thought in a bushel of chaff. The leading exponents of Marinism in Germany were HOFMANN VON HOFMANNSWALDAU (1617–79) and CASPER VON LOHENSTEIN (1635–83), both highly respectable officials of Breslau. The immorality of their writings, of which rather too much has been made by modern critics, was at any rate not a matter of personal character but of literary dilettanteism; perhaps also, to some extent, of reaction against the dryness and didactic solemnity of Opitz. They followed a fashion which seemed to them piquant—they being men of the world intent on amusing themselves with verse-making—and they had not the taste to see that the fashion was bad. What dooms them to an evil notoriety is not their immorality but their emptiness. The best work of Hofmann is found in his *Helden-Briefe*—imaginary love-letters which are supposed to pass between famous lovers who have defied or are about to defy the moral law. The preface states that the style is " fluent, easy, and pleasant rather than pompous, Ovid having been taken as a model "; that " not much will be found in the way of pagan gods, forced hyperboles, and other familiar school tricks." And, indeed, the alexandrines do flow smoothly, and the situations are poetically realized. But the heat of lawless passion is very tamely rendered.

When Hofmann died his friend Lohenstein delivered a funeral oration which began as follows:

" The Great Pan is dead! In these words an excited voice cried out from the island of Paxis, in the time of the Emperor Tiberius, to an Egyptian named Thamus who was sailing by, commanding that he carry the news of this death to the land of Palodes. The hair of Thamus stood on end; all who were in the ship began to pray. . . . Would to God that this voice of woe had sounded only on an Egyptian ship that was once coursing over the Ionian Sea and has now long since rotted, and that the ship of this city had not lately, on the seventeenth of April, been convulsed by panic terror! "

This is Lohenstein in a nut-shell—his style, his taste. He wrote half a dozen metrical tragedies, a quantity of miscellaneous verse, and a huge prose romance, *Arminius*. His prose is decidedly better than his verse, but in both he is pedantic and turgid. The indecency of his plays, so his editor Bobertag thinks, is ascribable not to pruriency, but to sheer lack of taste, combining with a natural appetency for the horrible and revolting. That his writings should have had a considerable vogue for half a century is in itself an instructive comment on the literary conditions of the time.

While Lohenstein and Harsdörffer and their kind were unconsciously making the very name of poetry ridiculous, there was one species, the religious lyric, that escaped the prevailing blight, being safeguarded in some degree by its association with song. Frigid pedantry is not readily singable. What Lutheranism had to offer in the way of divine consolation in the dark days of the great war found classical expression in the hymns of PAUL GERHARDT (1607–76), the most eminent of German

psalmodists. Trust in God as the one sure reliance in
life's adversity; assurance that He doeth all things well,
appearances to the contrary notwithstanding; the blessedness of the Christian hope; gratitude for the sacrifice on
Calvary; the pathetic appeal of the " wounded, bleeding
head "—such are Gerhardt's characteristic themes. He
has none of Luther's militancy, more of tenderness and
self-abasement. His voice is the voice of German Protestantism chastened by terrible suffering, yet humbly and
hopefully kissing the rod of the Chastener.

In comparison with Gerhardt at his best the modest
muse of SIMON DACH (1605–59) seems a little cold
and conventional. This is due in part, however, to the
" occasional " character of his poems; for the most of
them came from an external impulse. Dach was the leading light of a literary society at Königsberg, and acquired
such reputation that he received orders from far and near
for obituary and gratulatory verse. While the greater
part of his work is rather tame and perfunctory, there are
a few songs that please by their simple naturalness. One
of his made-to-order wedding-songs, the Low German
Anke von Tharau, is so fresh and hearty in its denotation of a love that shall hold out in wedlock against all
the whips and scorns of time, that Herder was quite justified in giving it a place among his folksongs.

While the religious lyric of Gerhardt and the other
Protestant psalmodists was but little affected by the con-
temporary drift of secular poetry, this drift is clearly
discernible in the songs of the Jesuit father FRIEDRICH
SPE (1591–1635), a man honourably distinguished in
German history by his opposition to the witch-burning

mania. As a poet Spe is best known by his *Trutz-Nach-tigall*, a lyric collection published after his death by one of his confessional disciples. He gave it the curious name *Match-Nightingale*, because " it matches itself against all nightingales in sweet and delightful song, and that, too, in truly poetic fashion." The character-istic note of Spe's poetry is love of the Saviour borne in upon the soul by the voices of nature, and expressing itself in erotic imagery. The bride of Christ, " wounded with a thousand sweet arrows," walks abroad in the ver-nal wood and seeks her " fair hero, Jesus." His name is echoed back to her by the zephyrs and the gurgling brook. She implores her sister nightingale to " exhaust her art " in calling Jesus to the arms of his longing bride. A number of poems have the setting of the eclogue or pastoral, the shepherds Damon and Halton vying with each other in singing the praise of the Beloved. All this sensuous eroticism and literary conventionality in deal-ing with religious emotion are somewhat repellent to more modern taste; the more so as the verse of Spe is a monotonous repetition of the same scenery, thoughts, feelings, images. Yet there is no reason to question his sincerity, and some of the songs charm by their intimate feeling for the aspects and messages of the outdoor world. In his treatment of metre Spe, too, was a reformer, inde-pendently of Opitz. His verse-forms are numerous, and they flow smoothly. In his preface he observes that " the quantity, that is, the length and brevity of the syllables, is generally taken from the accent; those syllables on which the accent falls in ordinary pronunciation being counted as long, the others as short."

One sees from the work of Weckherlin and Spe that a tendency toward metrical reform was in the air. No doubt it would have done its work in a short time even if Opitz had never written his *Book of German Poetry*.

CHAPTER XI

THE disastrous effects of the Thirty Years' War are not fully summed up in the tale that historians tell of burned cities and villages, of diminished population, ruined industries, impoverishment, and demoralisation. Bad as these were, the hurt to the national spirit was perhaps even worse. The hapless land that had so long been the battle-ground of Europe now became its laughing-stock. From the point of view of that international public opinion which humanism had created, Germany was a land of quarrelling priests and prosing pedants—a land politically helpless and artistically sterile. The outside world had not been greatly impressed by the literary achievements of Opitz and his retinue, and easily convinced itself, with Père Bouhours, that a German could not possibly have *esprit*. Worst of all, the Germans virtually accepted a position of pupilage. After the war, while Latin continued to be the language of scholarship, French became more and more fashionable among the gentry and the wealthy *bourgeoisie*. Gentlemen and ladies received their education in French, spoke French to one another, read French books, aped French customs. What was most needed, before there could be any healthy development of letters, was a general quickening of national self-respect. This came with the world-amazing victories of the great King of Prussia.

But while the interval between the Peace of Westfalia and the Second Silesian War is in the main an unrefreshing period of artificiality and imitation, the desert is not without its oases. In the first place there is Grimmelshausen's *Simplicissimus*, which is thoroughly German and essentially original. It is the work of a virile realist who had lived much and was interested in life for its own sake; and while not free from the discursive pedantry in which the age delighted, it is, at any rate, readable—the most readable prose of the century. It is by no means to be inferred that Grimmelshausen was unaffected by literary tradition; on the contrary, he read omnivorously, and drew hints from many literary sources.

Down to about the middle of the seventeenth century the German reader of fiction had fed mainly on imported products and weak imitations of them. There were three types, each with its variations. In the first place, there was the romance of heroic gallantry, which had derived from *Amadis de Gaul*, and taken on a deeper tinge of sentimentalism under the influence of the pastorals. Then there was the political romance, to which an impulse was given in Germany by Opitz through his translation of Barclay's *Argenis*. To this type belonged the patriotic but stilted and interminable *Arminius* of Lohenstein, admired of many for its colossal erudition. And then there was the picaresque novel, or romance of roguery, from Spain. The type made its appearance on

German soil in 1615 in an adaptation from the Spanish
by the Munich scholar Albertinus. It bore the title:
"Der Landstörzer (Vagabond), called Gusman von Alfa-
rache or Picaro: his marvellous and diverting life, how
he visited nearly every place in the world, tried all sorts
of service, rank and office, did and endured much good
and evil, got rich and poor and rich again, fell into abject
misery, and finally changed for the better." The picaresque novel was a sort of parody of the older romance
of knighthood. It owed its popularity, in Germany as
elsewhere, to the growing sense of something effete
and ridiculous in the old ways and ideals of chivalry
—the feeling that gave birth to Don Quixote. The
plebeian rogue was an adventurer like the lordly knight
of old, his weapons being shrewd wit and native
cunning, instead of lance and sword; the goal of his
effort being not a royal crown, but food and drink and
shelter.

As for the heroic sentimental romances, the recipe by
which they were made in Germany called for a turgid
hyperbolic style, a princely hero of wonderful pedigree
and invincible prowess, a series of incredible adventures,
and, above all, a far-away setting of which the author
could know nothing except from books. Take, for example, the opening of Ziegler's Asiatic Banise, which, to be
sure, comes after Grimmelshausen, but illustrates well
enough the literary trend now under consideration. It
was published in 1688 and often reprinted. The scene is
Farther India. Balacin, the exiled landless Prince of Ava,
has just heard of a massacre perpetrated in the city of
Pegu by the tyrant Chaumigren. He is concerned about

the fate of the adorable Princess Banise. Quite alone he wakes from a night's sleep on the heights overlooking Pegu and soliloquises thus:

" May lightning, thunder, and hail, as the avenging instruments of a righteous heaven, annihilate the glory of thy gilded towers, and may the vengeance of the gods destroy all the inhabitants of the city who helped to bring about the fall of the royal house, or did not with their very best endeavour, even with the proffer of their blood, try to avert it! Ye gods! Could my eyes become thunder-charged clouds, and these tears terrible floods, I would hurl a thousand bludgeons, like fireworks of a righteous wrath, at the heart of the cursed bloodhound, and verily I should not miss him! "

It is Grimmelshausen's distinction to have seen the foolishness of that sort of thing, and the advantage, to a writer of fiction, of leaning somewhat on his own observation of life. He was, however, not the first to hit on the idea of introducing an element of autobiography into a fictitious narrative, having been anticipated in a way by his older contemporary, HANS MICHAEL MOSCH-EROSCH (1601–69), who wrote under the pseudonym of Philander von Sittewald. Moscherosch was an Alsatian scholar of Spanish extraction, who suffered grievously at the hands of marauding soldiers. He was a member of the Fruit-bearing Society, in which he bore the name of the Dreamer. His most important work is his *Gesichte*, which began as a free translation of Quevedo's *Sueños*, but was continued independently. These *Visions*—the title really means *Things Seen* or *Aspects of Life*—are tediously diffuse and badly over-

weighted with recondite pedantry, but contain scattering
grains of wheat in the way of shrewd observation and
satiric humour.   The best of them, which is quite independent of Quevedo, is the one entitled *Soldier Life*.   It
tells how Philander was at one time pressed into a gang
of marauders and compelled to witness and in a sense
to participate in their brutal operations.   Underneath the
cobwebs of pedantry there are some rather telling pictures of the time, but there is nothing like an elaborate
or sustained fiction.   To provide this was reserved for
the author of *Simplicius Simplicissimus*.

The details of the life of JOHANN JAKOB CHRISTOPH
VON GRIMMELSHAUSEN are almost entirely matter of
inference.   He must have been born about 1625, and is
known to have died in 1676.   While a mere child he
was picked up by Hessian soldiers and taken to Cassel,
whence he soon drifted into the life of a soldier of fortune.   After the close of the war he settled at Renchen,
in the Black Forest, as magistrate and man of letters.
By much reading he endeavoured to make good the
defects of his early education.   In this way his style gradually took on an excess of pedantic ballast; but where
he is at his best, that is, where he draws on his own
variegated experience, he writes with a freshness of
humour and a power of vigorous portraiture such as
are not elsewhere found in the literature of the time.   His
general attitude toward the heroics of chivalry is similar
to that of Cervantes, but he had not the great Spaniard's
imaginative power, and his method of approach is altogether different.

Simplicissimus, the most important of Grimmelshausen's numerous writings, purports to be the auto-biography of a "singular vagabond" named Melchior Sternfels von Fuchshaim. The hero introduces himself as the foster-child of a poor peasant living in the Spessart Wood, and contrasts the situation humorously with the noble castles and knightly pursuits of conventional romance: "Instead of pages, lackeys, and hostlers, my sire had sheep, goats, and pigs, each dressed elegantly in his own natural livery; and they often waited upon me on the chase until I drove them home. His armoury was well provided with ploughs, mattocks, axes, hoes, shovels, dung-forks and hay-forks, wherewith he practised every day; for hoeing and digging were his *disciplina militaris,* just as with the ancient Romans in time of peace; the yoking of oxen was his captain's *commando,* drawing out manure his science of fortification, holding the plough his strategy, cleaning out the stable his knightly diversion, his tournament." One day the place is devastated by a band of soldiers. The boy flees to the woods and falls in with an old hermit, with whom he stays a long time, learning something of God and religion. After his benefactor's death he becomes first the fool, then the trusted page of the Swedish governor of Hanau, who dubs him Simplicius Simplicissimus. Presently he is carried off by marauding Croats and involved in the wild life of the vagabond soldiery. He learns to rob, as if that were the natural order of the world, is captured by the Swedes, finds a treasure, puts on the style of a gentleman, marries, leaves his wife, goes to Paris and struts among the ladies there as Beau Alman. Returning to Germany, he is wofully disfigured by small-

14

pox, comes to want, recuperates his fortunes as peripatetic quacksalver, and then takes to soldiering again. After the death of his partner, a bloodthirsty outlaw named Olivier, he finds his way back to the home of his childhood, where he learns that the hermit who had once befriended him was his own father. He now becomes studious, repents of his sins, and thinks to become a hermit like his sire. But the love of adventure carries him away again. He wanders three years more, drifting even as far as Asia. At last he returns to his books—world-weary and prepared to embrace the meditative life in earnest.

This story, published in 1669, is the one prose classic of the century. It was highly popular from the first, though erudite critics pronounced it rubbish. Did Grimmelshausen blunder into his brilliant success or come to it by superior insight? The question is debatable, because he began with exotic love-romances no better than those of his contemporaries, and he never publicly assumed the rôle of a literary reformer. Indeed, so carefully did he guard his anonymity that a century and a half elapsed before it was known who wrote *Simplicissimus*. And even in this his best work there are arid stretches, as if the author were, after all, distrustful of his realistic gospel and ambitious to shine by his learning, like other men. But for the most part he gives an impression of writing with his eye on the object. The atrocities of the war, the humours of vagabondage, the coarseness of a dissolute society, the manners and customs and superstitions of the people—all this is pictured with vivid realism and artistic impartiality. There is no preaching or posing. We get the naked truth at the darkest period of German history.

One of the imitators of Grimmelshausen was the voluminous CHRISTIAN WEISE (1642–1708), a learned schoolmaster who flooded the market with text-books, plays, and satiric tales. His " romances " pertain to the earlier part of his career, and were meant to furnish an antidote for the turgidity of the later Silesians. The best of them is the *Three Worst Arch-fools in all the World*, which was for some years a favourite of the reading public. Weise was possessed by the good idea that fiction might well deal with every-day life in natural language. But he was only a garrulous pedagogue, without literary skill, and without breadth or depth of experience; so that his battle with his enemies presents the rather unrefreshing spectacle of a contest between pedantic triviality and pedantic pomposity. During the last thirty years of his life he was rector of the gymnasium at Zittau, where he wrote more than fifty plays, to be performed by his pupils. It was the custom of the school to devote three days of each year to a dramatic festival; on the first day a biblical play was given, on the second a serious historical drama, on the third a humorous performance. The industrious rector met the entire demand with his own pen, and many of his plays were performed at other schools than his own. He was regarded in Saxony as a very remarkable man. A performance lasted some five hours and employed a large number of characters—presumably all the capable boys in the school. Weise's plays are now appallingly dull reading, but it is worth noting that, a century before Lessing, the Saxon schoolmaster essayed a genuine German comedy, with characters based to some extent on the author's observation, and with plots that were invented outright.

What one misses in these writers, and also in the influential preachers and moralists of the period, is good taste and enlightenment. Everywhere ponderous learning and a mania for recondite quotation; but along therewith gross superstition, pitiful narrowness, and a lacking sense of form, fitness, and proportion. Religion itself appears at this time rather unlovely. Protestantism was tending to become a fossil form or a petulant war of doxies, with no power to touch the heart or the imagination. The Bible, literally understood and valued in all parts alike, was the only thinkable standard for the regulation of life. What was needed for literature was a freer play of intelligence, a quickening breath of scepticism, inquiry, and discussion. These things might not be able to take the place of genius, but they could prepare the way for genius by educating the public taste.

It is thus that the character of CHRISTIAN THOMAS (1655–1728), the father of the German *Aufklärung,* acquires importance in literary history, though he was a jurist and produced no works of the imagination. As a young professor of law at Leipzig, Thomas endeavoured to ground his science rather on man's moral nature than on the biblical tradition. He had an independent, sceptical mind, and the temper of a reformer. In the winter of 1687–88 he did an audacious and unheard-of thing : he gave a public university lecture in the German language. His theme was the burning question of imitating the French. " How is it," he said, " that when one of us Germans goes to France, though he be properly dressed and can reason cleverly of a French roast or fricassee, speak the language properly, and make his bow like a born Frenchman—how is it that he is nevertheless generally laughed at as a silly sheep, whereas the French, when they come to us, commonly win love and admiration? It must be that in our imitation we have not yet hit the mark." This led to an analysis and eulogy of the French conception of the *honnête homme, homme savant, bel esprit, homme de bon goût*, and *homme galant*—all combining to produce the *parfait homme sage*.[1] From this Thomas went on to argue that French leadership was to be frankly accepted, but in its spirit, not in its externalities. His doctrine pointed to the secularisation of letters, and the enlistment of them in the service of man as a social being. In his lectures and Latin writings Thomas attacked some of the Christian foundations. In 1688 he started a literary periodical—the pioneer enterprise of its kind in Germany. When the theologians made it too hot for him at Leipzig, he found a refuge at the new Prussian university of Halle, where he taught for nearly forty years, an able exponent of those specifically North-German ideas and tendencies which were to find their strongest expression in Lessing and Friedrich the Great. Through these men and their respective followings with pen and sword, it was fated that Germany should first learn what France had to teach, then beat her in battle, and finally cast down her literary idols.

---

[1] See the *Festschrift der historischen Commission der Provinz Sachsen zur Jubelfeier der Universität Halle-Wittenberg am 1. bis 4. August,* 1894.

The leading apostle of French taste in the first half of the eighteenth century was Gottsched, and the great tragedy of Gottsched's life was the final collapse of his prestige under the impact of new ideas that came in part from England. His reformatory efforts were centred mainly on the drama, though he also meddled with the general theory of poetry. He was a man of the same type as Opitz, that is, a scholar without creative genius, but with a strong desire to pose as a lawgiver. The important difference between the two is that, while Opitz could only reflect the comparatively feeble light of the Pleiad, Gottsched is irradiated by the great luminaries of the age of Louis XIV. His controversy with the Swiss group headed by Bodmer must receive some attention presently, though it was only a logomachy of theorists. First, however, it is necessary to turn back and follow up the history of poetry.

In the closing years of the seventeenth century the very name of poet fell into a certain disrepute. It was the era of the occasional poem. The example of Weckherlin and Opitz had been imitated until every nobleman had his poetic hanger-on who furnished verses for all possible occasions, taking his pay in money, food, or favour. His status might be a little better or a little worse than that of a court jester or a mountebank. The *bourgeoisie* aped the gentry, and it came about finally that the price of " poetry " was a regular item in the cost of a well-conducted funeral, wedding, or betrothal. Thus the land was flooded with bad verse, and " poet " came to signify a disreputable pursuer of the thrift that follows fawning. The blight of the time was windy insincerity expressing itself in metrical buncombe. Such conditions naturally beget satire, and satire was forthcoming in abundance. The Baron VON CANITZ (1654–99), a successful diplomat and a gentleman of high personal character, raised his voice in rather tame alexandrines against the literary and social follies of the age, and his reformatory effort was continued in the more trenchant verses of BENJAMIN NEUKIRCH (1665–1729), the father of German literary criticism. In a preface Neukirch castigated the "bunglers who bring in Venus at every wedding, belabour Death at every funeral, and in extreme cases sing to Phyllis a death-song which is often deader than the singer and colder than his mistress." He contended that " only those should attempt poetry whom Nature had chosen thereunto," and only those " who had seen with their own eyes and felt in person that of which they would write." This was quite revolutionary doctrine. In his satire on *Foolish Poets* Neukirch has something of the bitter tang of Juvenal. There is power and there is truth in his picture of the literary *misère*. It is the work of a man who wrote satire not to amuse himself but to ease his mind.

The one poetic genius of the period was the unfortunate JOHANN CHRISTIAN GÜNTHER (1695–1723), who wore himself out with dissipation and remorse at the age of twenty-eight, but not until he had won the compensating guerdon of a poet's immortality. Günther was the son of a narrow but otherwise respectable Silesian doctor who detested the name of poet. His son's early addiction to verse-making led to angry remonstrance, and this to an implacable bitterness which repulsed every advance of filial affection. This was one part of the sad fatality of Günther's life; the other and larger part was his own lack of ethical stability. He was compounded of saint and vagabond. A passionate lover, he could not keep troth, and yet was too little of a worldling to be able to lord it successfully over his own conscience. As a student he led a wild life. His excesses brought him loathing and mental torture, yet he had not the strength to resist the next temptation. His vehement nature chafed under the restrictions of the social code, and he became a wanderer. And so, like a helpless plaything of mood and passion, sinning and sinned against, joying and agonising, he stormed through his brief pilgrimage —unable, as Goethe said of him, to tame himself. This is what is expressed in his best verse, and expressed with a sad sincerity and artistic power nowhere else to be found in contemporary German writers. His verses to Lenore are the best love-poems that any German had written for five hundred years. In Günther we begin to scent the morning air of a better day to come.

To break the evil spell that had come upon German letters in consequence of a false conception of the nature of poetry, Günther's passionate verse, born of a genuine experience, was worth more than volumes of satire and disquisition. But talent that falls much short of genius may sometimes render service by pointing the way to new vistas; and this was the fortune of BARTHOLD HEINRICH BROCKES (1680–1747), a man greatly esteemed in his day as a poet of nature. To the men of the seventeenth century nature had been little more than a sealed book. One finds in Opitz, to be sure, a mild expression of the satisfaction to be had by the weary bookworm in going out of doors; and in Logau a hearty eulogy of country life as contrasted with the multifarious badness of cities and courts. In Father Spe, too, there is honest delight in nature, but it is little more than an echo of the old mediæval delight in spring flowers and singing birds. In the exsufflicate style of Lohenstein and his kind there was of course no room for the love of any common thing whatsoever. As for Brockes, it cannot be said that he came to his apostleship by any sudden flash of insight. After studying law and travelling abroad he settled in Hamburg, his native place, as a gentleman of leisure and a cultivator of the æsthetic amenities. A passion oratorio which met with great success and was set to music by some thirty different composers, including Händel, made him famous; and his renown was still further increased by a translation in alexandrines of Marini's *Strage degli Innocenti*. Then he saw his mission. "Having observed," he said, "that poetry, unless it should have some useful purpose, was only an empty play of words, deserving of no great esteem, I exerted myself to find subjects from which mankind might derive edification along with permissible pleasure." He set about proclaiming the glory of God by writing minute metrical descriptions of His handiwork. The prodigious success of the first volume of his *Earthly Pleasure in God* (1721) fortified him in his pious endeavour, and he went on and on. The *Earthly Pleasure* at last spun itself out to the ominous length of nine volumes.

From our present point of view the verse of Brockes is not so much poetry of nature as a defence and illus-

tration of the thesis that one *ought* to enjoy out-of-door
things, and to take pleasure in very minute observation
of them, because they are the work of an all-wise and
loving Creator. There is no mystery for him, no communing with the unfathomable: everything is good and
beautiful and wisely ordered for man's comfort and
delectation.

> *Mich erquicken,*
> *Mich entzücken,*
> *In der holden Frühlingszeit*
> *Alle Dinge, die ich sehe,*
> *Da ja, wo ich geh' und stehe,*
> *Alles voll der Lieblichkeit.*

Thus sang Brockes at his best. " And eke the lynx is fair
and harmful; he is full of predatory lust, yet he, too, is
nevertheless a useful animal "—thus sang Brockes at his
worst. From this it is a far cry to the nature poetry
of Goethe and the Romanticists; yet Brockes must have
his meed of credit, for he was the first to cultivate intimacy with the works and moods of nature and to describe
them with great minuteness. He begat the generation
of sentimental landscape poets who presently drew the
fire of Lessing's *Laocoön*.

Toward the end of his life Brockes translated Pope's
Essay on Man and Thomson's *Seasons,* but ere these
translations were published another and more important
stream of English influence was coming in by way of
Switzerland. In the year 1721 a number of Swiss scholars under the leadership of JOHANN JAKOB BODMER
(1698–1783) organised a literary society at Zürich and

began to publish a journal. An era of superabundant journalism now set in. The example of Christian Thomas had already been followed here and there, and from this time on the periodicals multiplied with amazing rapidity in all parts of Germany. The most of them, the so-called moral weeklies, were short-lived and intellectually flimsy; but they enlarged the horizon of the people, and gradually popularised literary discussion. Bodmer's magazine, called *Discourses of the Painters,* because the contributors took the names of well-known artists (Rubens, Holbein, etc.), was avowedly patterned after Addison's *Spectator.* In point of literary charm and ripeness of judgment the *Discourses* fell far short of their model, but they introduced the pregnant idea of criticism as an art. By his study of Addison, Bodmer was led naturally to Milton, whose *Paradise Lost* he began to translate into German prose. The translation was published in 1730, and eight years later came a formal defence of Milton's art in a *Critical Disquisition on the Wonderful in Poetry.* This was the proximate cause of the breach with Gottsched, who was now in the height of his glory as literary dictator.

JOHANN CHRISTOPH GOTTSCHED (1700–66) began to lecture on philosophy at the University of Leipzig in 1725. His philosophy was the system of Leibnitz, as reduced to excessive simplicity by Wolff—in other words, a rationalism that left no room in the world for mystery and wonder. He was a man of practical bent and of high patriotic ideals. He saw that the state of the German drama was deplorable, that bad taste was rife in much of the recent literature, and that, in view of the prevalence of dialect in printed books, and of wide-spread uncertainty as to the requirements of the literary standard, there was need of an authoritative treatise on the High German language. It was borne in upon him that he himself was the man to set all these things right. And in part he was. He attacked his problems vigorously, and prosecuted his reforms with tireless energy. As professor, first of poetry and then of logic and metaphysic; as leader of the local German Society; as editor of various journals; as author of textbooks and treatises; as translator and adapter of plays for the Leipzig theatre, he worked always for clearness of thought, regularity of form, and good taste as he understood it. And he had his reward. By 1740 Leipzig was the acknowledged centre of German culture, and Gottsched was its prophet.

What Gottsched understood by good taste, however, was nothing more than strict conformity to rule. He looked on poetry as a child of the understanding, a branch of scholarship. The important elements were moral utility, lucidity, regularity, and rhetorical point. The ancients were, of course, the ultimate source of authority, but he thought the French had understood the ancients best and had followed them most faithfully; wherefore the French practice was to be regarded as canonical. For several years Gottsched maintained cordial relations with the Swiss " painters," notwithstanding their seditious talk about such things as fancy, imagination, passion, the wonderful, the sublime. After all, there was agreement on the fundamentals : namely, that poetry was imitation of nature, having for its purpose the betterment of morals; that Opitz was a very great poet, and that the later

Silesians were to be condemned. But when Bodmer's defence of Milton appeared, it seemed to Gottsched to open the gate for any sort of bizarre and fantastic extravagance. He reviewed the book sharply; there was a sharp reply, and then came rejoinders of increasing bitterness. The feud attracted the attention of all Germany. In time public opinion turned against Gottsched and in favour of the Swiss school. The dictator's name passed into a by-word. He was called the great dunce. It became an accepted dogma that he had been all wrong, his adversaries essentially right.

But the rightness of the Swiss school consisted simply in their theoretic insistence on the value of certain elements in poetry. When it came to applying their principles in imaginative work they proved even more impotent than the Gottschedians, and what came of their efforts was nothing but tedious and insipid didacticism. All his life long Bodmer continued to emit epics, tragedies, comedies, and descriptive and didactic poems, in serene indifference to the fact that no one read them. His best title to fame is really his effort to rouse interest in mediæval German poetry. He published specimens of the minnesingers and of the *Nibelung Lay*. But the time was not ripe for these studies to bear fruit.

To have turned the German mind in the direction of England, and thus to have prepared the way for a new poetry of emotion and sentiment, is the great service of Bodmer and his friends. And yet it is quite thinkable that the influx of English ideas might have come about just the same without him, for other minds were beginning to feel their attraction. Back in 1682 a blank verse translation of *Paradise Lost* had been published at Zerbst, but without drawing attention. Bodmer's prose version and defence did draw attention. In 1720 the first translation of *Robinson Crusoe* appeared, and was so eagerly read that five editions were called for during the year. Then came a perfect flood of imitations, bearing such names as the German Robinson, the Italian Robinson, the French Robinson, the Clerical Robinson, the Medical Robinson, the Saxon, Silesian, Swabian Robinson, and so forth. Within a few years industrious scribes had provided a Robinson for nearly every country in Europe and for the most of the German principalities. As early as 1728 the journals begin to refer to Edward Young, whose *Night Thoughts* and *Conjectures on Original Composition* were destined in time to exert considerable influence. The translations by Brockes from the English have already been referred to. In short, by the middle of the century the names of Milton, Addison, Pope, Thomson, and Young were fairly well known in Germany, and the German mind had been prepared, as well as the English, for Richardson, Bishop Percy, Ossian, and Sterne. But Shakespeare as yet was virtually unknown.

From England came the quickening impulse that made a poet of the young ALBRECHT HALLER (1708–77), the Swiss savant who in time won European fame for his services to physiology, botany, and anatomy. In his early youth Haller was an admirer of Lohenstein, and wrote great quantities of verse—pastorals, tragedies, epics—in the diffuse and inflated style of the Second Silesian School. After taking his degree at Leiden he went to England and there learned to admire the philosophic terseness of Pope. Might not something of the kind be possible in his Swiss German? On returning home he made a tour in the Alps, and presently published (1732) a little volume which he modestly called an *Attempt at Swiss Poems*. Its key-note, as Max Koch observes, is found in a sentence which Haller had recorded in his diary of travel (he wrote his diary and letters in French, his scientific works in Latin) : *Heureux peuple que l'ignorance préserve des maux qui suivent la politesse des villes!* The most important of the *Swiss Poems* is one in forty-eight ten-line stanzas entitled the *Alps,* in which he glorifies the simple and innocent life of the Swiss farmers, describing them as disciples of nature, true sages, happy in their poverty and content-ment, and blest in their freedom from all the luxury, envy and vice of cities. Incidentally, he describes Alpine scenery in some detail, but only as a matter-of-fact set-ting to the simple life he commends, and not at all for the sake of its intrinsic beauty or its power to uplift the soul. His feeling is rather that the Alpine regions are unpleasant and forbidding, a hard place in which to live, but the home, nevertheless, of virtue and wisdom. Hal-ler was not a landscape poet of the school of Thomson, but a philosophic poet of the temper of Pope, only far more devout. The feeling for the romantic beauty and uplifting power of the mountains comes later—with Rousseau, whom Haller detested. But the young Swiss savant was nevertheless a precursor of Rousseau in the attack on civilisation as a process involving corruption of the human heart. In the history of German poetry Haller's importance consists in his having effected a new combination: the combination of emotional warmth, terseness of expression, and philosophic pregnancy.

The most important of the landscape poets who continued the line of Brockes, Haller, and Thomson was EWALD VON KLEIST (1715–59), author of *Spring.* Kleist was a Prussian soldier whose early experience predisposed him to pensive poetising. During his monotonous garrison service at Potsdam, between the two Silesian Wars, he diverted himself with country walks, which gave a basis of reality to his musings on man and nature. He planned a poem on the seasons, intending to call it *Landlust,* that is, *Pleasure of Country Life,* but completed only a part of the first book, which was published in 1749 under the title of *Spring.* The form is the ancient hexameter, preceded by an unstressed syllable. It began, in the first edition:

Receive me, ye hallowèd shades, ye dwellings of sweet emotion,
Ye lofty arches of verdure and darksome slumberous zephyrs.
Who oft for the lonely bard have lifted the veil of the future,
And oft have opened for him the azure gates of Olympus
And shown him heroes and gods,—receive me and fill my being
With sadness and sweet repose !

It was Kleist's purpose to describe the aspects of nature and of country life as they had presented themselves to his eye, but the lyric element of joy in nature as a relief from the madding crowd is by no means lacking. Lessing, who became Kleist's dear friend, thought there was too little of epic recital in proportion to the descriptions. We have his word that if Kleist had lived to revise and complete the poem, he would have supplied an element of narrative and made the " pictures " evolve and follow one another in a natural order.

As to the work of Gottsched and his disciples, there is not very much to be said. The pitiless logic of events doomed him to be made the scapegoat of a discredited order of ideas; but the contempt that was heaped upon him in his later years and in after time did him much injustice. For, after all, the ideas for which he stood were not so bad. One cannot read much in the literature of the preceding epoch without coming to the conclusion that a stout plea for good taste, lucidity, and reasonableness was neither superfluous nor untimely. Gottsched made the plea, and made it with much effectiveness. Had he never written a verse, or meddled with the theory of poetry, or tried to legislate for poets, he would still be entitled to an honourable place in the history of German scholarship and the German drama. It is true that Lessing once expressed the opinion, in the ardour of reform, that it would have been better for the German drama if Gottsched had never concerned himself with it at all. But this was going a little too far. Gottsched found the drama in the form of a vulgar show completely dissevered from the intellectual life of the nation. For a hundred years no real progress had been made in the histrionic art, unless it be that women had come to be employed for the parts of women. The strolling companies of players were to a great extent social pariahs, without artistic ideals. The plays were generally cobbled together by the actors, the parts were largely extemporised; while the clown, with his irrelevant antics

15

and indecencies, was always the central attraction. It was Gottsched, more than any one else, who put an end to such conditions and elevated the drama into a form of art which could be taken seriously by intelligent people. By his co-operation with the Neuber company at Leipzig, by interesting himself in the plays that were to be given and in the acting of them, by providing a repertory of translations and adaptations, he gave the Germans their first theatre worthy of the name. The dramatic art could now develop hand in hand with the histrionic. To have done this is a work of such far-reaching importance that Clio can afford to pardon Gottsched for his pedantic insistence on the French rules, and for having written a *Cato* which is " faultily faultless, icily regular, splendidly null."

In the year 1745 a group of ambitious young writers who had been in the main friendly to Gottsched, but had grown weary of his acrimonious controversy with the Swiss school, united in issuing the *Bremen Contributions*. It was so called because the publisher was a Bremen bookseller; the real home of the enterprise was Leipzig. The most important contributors, if we have regard to later distinction in letters, were Elias Schlegel, a dramatist of considerable talent; Ebert, religious poet and translator of Young; Cramer, author of *Spiritual Odes and Songs;* Zachariæ, humourist; Rabener, satirist; Gellert, fabulist; and lastly, Klopstock. This was, for the time, a somewhat remarkable galaxy of talent; and the new journal, which excluded all polemic, invited original productions and was very carefully edited, soon became a power in the land. At least it won a prestige

such as no preceding magazine had enjoyed. Nevertheless, it aimed at nothing higher or deeper than correctness
of form, combined with clearness and good logic. The
doctrine that the final purpose of poetry is the betterment of morals was fully accepted, and the fable, as a
type at once moral and fanciful, was in high favour. The
pattern of the group was Hagedorn, whose manner,
forms, and choice of subjects were imitated.

FRIEDRICH HAGEDORN (1708–54) is best characterised as the antipode of Haller. In his youth he, too,
sojourned for a while in England, acquiring a perfect
mastery of the language. In 1732 he settled in Hamburg
as secretary of the " English Court," an old commercial
company; and in this comfortable berth he spent the
remainder of his days. His temperament inclined him
to an easy-going life, to convivial pleasure, and a *carpe
diem* philosophy. His favourite author was Horace.
While Haller is grave and thoughtful to the point of
heaviness, Hagedorn is light, cheerful, fluent. He makes
no great demand on intellect or emotions, but is still
readable for his good sense, the pleasant flow of his verse,
his graceful turns of expression. His specialty was the
fable, a form in which he is hardly inferior to Gellert.
But he also wrote moral and satiric tales, anacreontics,
odes, epistles, epigrams. He sang of love and friendship
and wine and kisses; of roses and nymphs and shepherdesses; of the excellence of moderation. But his songs
have as little of spontaneity as his satire has of sting.

Except Klopstock, the most important member of the
group that wrote for the *Bremer Beiträge* was CHRIS-
TIAN FÜRCHTEGOTT GELLERT (1715–69). The son of

a Saxon clergyman and always worthy of his pious
baptismal names, he spent the last quarter-century of
his life in the service of the University of Leipzig, lec-
turing mostly on poetry and rhetoric. Though frail of
body and subject to hypochondria, he achieved remarkable success as a writer, especially with his metrical fables
and tales. The Æsopian fable was just then in high
favour and taken very seriously. Even Lessing thought
it worth while to write a disquisition on the fable, and
to illustrate his theory with original specimens, some in
prose, some in verse. But all the other fabulists were
eclipsed in public favour by Gellert, whose vogue was
comparable to that of La Fontaine in France. By the
clarity of his style, the smoothness of his verse, and the
unimpeachableness of his common sense, he quite won
the hearts of a generation which held everywhere—in
Zürich as in Leipzig—that the final purpose of poetry
is to improve morals. His *Fables and Tales* (1746–48)
were reprinted in numberless editions, made their publisher rich, and remained for several decades the popular
ideal of edifying literature. Aside from these, Gellert
wrote several light comedies of very thin substance, and
led the procession of the imitators of Richardson, of
whom he had a very high opinion. In a metrical eulogy
he extolled "the Briton Richardson" as the "creative
spirit who had taught us to feel the charm of virtue";
whose works were at once "nature, taste, and religion";
who was "more immortal than Homer." Gellert's *Swedish Countess* (1747–48) is an attempt at moral family
fiction in the vein of Richardson. The heroine, with her
obtrusive virtuousness and religiosity, her moralising and

sentimentalising, is a person of very much the same sort
as Pamela and Clarissa.   On the other hand, the story
and the technic have little suggestion of Richardson.[1]
The German tale is a complicated tissue of strange adventures and incredible happenings—illicit connections,
double marriages, incest, and other crimes—which show
that Gellert was quite under the spell of the older romances and very far from supposing that reality could
be made interesting.

---

[1] The history of Richardson's influence in Germany is ably
treated by Erich Schmidt, *Richardson, Rousseau, and Goethe*,
Leipzig, 1875.

CHAPTER XII

As was implied at the beginning of the last chapter, the dawn of the great era in German literature is coincident with the rise of Prussia as a military world-power. The coincidence is not accidental, though it is no doubt possible to make too much of it. Of the six most eminent writers of the century, Wieland and Schiller were Swabians, and Goethe was of the imperial city of Frankfort. Herder and Klopstock were indeed born on Prussian soil, but they did not long remain Prussian subjects. None of the five concerned himself to any great extent with contemporary politics, and what they wrote might seemingly have been written if Friedrich the Great had never fought the Second Silesian War, or had been defeated. It was only Lessing who was greatly and directly affected by the struggle. Still, there is no room for doubt as to the fundamental rightness of Goethe's saying that it was the Seven Years' War which first brought real import into German literature. It caused an emotional awakening—a storm of anxiety, grief, pride, and exultation. Hearts were made to beat faster, while tongue and pen could occupy themselves with more exciting matters than the literary squabbles of the preceding decades. How thin and unreal must the old issues have seemed to a people that had lately heard the news of Rossbach!

Moreover, the war gave a powerful impulse to national sentiment. Although the King of Prussia warred in part against men who spoke the German language, and although a united Germany under Prussian leadership was not as yet even dreamed of, Friedrich II became something like a national hero. For he had warred also against France and Russia, and had beaten them in hard-fought battles. He was felt to be the representative of a new Germany of the North, which must henceforth be reckoned with by the great powers. His pluck and prowess stirred the blood even of South Germans who could not approve his policy or sympathise with his ambition. They felt that, after all, he had invested the German name with a fresh lustre and dignity. All this tended, in the domain of letters, to increase the nascent impatience of French leading-strings, and to prepare the way for a generation of writers who should be aggressively, enthusiastically German.

Even before the outbreak of the Seven Years' War a phase of this militant Teutonism is seen in the young FRIEDRICH GOTTLIEB KLOPSTOCK (1724–1803). While yet a lad, and before leaving the preparatory school at Pforta, Klopstock became deeply interested in epic poetry. He read *Paradise Lost* in Bodmer's prose, and his devout and patriotic soul was grieved that his native land had no such great religious epic. Might not the need be supplied? He chose the Redemption for his theme, but the question of form was difficult. There was no helpful tradition. The form most in vogue for a long poem of

any kind was the alexandrine; but Klopstock, thoroughly
schooled in the Greek and Roman poets, soon convinced
himself that rhyme was an ignoble modern jingle, un-
worthy the holy muse of Zion. Blank verse had no
standing. At last he began in prose, while studying
theology at Jena, but presently decided in favour of the
ancient dactylic hexameter. In 1746 he went to Leipzig,
where he became acquainted with certain members of the
coterie who were behind the *Bremer Beiträge*. He began
to contribute odes of friendship in rhymeless antique
metres, and ere long was induced to publish the beginning of his epic. The first three cantos appeared in
1748 and made a prodigious sensation. The name of
Klopstock became the symbol of a new order of poetry
and a new conception of the poet's calling.

The commotion caused by Klopstock in literary circles
can only be understood, at this distance in time, by comparing him with the facile rhymesters who preceded him.
Take, for example, Hagedorn, the most eminent and beloved of them all—Hagedorn, with his suave Epicurean-
ism, and his placid ditties of wine and kisses and song
and jest. He begins an *Ode to Poesy* very significantly
with the line:

O playmate of my idle hours!

In the wake of Hagedorn came Gleim (1719–1803), and
after him a whole flock of anacreontic poets, babbling
of Bacchus and Amor, rose-crowned heads, bibulous joys,
and endless osculation. They were by no means frivolous men, but they put on the mask of frivolity by way
of asserting their independence. They regarded poetry

as a matter of graceful feigning, or a trick of dressing up common sense in some kind of pleasant allegory, and presenting it in smooth and lucid verse. This is the whole art of Gellert, who was revered by multitudes as the greatest poet and most helpful moralist of his day.

In contrast with all this, Klopstock appeared as a consecrated singer, completely possessed and permeated by the sacred majesty of his theme. Listen to his invocation:

But, O Deed which alone on high the Allmerciful knoweth,
Dareth Poesy near even thee from her shadowy distance?
Hallow her, O my Creator, before whom I here bow in worship,
Guide her to me, thy disciple, in all her glorified beauty,
Full of immortal power and full of divine inspiration.
Give her thy fire, O Thou who seest the depths of the Godhead,
Thou who hast fashioned man of the dust and made him thy Temple.
Pure be the heart! Thus may I, albeit with only the trembling
Voice of a mortal, yet dare to sing the blessed Redeemer,
Treading the awful path alone with venial stumbling.

For the author of these lines poetry was evidently not the playmate of idle hours, but the whole man, energised for a supreme effort. The sonorous dignity of his verse, his profound seriousness, the daring sweep of his imagination, the fervour of his religious feeling, his pregnant, thought-compelling diction, had the effect of a revelation from higher spheres. There was, of course, adverse criticism, but the aspiring youth of Germany turned to Klopstock as the coming man.

And his odes reinforced the impression of lofty seriousness made by the opening cantos of the *Messiah.*

Friendship, love, tears, patriotism, poetic ambition, were here treated as high and holy matters, fit to engage, like religion, the deepest emotions of the soul. He addressed his friends of the *Bremer Beiträge*—Ebert, Cramer, Giseke, and other quite ordinary folk—in perfervid Alcaic strophes bristling with strange mythologic names which were supposed to be ancient German, but were really a mixture of Celtic and Old Norse. The public began to hear of Iduna and Braga and the fountain of Mimer, and of ancient bards inhabiting the German forests and emitting " lawless songs " of intense emotion. In his imagination Klopstock draped himself and his friends in the costume of these bards, who had drawn their inspiration from their own souls, from nature and the fatherland, from ethnic tradition and the elemental feelings of love and friendship. Insensibly this dream of the bards blended with the intoxication of a new hope for German poetry—a hope to be realised by a return to the old ways and the old sources.

In 1751 Klopstock went to reside in Copenhagen as a pensioner of the Danish government. He had no duties to perform in return for his stipend, except to complete his great poem for the benefit of mankind. Such an unprecedented honour bestowed on a German poet by a foreign king, at a time when Friedrich of Prussia took not the slightest interest in German letters, increased the prestige of the *Messiah* and its author. But as the poem advanced slowly to completion, and new instalments were published from time to time, the interest fell off; and when the last of the twenty cantos appeared, in 1773, there was no excitement over them. Klopstock was still a name to conjure with in certain quarters, but more for what he represented as a lyric poet than for the pleasure of reading his supernal epic.

To-day it is almost impossible to read it at all as a whole. There are noble passages that fascinate in their own way—not at all the way of Vergil or Milton—but they are not numerous enough to sustain one through the twenty thousand lines of a narrative which in the main lacks objective human interest. Klopstock's hero is not the Jesus of the synoptic gospels, but the Messiah of theological tradition—a conception with which poets have always found it difficult to operate. The attempt to blend the anthropomorphism of the primitive church with metaphysic and spiritual religion results in baffling the reason without satisfying the imagination. Klopstock's vague and vasty heaven is quite unthinkable, while his angels and seraphs and thrones and choiring cherubim, who have nothing to do but express ecstatic emotions, soon become wearisome. The devils in hell are somewhat more interesting, but they too are only conduits of emotion, for one knows that their rage against Omnipotence is foredoomed to futility. As for the legion of human or quasi-human beings that are introduced, they feel intensely and express themselves in noble language, but they are mere voices; they have no individuality, they do nothing of importance, and their feelings reduce to a few simple types. The consequence is an intolerable monotony. Withal the *Messiah* is very prolix. The narrative begins just before the arrest and betrayal of Jesus, and ends with the ascension. The crucifixion is over in the tenth canto. Such a scheme involved the overloading of the poem with a great mass of details which are not vitally related to the main argument, and tend rather to obscure and confuse it. The simple pathos of the laconic gospel story makes a much more powerful appeal to the devout imagination.

As a lyric poet Klopstock was nobly endowed, though he lacked the qualities that make for a lasting popularity. His odes, which are on the whole his best title to fame, are the expression of sincere feeling and pregnant thought. If they now seem artificial it is partly due to his exotic forms. In substituting the metres of Horace for the rhyme which he regarded as ignoble, Klopstock broke with all the traditions of German verse, and offered something strange and difficult. It became necessary to " scan " his effusions by the aid of a metrical scheme. To the unlearned, whose ideas of lyric poetry were associated with song, the unsingable odes of Klopstock could hardly seem anything more than a curiously artificial kind of prose. His Alcaics and Sapphics made no music in the heart. One of the best of his short poems is the *Ode to Fanny*, such being the name of a young woman whose rejection of his youthful love threw him back on the melancholy hope of a union in heaven. But what can the lady herself, or the other women who were now beginning to form a very important part of the literary public, have made of such verses as these:

> *When thou shalt stand there, wakened in loveliness,*
> *Then I shall join thee, lingering only till*
> *A seraph takes me by the hand and*
> *Leads me away to thee, immortal.*

Then shall thy brother, fondly embraced by me,
Come to thee, too, the while I tearfully—
  O happy tears of the life eternal—
    Call thee by name and stand beside thee.

And then, too, Klopstock's favourite subject-matter soon fell into a sort of disrepute. His own enthusiasm for the ancient Germans, as he imagined them—a rugged, emotional, self-sufficing people, passionately fond of poetry—was perfectly genuine. But his style was taken up by imitators for whom the exploitation of the bardic age was simply the newest fashion, and they made the fashion ridiculous. A new sentimentalism, which held with the young Goethe that feeling is everything, possessed itself of Klopstock's apparatus and used it for an emotional debauch. When the reaction came, and especially after plodding scholarship had shown that Klopstock's idea of the ancient Germans was quite unhistoric, it was patent to every one that the " bardic roar " which he had started was only an odd aberration of taste. With the highest of motives he had sought to regenerate German poetry by a return to ancient national sources of inspiration; but in so doing he had pictured a past that was very largely spurious, and had employed forms that were altogether un-German.

Aside from his odes and his epic, Klopstock wrote three biblical dramas: the *Death of Adam* (1757) in prose, *Solomon* (1764) and *David* (1772) in blank verse. The first attracted considerable attention in France (Goedeke chronicles no less than eight French translations and imitations), and was done into Danish,

Italian, and English. It is, however, without dramatic
life. And the same may be said of the other two, which
are interesting chiefly as early experiments in the metre
which was to prevail in the coming classical drama.
Much more important historically are the three *Bardiete*,
as they were called, on account of their "bardic"
choruses: *Hermann's Battle* (1769), *Hermann and the
Princes* (1784), and *Hermann's Death* (1787). Although professedly written for the stage, they are dramatically impossible, being little more than connected
gusts of emotion. The language is a tense and pregnant prose, into which Klopstock threw all the ardour
of his love for the ancient fatherland. What is represented is very unreal, even unhuman; but some of the
lyric passages, if one can but make his peace with their
exotic form, are superb in their intensity and rugged
force. To be sure, it was a spurious mythology with
which Klopstock undertook to displace the Greek and
Roman gods; but his purpose of drawing attention to
Germanic antiquity, asserting its value, and making it
available for the higher poetry, was altogether laudable.
His mistakes were soon corrected, but his literary patriotism bore abundant fruit in the time to come.

All his life long Klopstock took himself very seriously; so seriously, indeed, that he sometimes made himself the target of gentle derision. But his name is justly
venerated in Germany, albeit his works are now but little read. It was he who rescued German poetry from
prettiness, frivolity, and shallow intellectualism, and
made it the energetic expression of intense and elemental
feeling. But for him it might never have occurred to the

young author of *Götz von Berlichingen* to say that what makes a poet is a heart completely filled with one emotion. And what is no less important in literary history, he invested the name and calling of the poet with a new lustre. Before him, to be a poet was to know the rules of metrical composition; after him, it was to possess a mysterious and supremely enviable gift called genius.

For the Klopstockians man at his best was a creature consisting of sublimated feelings. They made him a seraphic spirit, a rapturous friend, a fervid patriot, as the case might be; but of his sensuality and his practical intelligence they took little account. A reaction against this excessive emotionalism, with its imperfect and distorted account of human nature, was inevitable. The sensual man presently found a champion in CHRISTOPH MARTIN WIELAND (1733–1813), though not till after he, too, had passed through a stage of fervid religiosity.

Wieland was a Swabian, born near Biberach. As the diligent pupil of a pietist school, in which rather too much was made of religion, he suffered acutely from doubt. At the age of seventeen he fell in love Platonically with his cousin, Sophie von Gutermann (afterward Frau von Laroche). While walking with her of a Sunday afternoon, after hearing his father preach on the text, God is love, he suddenly conceived the idea of a philosophic poem on the *Nature of Things*—a poem that should refute Lucretius and all the false philosophers, and exhibit the world as the perfect work of a loving God. The plan was quickly executed, and the poem, in six books of alexandrine verse, was published in 1751. Then came—all in 1752—a descriptive poem called

Spring, a series of twelve *Moral Letters in Verse,* an *Art of Love,* in opposition to Ovid, and a collection of seven poetic tales, mostly with an Oriental setting. All these youthful productions are characterised by a supernal conception of virtue and love, and a facile verbosity of style. Love is glorified as a Platonic affinity of beautiful souls. The object of poetry is to recommend virtue and innocence. On the other hand, amid all the gushing sentimentalism of adolescence there appears a serious effort to treat the wisdom of the sages as something to live by; in other words, to arrive at a practical philosophy of life. In his early youth, Wieland's favourite author was Xenophon, his ideal of character, Socrates.

In 1752, having finished his university studies at Tübingen, Wieland went to live with Bodmer, who had lately had Klopstock for a guest, and had fallen out with him because that seraphic singer evinced an unseraphic fondness for young persons of the female sex. Wieland, at this time himself a very ardent Klopstockian, made no such mistake. For two years he shared Bodmer's narrow, desiccated life, living in his house, taking part in his English studies, poetising in the biblical Bodmerian vein. The fruits of this pious intercourse were a hexameter poem, the *Trial of Abraham,* a series of nine *Letters of the Dead to Surviving Friends,* also in hexameter, and a number of lesser things in the way of prayers, odes, and hymns. A little later came two publications in prose: *Sympathies,* wherein the ideally beautiful soul was made to pour out its angelic emotions in communion with a kindred spirit, and *Feelings of a Christian,* a collection of high-keyed fantasies which were afterward reprinted under the name of *Psalms*. Lessing criticised them rather sharply as not being a sincere expression of religious emotion, but only brain-spun extravagances of the imagination. The criticism is just, but needs some explanation; the more as it applies with equal force to the most of Wieland's early work. His mind was naturally chaste, he was an eager student of Plato, and he associated mainly with pious folk who looked on the sexual instinct as a lure of the devil. And thus the amiable sentimentalism of youth, nourished by the reading of Young's *Night Thoughts* and Richardson's novels, combined with Platonic idealism and with vague notions of a pre-established harmony to furnish him with a peculiar style, which may best be described as *Schwärmerei* of the imagination. He had not yet found the middle way between seraphic dreams and common sensualism. But with all their sublimated sentiment, which makes them seem hollow to a more matter-of-fact age, the literary effectiveness of some of these early writings is unmistakable. One is not surprised that Wieland soon began to find translators, and became, while yet a young man, a literary personage of international repute. What he needed was a larger contact with human nature, and this soon fell to his lot. After leaving the house of Bodmer he remained five years more in Switzerland, and a change in his general attitude toward life was already setting in when he was called back to his native Biberach as town councillor.

At Biberach, or rather at the near-by castle of Warthausen, Wieland found his quondam sweetheart as the wife of Frank Laroche, who was employed as overseer

16

of the estates of Count Stadion. This gentleman was an elderly statesman who had lately retired from the service of the Elector of Mainz and taken up his abode at Castle Warthausen. Intellectually Stadion was in the fullest sympathy with the Age of Reason. His favourite writers were the French and English deists. In this circle, where the tone was that of society in the great world, where common-sense was held in high esteem, and all imaginative fervours had to run the gauntlet of sceptical criticism and raillery, Wieland was soon at home. He browsed freely in the Count's well-stocked library, and his philosophy of life rapidly took on the colour of his new associations.

By way of Voltaire, curiously enough, he was led to Shakespeare, and set about translating him. For this task he was but poorly equipped. His knowledge of Elizabethan English was imperfect, the theatre was almost a sealed book to him, and he had very little dramatic insight. It is true that he had adapted from Nicholas Rowe and published under his own name a piously solemn tragedy *Lady Jane Gray;* but this had been a religious more than a dramatic enterprise. Worst of all, he had no adequate conception of Shakespeare's genius, but looked at him through the distorting medium of contemporary French criticism. In translating he not only converted verse into prose, which was quite pardonable, but he omitted, transposed, altered, and padded, until the result was often mere travesty. Nevertheless, his translation of twenty-two plays, which appeared between 1762 and 1766, served a useful purpose in connection with the dawn of Shakespeare on Germany.

His next undertaking, the prose tale *Don Sylvio von Rosalva,* was a sort of pendant to *Don Quixote.* Wieland's hero, like him of La Mancha, is a Spanish knight who suffers from an imaginative obsession, due to his reading, which causes him to move about in a world unrealised. The obsession is an obstinate belief in fairies, coupled with a proneness to find them everywhere. The book is mostly fantastic fooling. The inventions are rather puerile, the humour has a suggestion of being pumped up from a scant supply, and one at least of the interwoven stories is rather indecent. On the other hand, the style, with its light touch, its perfect lucidity, its gracefully turned periods, and its badinage of the *bel esprit,* is something quite new in German letters. One has a feeling that when the instrument shall be turned to a somewhat worthier purpose, Germany will have its first great prose stylist.

It was turned to a weightier and worthier purpose in *Agathon* (1766), the first of the German cultural romances. The hero is a Greek of the time of Pericles, who grows up among the priests and priestesses of Delphi, becoming an idealist and a dreamer of fine dreams. With a chaste maid named Psyche, who afterward turns out to be his sister, he has an ecstatic experience of Platonic love. Then he goes to Athens, takes a hand in politics, is banished, captured by pirates and sold into slavery at Smyrna. His purchaser is a middle-aged sophist Hippias, who tries to indoctrinate him with sensualistic philosophy. Agathon is proof against the arguments of Hippias, but not against the charms of the lovely hetæra Danaë. When he learns, however, that he

is not the first of her lovers, he flees in disgust to Syra-
cuse, where he becomes the chief adviser of the tyrant
Dionysius. A new turn of Fortune's wheel drives him to
Tarentum, where he finds Danaë and learns that she has
turned virtuous. So lovely is her character that she con-
verts him to her views. Finally he becomes acquainted
with the sage Archytas, who expounds to him the true
(eighteenth century) philosophy of life. The main
points are that materialism is false and dangerous; that
man needs a religion; that enlightenment is the one sure
hope of better times and better men; that all *Schwärmerei*
of the imagination is a disease, and that " the best prophy-
lactic against this disease is the performance of our duties
in civil and domestic life."

Wieland had now found his mission: to deal indirectly with the problems of modern culture, while nominally portraying the life of Ancient Greece, the Orient, or
the Middle Ages. In discoursing of Ancient Greece,
with its conflicting systems of philosophy, its hetærism,
and its love of sensuous beauty; or in laying his scene in
the far-away lands of Oriental and mediæval romance,
he was able to treat of sexual love with a frankness that
might have been offensive but for the indirectness of his
method. Indeed, some were shocked as it was, imagin-
ing that the seraphic Wieland of 1750–60 had turned
satyr. But this was to misconstrue him. If the reaction
against his youthful *Schwärmerei* sometimes carried him
too far in the direction of frivolity and lubricity, he at any
rate never ceased to be an honest searcher after wisdom.
The idea that lay nearest his heart in the second period of
his career, aside from the general inculcation of the social

ideals of the Age of Reason, was that sexual love, which he had now come to look on as a part of nature's wise order, must be saved from animalism by the sense of beauty. This is the burden of the poem *Musarion* (1768), a little masterpiece of sensuous colour and graceful persiflage. Musarion is a fair and voluptuous, yet wise and temperate hetæra, who takes the splenetic Phanias under her tutelage and teaches him the art of love as a philosophy of the graces. The substance of her doctrine is contained in the lines:

> *Das Schöne kann allein*
> *Der Gegenstand von unsrer Liebe sein;*
> *Die grosse Kunst ist nur, vom Stoff es abzuscheiden.*
> *Der Weise fühlt. Dies bleibt ihm stets gemein*
> *Mit allen andern Erdensöhnen;*
> *Doch diese stürzen sich, vom körperlichen Schönen*
> *Geblendet, in den Schlamm der Sinnlichkeit hinein,*
> *Indessen wir daran, als einen Wiederschein,*
> *Ins Urbild selbst zu schauen uns gewöhnen.*[1]

Wieland's facility with the pen, notwithstanding his laborious filing, was phenomenal. In the one year, 1770, he published a poem in six books, called the *Graces,* a good-sized volume of *Dialogues of Diogenes of Sinope,* and two volumes in the rambling, whimsical style of Sterne, these last directed more particularly against Rous-

---

[1] In English prose : The Beautiful alone can be the object of our love. The great art is simply to separate it. from matter. The sage feels. This he always has in common with the other sons of earth : but while they, dazzled by corporeal beauty, plunge into the mire of sensuality, we accustom ourselves to see in it, like a reflection, the prototype itself.

seau and his views of the state of nature. The next year
brought the *New Amadis*, a comic poem in eighteen cantos. It goes without saying that books produced so rapidly could not contain much meat. Nevertheless, they
were well written and entertaining, and they presented
the reigning philosophy of enlightenment with just the
spice of cynicism needed to captivate a too self-compla-
cent generation. The result was that the classes which
had previously read nothing but French books were to a
great extent won over by Wieland for German literature.
It is significant that his *Agathon*, his *Musarion*, his *Dialogues of Diogenes*, and his *Graces* were all promptly
translated into French.

The publication of the *Golden Mirror*, in 1772,
proved a turning point in Wieland's life, since it led to
his settlement in Weimar. The book is a serio-fantastic
affair, with an Oriental setting suggested by the *Arabian
Nights*. It purports to be a history of the extinct dynasty
of Sheshian, prepared by wise men for the entertainment
and instruction of the Hindu prince Gebal. The fiction
is that every night, after he has gone to bed, the sultana
Nourmahal reads to him from the history until he yawns
three times. The sage Danishmend and a girl called
Mirza attend the readings and have their say with the
others. Such a setting made an opportunity for all sorts
of comment on kingship and statecraft. It was a favourite idea of the age that the happiness of a people depends
mainly on the wisdom and goodness of its ruler : hence
the keen interest taken in the education of princes. Wieland's contribution to the subject attracted the attention
of the dowager Duchess Amalia, of Weimar, and sug-

gested to her that he would be a desirable tutor for her son Karl August, then a boy of fifteen. Her offer was accepted, and when the young prince succeeded to his dukedom three years later, he took care to retain Wieland at Weimar—the first of the group that was to render the little Thuringian city for ever illustrious.

Wieland's tergiversation and his pronounced sympathy for foreign ideas drew upon him the hatred of certain devout and patriotic youth who revered the name of Klopstock. In 1772 a number of them who were students at Göttingen formed a society for the cultivation of poetry, friendship, manly virtue, and love of country, in what they supposed to be the genuine style of the ancient forefathers. Their own usual name for the sodality was the Grove (*der Hain*), but in after years it came to be known as the *Hainbund*, or Sylvan League. The leaders were CHRISTIAN HEINRICH BOIE (1744–1806), who had lately founded the Göttingen *Musenalmanach* on the model of a French *Almanac des Muses*; JOHANN HEINRICH VOSS (1751–1826), to whom Boie soon transferred the editorship of his poetic annual; the melancholy LUDWIG HÖLTY (1748–76), and the two Counts STOLBERG (CHRISTIAN, 1748–1821, and LEOPOLD, 1750–1819). A letter of Voss, afterward well known by his idyls and his translation of Homer, describes a meeting which took place July 2, 1773:

" Above there was a vacant arm-chair for Klopstock; it had his complete works on it, and was decorated with roses and gilliflowers. Under the chair lay Wieland's *Idris* torn to shreds. Cramer now read aloud from the *Songs of Triumph*, and Hahn a few odes of Klopstock that had reference to Germany. The pipe-lighters were made of Wieland's writings. Boie, who does not smoke, was obliged to light one with the rest and stamp on the torn *Idris*. Afterward we drank in Rhenish to the health of Klopstock, to the memory of Luther and Hermann, then to the health of Ebert, Goethe (probably you do not know Goethe yet), Herder, and others. Klopstock's ode *Rheinwein* and some others were read aloud. Now the talk waxed warm. With hats on our heads we spoke of freedom, Germany, virtue, and song, and you can imagine how. Then we ate, drank punch, and finally burned Wieland's *Idris* and his picture."

It is patent from this description that the youthful leaguers were not lacking in enthusiasm for the regeneration of their country. They proposed, as one of them phrased it, to "stem the torrent of vice and slavery." And, indeed, while they soon dispersed and went their separate ways, with waning admiration for Klopstock, they did actually further in some degree, by the poems they contributed to the Göttingen *Musenalmanach*, the cause they had at heart. They did not fully share their hero's antipathy to rhyme. While they turned out enough and more than enough rhymeless odes in the Klopstockian style, they also cultivated more popular forms suggested by German folk-lore or by such glimpses of the minnesong as were then obtainable. Hölty wrote several ballads, as well as simple and singable songs of love, friendship, nature, and the fatherland. Count Friedrich Stolberg glorified Freedom in fervid stentorian odes and dithyrambs, but he also sang of mediæval knights and of a German lad who demands a sword that he may die for his country and be worthy of the fathers. Both Hölty and Stolberg are in a way precursors of romanticism. Voss, on the other hand, made a specialty of the idyl, a genre in which the Swiss writer SALOMON GESSNER (1730–88) had lately achieved a more than national renown. The prose idyls of Gessner, with his vague Arcadian landscape, his tender shepherds and shepherdesses, and his sentimental pictures of golden innocence, appealed strongly to the rococo age, which was far enough from caring about actual shepherds or any other humble folk as they really were. But Voss brought the idyl down from the clouds by depicting scenes and characters from the Low German life that he shared as a schoolmaster at Eutin. His usual form is the hexameter, and he sometimes uses dialect to increase the effect of realism. He was not an inspired poet, but his work, with that of his Göttingen confreres, is historically important because of its self-reliant, home-staying Teutonism.

This spirit was now working in many minds and drawing strength from three English books that had lately been published. Young's *Conjectures on Original Composition*, published in 1759 and twice translated within a year, precipitated a wholesome discussion of genius *versus* imitation; Macpherson's *Ossian* (1762–65) seemed to reveal a new national poet of peculiar and fascinating type, while Percy's *Reliques* (1765) brought welcome proof that the poetic gift was not a matter of learning and refinement. The old English or Scottish ballad, with its vigour and heartiness, its traditionary folk-lore, its frequent appeal to the sense of mystery, began to seem a far finer thing than the fashionable effusions of wit and sentiment.

Among the men who caught the new infection was GOTTFRIED AUGUST BÜRGER (1747–94), a Göttingen poet, but not of the League. In his youth he nearly made shipwreck of his life by dissipation; the best years of his manhood were darkened by sin and sorrow and disgrace, and his end was pathetically sad. But while ethically unstable and doomed to a life of suffering, he understood the language of passion and had a keen sense of certain long-neglected poetic values. This fitted him to be a harbinger of the coming " renascence of wonder." His weird and haunting *Lenore* (1774) opened a new era in ballad poetry. The spookiness and horror which were here woven into a tale of the time of Friedrich the Great had been common enough in the folksongs of the fifteenth and sixteenth centuries, but the old ballads had all been forgotten in the age of enlightenment and gallantry. No one knew of their existence. Thus Bürger's eerie ballad, with its perfect verse-craft, its dramatic vividness, and its onomatopœic

> *Und hurre hurre, hop hop hop!*
> *Gings fort im sausenden Galopp,*

describing the midnight ride of the Bride of Death, came as a revelation of new and strange possibilities. Bürger never afterward achieved anything quite so good as *Lenore*, though many a stirring song and lusty ballad, and some admirable sonnets, came from his pen. His average merit is high, but he was capable of dropping into repulsive vulgarity.

CHAPTER XIII

LESSING AND HERDER

GOTTHOLD EPHRAIM LESSING (1729–81) is the first German example of a man of letters in the grand style. Of the poet's peculiar gift he had, as he himself clearly perceived and frankly admitted, but a small share. He belongs to the knights of intellect, to the order of Erasmus and Voltaire. He wrote a great verse drama, but its greatness does not reside in its poetic quality. In an age of emotional expansion and effervescence he kept his head. His learning was vast, but in early life he discovered the danger of pedantry, and thereafter took care to guard against it. He held his scholarship in strict subjection to the Man Thinking. Whatever subject he took up he illuminated, if he did not always convince. The fine independence of his mind and his life is in itself a precious tradition; his very character a sort of classic.

The earliest writings of Lessing, consisting of prose comedies, epigrams, fables, anacreontics, and other poetic trifles in the reigning Saxon manner, contain but little that foretells the coming man. Born at Kamenz and schooled at Meissen, he entered the University of Leipzig in the fall of 1746, ostensibly to study theology. Like Klopstock he had come from school well stuffed with

Latin and Greek, and ambitious of literary distinction;
but unlike him he had not hitched his wagon to any particular star. All the possibilities were open. In Leipzig
he presently discovered, to quote his own words, that
" books might make him learned, but could never make
him a man." He was appalled at his own awkwardness
and ignorance of social forms. So he took up riding and
fencing, and in other ways set about acquiring the style
of a Saxon gentleman. By his cousin Mylius, a talented
freethinker who was earning a precarious living by
means of miscellaneous journalism, he was introduced to
Madam Neuber and her Thespians. Soon he was at
home before the scenes and behind. While at school in
Meissen he had written a comedy wherein a conceited
young pedant was made ridiculous. He now revised it,
and early in the year 1748 the *Young Scholar* was put
on the boards with success. The much-experienced
Neuber, whose word was just then weighty in matters
theatrical, spoke of its author as the German Molière.

This was enough, provisionally, for a youth of nineteen to steer his course by. Lessing's mind now began
to teem with dramatic projects, and during the next two
years four of them were carried to completion; namely,
the *Misogynist*, the *Old Maid*, the *Jews*, and the *Free-
thinker*. Taken as a group, they belong to an era that
was closing. The characters, situations, intrigues, and
technic were derived by Lessing in the main from his
reading of the French *Théâtre Italien*, Regnard, Mari-
vaux, Destouches, and Holberg. Curiously enough, the
influence of Molière is hardly discernible. Everything
smacks of a conventional and borrowed art. Important

characters bear such alien surnames as Damis, Chrysander, Valer (Valerius), Adrast, Theophan, Lelio, Wumshäter (Woman-hater). There is always a *fille d'intrigue* called Lisette. The distinguishing merit of the plays is their lively, close-knit dialogue. In two of them a serious purpose is discernible: in the *Freethinker* to satirise the fanatic enemies of religion, in the *Jews* to plead for a more tolerant attitude of public opinion toward the sons of Israel.

In 1748, the Neuber company having disbanded, Lessing migrated to Berlin to try his fortune, with his friend Mylius, as journalist and literary free lance. During the next few years he busied himself mainly with studies in classical philology and modern literature, more especially with the history and theory of the drama. His reading took a wide range in Greek, Latin, Italian, Spanish, French, and English. As the friend and pupil of Voltaire's secretary, Richier de Louvain, he came into personal relations with the distinguished Frenchman, who had not yet quarrelled with his royal host at Berlin, and was regarded in court circles as the greatest man of the age. Lessing admired Voltaire greatly, but was not the man even in his youth to suspend his critical faculty before any terrestrial fact whatsoever. The coming author of *Nathan* was already applying this faculty to religion. He had drifted far in the direction of the fashionable deism, but his pugnacity was aroused no less by the over-confident enemies of Christianity than by its orthodox defenders. As he said afterward: " The more rigorously the one side tried to prove their Christianity, the more doubtful I became: and the more arrogantly and triumphantly the other side undertook to trample it under foot, the more I felt inclined to maintain it, at least in my heart."

The first work of Lessing that is historically important is *Miss Sara Sampson*, written in 1755. By way of accenting the fact that it dealt with ordinary folk and not with sceptred kings, he called it a "bourgeois tragedy." With almost equal distinctiveness he might have called it a prose tragedy, a domestic tragedy, or a lacrimose tragedy. It was a challenge to the conventional dogma which associated the idea of tragedy exclusively with the form and style of the French type. "A bourgeois tragedy," exclaimed Lessing, "great heavens! Is there a word of any such thing in Gottsched's *Critical Poetics?*" The play is essentially the child of its author's reading and theorising. Some twenty years before (1732) Lillo had dressed up a "tale of private woe" in his *George Barnwell,* proposing that tears of sympathy should supply the place of the "absent pomp." The successful experiment interested Lessing. He took hints from Lillo, Congreve, Richardson and Swift, and evolved a play in which a sentimental English girl, having run away from her country home and her kind father with a plausible reprobate who promises to marry her, is poisoned by the former mistress of her lover, who thereupon commits suicide. A generation accustomed to weep over the heroines of Richardson wept also over *Miss Sara*. The play has its good points, but the characters, with the exception of Marwood, the jealous mistress, are rather tiresome, because of their mawkish and long-winded sentimentality. This was foreign to Lessing's nature; it came from his reading. But while *Miss Sara* was soon almost forgotten, and Lessing himself spoke of it as a hunchback child not to be cured by surgery, it set a new fashion and made a breach in the ramparts of pseudo-classicism. Its fundamental situation, the man between two women, the one sentimental, the other passionate, recurs again and again in the dramatic productions of the ensuing epoch.

How different is *Minna von Barnhelm*, the first German drama which proved to have in it the stuff that lives on and on! The Seven Years' War evoked in Prussia a patriotism to which Germans had long been unaccustomed, save as they read about it in books. All at once the dream of antique heroism, of mighty effort for great ends, of willingness to die for the fatherland, seemed to realise itself before their face and eyes. The result was a general exaltation of feeling, a heightened sense of present values. In this Lessing shared. He wrote a one-act tragedy, *Philotas,* on the theme of patriotic self-sacrifice. Its setting, however, was antique, its matter without obvious bearing on present issues. By his residence in Berlin, the Saxon Lessing had become very much Prussianised. To be sure, his habit of seeing and taking the other side, wherever extreme partisanship lifted its voice, caused him to be set down in Berlin as a Saxon sympathiser. In Saxony, on the other hand, he bore the reputation of an arch-Prussian. And, indeed, he admired the Prussian king. Moreover, his best friends were Prussians, and the closest of them all, Ewald von Kleist, was a Prussian officer who fell at Kunersdorf. When Gleim, catching the patriotic infection, turned his back on ana-

creontic frivolities, and began to sing the victories of
Friedrich in stirring Chevy Chase stanzas, Lessing acted
as his poetic mentor; and on the publication of Gleim's
Songs of a Prussian Grenadier (1758), Lessing supplied
a laudatory introduction. A little later the critic-scholar
suddenly dropped his literary pursuits and became secretary to General von Tauentzien, the Prussian command-
ant at Breslau. Here it was, at the centre of military
operations, that Lessing, in daily association with military men, sharing their work, their ardours, and their
diversions, saw and lived the life which is reflected in
Minna von Barnhelm.

Minute study of *Minna von Barnhelm,* such as our
time is wont to bestow on the classics of literature, has
brought to light many traces of literary influence. But
these things are relatively unimportant. The salient historical fact is that here at last, and for the first time,
genuine German life was brought on the stage with captivating art. The characters are no longer bookish types
speaking a conventional language, but real men and
women, each with a distinct individuality, and all talking
naturally under easily supposable conditions. In the
motives and situations some concession is made to the-
atric convention, but broadly speaking the comedy is
without caricature in the direction of farce, and the sentiment never degenerates into mawkishness. But dramatic realism, lively movement and technical skill offer
no guaranty of immortality. Multitudes of good realistic
plays have been quickly forgotten, just because they were
too faithful to the life of their epoch in its trivial and
quotidian aspects. The perennial charm of *Minna von*

Barnhelm is due to the fact that the reader or spectator feels in it the pulse-throb, not only of human nature, but of human nature in a great and critical epoch. Peace had come after seven years of bitter internecine conflict; men were asking how the wounds were to be healed, and what the Prussian triumph might portend for Germany. Lessing answers with a pleasant and tactful work of art. The stiff-backed Prussian officer Tellheim is brought to his knees by the sprightly Saxon Minna, and the Saxon victory is so managed as to convey, without any preaching, a salutary lesson of laughter, peace, hope, and mutual understanding. There is no partisanship in *Minna von Barnhelm,* nothing to leave a sting. It could be played in Leipzig, or even in Vienna, as well as in Berlin. It was a national German deed.

Just before going to Breslau, Lessing had commenced issuing, in conjunction with his friends Nicolai, Mendelssohn, and others, a journal called *Letters Concerning the Newest Literature.* It ran from 1759 to 1765, and contained, in Lessing's contributions, the best literary criticism that had appeared in Germany up to that time. But urbanity was not one of its virtues. The idea was to emancipate criticism from the pettiness of cliques and factions, and tell the plain truth. But as the letters were largely devoted to mediocrities—incompetent translators, pretentious poetasters, and so forth—they now make the impression of a Hercules slashing among pygmies who might well enough have been left to the oblivion which Time mercifully provides for their kind. It is noticeable, however, that certain far-reaching ideas had already taken root in Lessing's mind; namely, that

17

the French classical tragedy was not so Greek as had been
supposed; that Shakespeare was more truly Greek than
the Frenchmen—more nearly akin to the German genius,
and hence a better model for imitation. To enforce these
ideas, with Aristotle in hand, and to drive them home
with clear analysis and superb dialectic, was to be the
task of the *Hamburg Dramaturgy*. But before he took
up that task Lessing put himself at the head of European
critics with his *Laocoön* (1766).

The purpose of the *Laocoön* was to delimit the prov-
inces of poetry and the plastic arts in such a way as to
prove the necessary futility of minute description in the
former and of symbolism in the latter. The subject had
been treated by several English and French writers, and
was closely connected in Lessing's mind with the new
Hellenism, which taught that the Greeks were the one
source of light and the final authority in matters of art.
If this was so, it followed that to understand the Greeks
properly was to arrive at final canons. Lessing accepted
this point of view, but there remained the problem of
making sure that the Greeks had been properly understood. The great apostle of the new Hellenism in Germany was Winckelmann, whose enthusiastic descriptions of Greek statues opened a new era in archæology
and art criticism. Why does Laocoön appear nobly calm
in the statue, whereas Vergil makes him shriek with
pain? Winckelmann's answer was: Because the statue,
like all Greek statues, bodies forth an ethical ideal of
" noble simplicity and quiet grandeur." Here Lessing
takes up his argument, contending that the sculptor was
not concerned with ethics, but with physical beauty. In

due time the following dogma is made to emerge from
the discussion: From the nature of the means they
respectively employ, plastic art is confined to the representation of things coexistent in space, that is, bodies; while
poetry must represent things sequent in time, that is,
actions. From this it follows that the descriptive poet
who tries to give a vivid impression of an object by
describing its parts one after the other, must necessarily
fail, because the mind can never synthetise the details into
an all-at-once impression.

The argument of the *Laocoön* is vulnerable at many
points. Lessing was hardly the man to be a law-giver
for the plastic arts, for of statues and paintings he had
seen but little. When he wrote the *Laocoön* his eyes had
never rested on a cast of the group, possibly not even on
a drawing of it. He puts painting and sculpture together
under the name of *Malerei,* as if they were the same
thing. He writes of poetry as if its only aim were to
produce a vivid mental image. Historical considerations
are entirely lacking. The eighteenth-century thinkers
had a sublime faith in the power of logical ratiocination;
and just as one of them would sit down among his books
and evolve a complete theory, say, of primitive society,
so another, with hand and eye quite unschooled, would
boldly expound the necessary principles of plastic art.
But after all, the *Laocoön* is one of the most stimulating
pieces of criticism ever written. The difficulty is in certain tacitly assumed premises. These granted, the clarity
and cogency of the reasoning are beyond praise. The
book did not purport to be a systematic treatise, but a
" ferment of thought "; and its importance is to be found

in the ferment of thought that it produced in other minds. Says Goethe, in speaking of its effect on himself and his contemporaries: " As by a lightning-flash the consequences of this splendid thought lighted up the way before us, and all previous criticism . . . was thrown away like a worn-out coat."

As in the *Laocoön*, so in the *Hamburg Dramaturgy,* which has the value of a classic treatise on the tragic art, though in form it was a weekly journal conducted in connection with the so-called Hamburg National Theatre, Lessing proceeds on the hypothesis that it is possible to arrive at absolute canons of art, and that the way to do it is to study the Greeks. The most important numbers are those devoted to Voltaire's *Semiramis, Zaïre,* and *Mérope,* Thomas Corneille's *Essex,* Pierre Corneille's *Rodogune,* and Weisse's *Richard the Third.* Lessing's attitude toward the Frenchmen is that of a keen and resourceful attorney for the prosecution. Voltaire is subjected to withering criticism, and even the great Corneille fares badly. Shakespeare is exalted. It is shown that the wonderful rules of the *haute tragédie* are in good part mere pedantries, based on a misunderstanding of Aristotle. But there is always the implication that, once the great Stagyrite is correctly understood, the whole matter is settled, because *his* rules were based on eternal facts of human nature. " I could easily settle with Aristotle's prestige," he wrote, "if I could do likewise with his reasons." The impression is produced that for Lessing the merit of Shakespeare was not so much in being Shakespeare as in being a better Greek than Voltaire.

That Lessing does not deal quite fairly with the

Frenchmen whom he assailed must be admitted. His gibes at Voltaire may be pardoned, since the greatness of Voltaire, as Lessing very well knew, does not reside in his tragedies. But it is different with respect to the elder Corneille, in whom all the world now recognises the representative of a noble and stately form of art, which had the same right to be, and to be itself, as had the art of Sophocles or of Shakespeare. But in Lessing's defence it must be said that he was not so much concerned to disparage the *haute tragédie* in itself as to shatter its false pretensions and disillude its German imitators. For it was not content to stand on its own merit as French, but paraded itself, at least in critical discussion, as Greek; and in Germany, where no Corneille or Racine had made his appearance, the reverence of the learned for a form and style conventionally supposed to be Greek had become a hampering superstition. The times demanded not so much a judicial appraiser as a liberator who should tear off the mask. Lessing tore it off.

The valedictory number of the *Hamburg Dramaturgy* contained Lessing's famous renunciation of the name of poet. He declared that he did not feel the living spring within him, and owed solely to his critical faculty whatever success he had had as a poet; wherefore it annoyed him to hear the critical faculty disparaged. " They say it stifles genius," he wrote, " and I thought I had got from it something that comes very close to genius. I am a lame man who cannot possibly be edified by a lampoon against crutches." *Emilia Galotti*, the second of his three most famous plays, could hardly be better described than by calling it a tragedy begotten of the crit-

ical intellect, but of a critical intellect so keen and so
perfectly disciplined as almost to deserve the name of
genius. The theme had haunted his mind for years.
Originally he had planned a Roman play on the Vir-
ginia story, with revolution following the daughter's
death by the hand of her father. Then he decided to give
the tragic incident a modern setting, and to leave out the
revolution. So Appius Claudius was converted into an
art-loving Italian prince who has tired of his mistress
and been set aflame by the fresh beauty of Emilia Galotti.
By means of a plot hatched in the brain of the prince's
superserviceable tool, Marinelli, Emilia's betrothed lover
is killed by pretended robbers, and she herself is " rescued " and taken to the castle of the prince. There she
is killed by her father on her own petition, not because
she is in any immediate danger from her pursuer, but
because she cannot trust herself to resist his seductive
wiles. To the prince nothing happens.

Aside from its dubious catastrophe, which is just a
little shocking, reason about it as one will, *Emilia Galotti*
is a fine example of close-knit dramatic construction.
The characters are lifelike, there is rapid movement, perfect motivation, and never a sentence that does not tell.
It was really a " regular " tragedy of a new type, since
the rules, in their essential import, were strictly observed.
It is thus in a sense the starting-point of the modern
tragic drama in Germany. Regularity was not to be the
shibboleth of the coming epoch, but Lessing's masterpiece of technic remained as a beacon to warn off from
subjective extravagance. Even in plays which disre-
garded the warning its influence is discernible. While in

form only the tragedy of an ill-fated girl in far-off Italy, it was closely related to the larger life of the time, because it was taken as a caustic comment on the ways of the German princelings. Thus it helped in more ways than one to swell the current of revolutionary feeling.

And now, leaving Lessing's greatest work for consideration in a subsequent chapter, let us turn to the man who first brought home to his nation the idea that merit in literature comes not by the imitation of models, however good, but by originality, native vigour, and fulness of expression.

It was not given to JOHANN GOTTFRIED HERDER (1744–1803) to create finished masterpieces of any kind. He had imagination, learning, historical insight, intellectual acumen and prophetic vision; but he lacked literary skill of the humbler sort—was not a good craftsman with the pen. His early writings, with which alone we are here concerned, are a shower of sparks struck from his mind as he read. He wrote in a fervour, digressing, rhapsodising, gathering in irrelevant material, and rarely giving his matter time to clarify and arrange itself into a luminous argument. He is thus fragmentary, chaotic, difficult to read. But he is full of substance. In his work are found, along with much that is confused and erroneous, the germs of the whole literary movement that began with Goethe's *Götz von Berlichingen* and ended with the decadence of romanticism. He is the real father of the historical method. It was he who first expounded, in a large and impressive way, the idea that poetry is everywhere the evolutionary product of national conditions, and that the criteria for judging it should be sought in that fact rather than in abstract and universal canons. He was the first apostle of the folksong and the founder of a new science of the Bible.

Herder was born at Morungen, East Prussia, studied theology at Königsberg, and then settled in Riga as teacher and preacher. As a student he read Rousseau and Hume, and discussed them with the young Kant, then unknown to fame. He also became acquainted with JOHANN GEORG HAMANN (1730–88), an eccentric poly-histor then living at Königsberg and immersed in the study of ancient and modern languages. Hamann had lived in England, having been sent there as a bookseller's agent; but he had no mind for business, took to dissipa-tion, and presently brought up in the gutter. Then he repented of his sins and found in the Bible the mainstay of his new-born soul. He began to study the Scriptures in Greek and Hebrew, divagated thence into Greek poetry and philosophy, delved into Arabic, and withal took a lively interest in English, French, and German literature. He taught Herder English, using *Hamlet* for a text-book. His oracular profundity gave him the sobriquet of the Magus of the North. By his multifarious studies, pur-sued with imaginative heat, he had acquired a keen sense of ethnic differences. Underneath all the differences, however, he found poetry of some kind as a universal fact of primitive culture. " Poetry," he writes in his *Æsthetica in Nuce*, " is the mother-tongue of mankind, just as gardening is older than agriculture, painting than writing, song than declamation, similes than syllogisms." Odd fancies were mixed up with his ideas of primi-

tive poetry. Thus he writes, again in the *Æsthetica*:
"The repose of our ancestors was a deeper sleep, and
their motion a reeling dance. Seven days they would
sit in silence or meditation or amazement, and then
ope their mouths in winged proverbs. The senses
and the passions speak and understand nothing but
images."

The half-truth that poetry is the mother-tongue of
mankind, is the germ of Herder's message. "It is certainly true," he says, "that long before there was any
prose, poetry had reached its greatest height. . . . The
first authors of every nation are poets, and the first poets
are inimitable. . . . In later times we have versified philosophy, but mediocre poetry." These sentences are from
the *Fragments on Recent German Literature* (1767–68),
which were in form a running commentary on the *Lit-
eraturbriefe* of Lessing. The general theme of the First
Collection is the relation of language to poetry. "The
genius of a nation's language," says Herder, "is at the
same time the genius of its literature." This led to a speculative account of the life and growth of language in general, thence to a consideration of the peculiarities of the
German language as compared with other languages. In
the Second Collection Herder paid his respects to the German imitators of Hebrew and Greek poets, arguing that
the essence of a nation's poetry can never be transferred to
the language of another people, because the poetry reflects
a psychic life that grew out of peculiar conditions of
time and place. The Hebrews, he says in effect, looked
out on a nature that was different from that which we
Germans know; their religion was not like ours, their

patriotism had another basis. The " roses of Sharon "
and the " cedars of Lebanon " mean nothing to a German ; to be effective, the poetry of nature must be poetry
of the nature that one knows and feels. So, too, the
Greeks had their own peculiar history, mythology, and
environment, out of which their poetry grew ; the attempt
to imitate them—this was shown by a series of penetrating comparisons—results in artificial productions which
are neither Greek nor German. Herder's counsel to his
countrymen was that, instead of trying to imitate the
Greeks, they make good translations of them, study their
spirit, and learn therefrom to be original, even as the
Greeks had been.

In the *Critical Forests* (1769) Herder subjected the
new *Laocoön* to a searching criticism which exposed
some of the weak points in Lessing's argument. The
most of the critique is occupied with matters of scholarship having no relation to the literary movement of the
time, but toward the end Herder took exception to Lessing's fundamental distinction between poetry and plastic
art. This was, it will be remembered, that the former
employs arbitrary signs successive in time, the latter
natural signs coexistent in space. Herder pointed out
that the essential nature of poetry could not very well in-
here in a quality which it shared with music, dance, and
ordinary speech. The distinctive thing about poetry, he
thought, was energy—the " power that resides in the
words and, though it first passes through the ear, works
immediately on the soul." But notwithstanding the difference in their point of view and their theoretic conclusions, the two men agreed in their opinion of tame

descriptive poetry. "Action, passion, feeling! I, too, love them in poetry beyond all things else," exclaimed Herder. "I, too, hate nothing so much as dead, stagnant description, especially when it takes up whole pages and poems. Yet I do not hate it with such deadly hatred as to condemn every detailed picture, even should it be painted as consisting of coexistent parts. . . . Nor do I hate it because Homer does thus and so, and not otherwise. If I have learned anything from Homer, it is that poetry works by its energy." So far as the ultimate nature of poetry is concerned, neither Lessing's formula nor Herder's has any great value; but the idea that it was power, rather than picturesqueness or sentiment, proved very captivating to the young writers who were about to be known as *Kraftgenies,* or power-geniuses. It was also interesting to hear that the Greeks were, after all, only the Greeks, and that their poets had never been sent into the world to furnish artistic norms for all men everywhere.

Next came the *Letters on Ossian and the Songs of Ancient Peoples,* and an essay on Shakespeare—both published in 1773. By this time Herder had resigned his position at Riga, spent some months in France, and made the acquaintance of Goethe, who was then studying law at Strassburg. The importance of the writings just mentioned is largely due to the fact that the ideas they contain were instilled, during Herder's memorable sojourn at Strassburg in 1770–71, into the mind of a man who could turn them to account creatively. Macpherson's *Ossian* and Percy's *Reliques* were received by Herder with great enthusiasm as the gospel of a new literary dispensation. In his judgment the newly discovered Celtic bard was quite comparable to Homer, and each was admirable because he had been the organ voice of his people. " I should like to remind you," he wrote, " that the poems of Ossian are *songs,* songs of an uncultured, sensuous people. . . . Know you that the wilder a people is, *i.e.,* the freer and more spontaneous in its action (for the word has no other meaning), the wilder, *i.e.,* freer, livelier, more sensuous, more lyrically energetic its songs must be, if it has any. . . . Homer's rhapsodies and Ossian's songs were, so to speak, impromptus, because in their time there was no knowledge of anything else. After Ossian came the minstrels—weak and distant followers, it is true, but still followers—until art came in and extinguished nature. Then men learned to torment themselves from youth up with foreign languages, learning syllabic quantities which no longer came naturally by ear; they learned to work according to rules which no genius accepts as rules of nature; to poetise subjects about which one cannot even think, still less muse or employ the imagination; to feign passions that we have not, and imitate psychic powers that we lack—until everything became falsehood, weakness, artificiality. . . . Poesy, which ought to be the most impetuous and self-assured daughter of the human soul, became the most uncertain, lame, and staggering."

The essay on Shakespeare was an impassioned protest against the absurdity of judging the mighty Briton by the canons of French tragedy. It begins with a comparatively calm account of the Greek drama, which is

explained as the natural product of Greek conditions. Its
purpose, we are told, was to stir the soul by an illusion
of reality, and this end it attained by very simple means.
In comparison with the drama of the Greeks, that of the
French is described as a " doll that lacks mind, life,
nature, truth." When the subject of Shakespeare is
reached, Herder becomes rhapsodic and tortures the
German language for superlatives. The drift of it all is
that Shakespeare substituted complexity for the Greek
simplicity, and that he, too, was effective—tremendously
so. He made a drama different from that of the Athe-
nians, because he had another tradition behind him, another life about him. He had the genius to express that
life in all its fulness, variety, rush, and pressure. His
plays are likened by Herder to the surging sea. The
seemingly disordered scenes are the " outline of a divine
theodicy." Shakespeare is the " interpreter of nature in
all her tongues." " What," vociferates Herder, after an
eloquent exposition of *King Lear,* " Shakespeare no dramatic poet ! He who embraces with his arm the hundred
scenes of a world-event; who orders it all with his eye,
filling it with one soul that breathes through it and gives
it life; and who carries along with him, I will not say
our attention, but our heart and all our passions, from
beginning to end ! "

Herder's enthusiasm for " wild " folk furnished him
with new criteria of poetic merit. They were strong feeling, sincerity, sensuousness. Where these were, he
thought he heard the voice of nature; and he found it
especially in the poetry of unlettered men, or of those
who, if lettered, had kept their souls unharmed by the

corroding influence of conventionality and refinement. From his point of view, then, the greatest poets, such as Homer, Ossian, and Shakespeare, had been at once folk-singers and poets of nature ("nature," of course, including human nature). Following up his idea and making no very sharp distinction in his mind between the natural, which was always good, and the artificial, which was always bad, he began to make a collection; his object being to show that poetry is indeed a wildflower that grows everywhere and flourishes best among rude and primitive men. His work was published in 1778 under the title *Folksongs,* which was wisely changed in later editions to *Voices of the Nations in Songs.* The selections were obtained from a great variety of literary sources, and were all translated into German in imitation of the original form. Under the heading " Far North " were included songs from Greenland, Lapland, Esthonia, Bohemia, Kamchatka. Then came the " Greeks and Romans," represented by Orphic hymns, songs of Sappho, Pindar, Simonides, a chorus from the *Antigone,* some songs of Catullus and Horace, and a few in monkish Latin. Under " Romanic " were embraced a few from the Italian and French, a large number from the Spanish. The heading " Northern " was made to cover songs from the Edda, Scottish and English ballads, lyrics of Shakespeare and some songs from the Danish. The sixth book was devoted to German songs, and among these were a few, hitherto unpublished, that had been collected by Goethe in Alsatia. Finally there was an appendix giving specimens of poetry from Madagascar and Peru.

That this famous collection contained very heterogeneous things is a matter of small importance. Its significance lies in the fact that it exhibited poetry as a universal fact of human nature and supplied new criteria
for judging it.

If Herder has appeared hitherto as a precursor of
romanticism, he is still more so in a pamphlet which he
published in 1775 under the odd and hardly translatable
title *Auch eine Philosophie der Geschichte*. It is a
vehement attack on the Age of Enlightenment, coupled
with an incidental defence of the despised Middle Ages.
" Can any one in the world fail to comprehend," he wrote,
" that light does not nourish mankind? That repose and
luxury and so-called freedom of thought can never make
the general happiness and destiny? I am far from
defending those everlasting national movements and
devastations, feudal wars, monkish armies, pilgrimages
and crusades; but I would fain explain them. And what
a spirit breathes in it all! Ferment of human forces!
Grand cure of the entire race by means of violent exercise! If I might use so bold a figure, Fate was winding
up the great clock that had run down (doing it, to be
sure, with much noise, and not expecting the weights
to hang quietly), and how the wheels did rattle!"
A little farther on, after a bitter characterisation of his
own epoch, he continues : " Be it as it may, give us back
for many reasons your reverence and superstition, your
darkness and ignorance, your disorder and rudeness of
manners; and take in return our light and our unbelief,
our nerveless coldness and refinement, our philosophic
flaccidity and human wretchedness!"

This by no means represents Herder's final attitude, but the booklet is significant—like Goethe's warm encomium of Gothic architecture, published two years earlier —of the coming change of feeling toward the Middle Ages.

CHAPTER XIV

THE time was at last ripe for the coming of the king.
But let his kingship be looked for in no one period of his
life, in no one phase of his work; rather in the totality of
his many-sided, finely balanced, and marvellously clear-
sighted genius.

GOETHE, christened Johann Wolfgang, was born at
Frankfort-on-the-Main in 1749 and died at Weimar in
1832. By his mother he was imaginative and artistic,
by his father precise, methodical, studiously observant of
his own ways. The blood that flowed in his veins was
full of opposing potentialities. In his youth he was as
capricious as an April day; now taciturn, distraught,
brooding over nameless woes; again jovial, hilarious,
ready for the wildest lark; one moment a sentimentalist
revelling in the joy of tears, the next a satirist turning
his weapons back upon himself, or a phlegmatic observer
surveying his own vagaries in the white light of reason.
He knew all moods, passions, enthusiasms. He had in
him the germs of a poet, a painter, a mystic, a rationalist, a scholar, a man of science, an administrator, a
devoted publicist.

The atmosphere of the Goethe household in Frankfort

was one of patrician refinement. The family lived rather simply in social contact with the best people in a commercial city of some thirty thousand inhabitants, where there was neither prince nor court. An æsthetic appeal was always present in the form of books, pictures, music, and reminiscences of Italy—a subject on which paterfamilias was fond of dilating. If there was wealth, according to the standards of the time, there was no exclusiveness, and no pampering of the children. The boy Wolfgang saw much of the plain people, and learned to love their language and their ways.

In the free city of Frankfort national feeling was at a low ebb. The burghers were proud of their position as a constituent of the empire, and when an emperor was to be crowned they crowned him with elaborate ceremonial. For the rest they cared little for the empire, and felt themselves nearer to Paris than to Vienna. Perhaps the most lasting impression made on the mind of the boy Goethe by the political conditions of his native city was a certain fond feeling for the picturesqueness of old local custom, and for the pomps and mummeries of public authority; in especial a habit of regarding the empire as a venerable symbol not to be taken very seriously, save with the poetic imagination. In the family disputes over the Seven Years' War—the mother's people were Austrian sympathisers—the boy sided with his father in favour of the Prussian king. The occupation of Frankfort by a French army in 1759 brought a host of new impressions. For the sake of his French, Wolfgang was allowed to attend the French theatre which the city's unwelcome guests provided for their own amusement.

From a French comrade of his own age, the son of one of the actresses, he quickly picked up colloquial French. He saw French comedies, occasionally a tragedy, and soon felt equal to the writing of a French play. He read Racine and Corneille, and tried to master the doctrine of the unities. But this task he soon gave up in disgust, concluding with precocious wisdom that the plays were better than the theory.

What is important in all this is that by the time he was twelve years old Goethe was an accomplished young Frenchman—at home in the French drama, and accustomed to look at all things theatrical from the French point of view. Later his mind underwent an anti-Gallic revulsion, but impressions had been received which must certainly be counted in with the totality of later influences that made it impossible for him, in the Napoleonic era, to take sides with the virulent haters of France.

In 1765 Goethe entered the University of Leipzig, registering, in accordance with his father's wish, as a student of law. He was a good Latinist, but no Grecian at all, had a smattering of Italian, and rather more than a smattering of English. Already poetry was his ruling passion. He had filled divers volumes with juvenile verse, and he had high hopes of light and leading from the Leipzig professors, especially from Gellert, who was then at the height of his popularity. But he was disappointed. No one took any interest in his poetic aspirations, and the academic mill was just then grinding no grist that he could assimilate as food. So he turned his back on it—with emotions that were afterward cynically recorded in *Faust*. In a few months he gave up hope and fell into a moping melancholy. Then came a distracting love-affair with Annette Schönkopf—the first in a long procession of terrestrial muses—which revived the dying lyric flame, and at the same time furnished the central motive for a little play, *Die Laune des Verliebten*.

Aside from juvenilia that may be neglected, the earliest phase of Goethe's lyric gift is seen in the recently discovered collection, *Annette*,[1] dating from 1767, and in the *New Songs*, published with music in 1769. The *Annette* poems are in the gallant, erotic vein. They reveal a youth occupied with the stirrings of sexual passion, and turning his hand to *petites poesies* in the conventional Saxon style. A model can be found for nearly every one of them. The personal note, if they have one, is a note of boyish knowingness. The *New Songs* have a like savour, but are more terse and more original in expression. These too, however, convey a suggestion of mental origin; of being a clever moralist's comment rather than a poet's cry. Love is treated, not indeed ignobly, but with little depth or delicacy of feeling. Yet they are realistic. Schiller's earliest love-songs tell of cosmic harmonies and the prenatal affinity of soul for soul; Goethe's of amorous dalliance, of the half-stolen, half-permitted liberties of the lover, of the dangerous pull of desire, and of the blessedness, for man and maid, of having resisted it. At the time, Goethe thought the songs artless and likened them to wildflowers growing by the

---

[1] First published by Suphan in the *Deutsche Rundschau* for July, 1895, and afterwards included in the Weimar edition of Goethe, vol. 38.

brook. But the effect of spontaneous artlessness is just what the reader of to-day does not find in them. That is a later development.

Die Laune des Verliebten, i.e., the *Lover's Wayward Humour,* is a pastoral in lightly tripping alexandrines that pulsate with life, notwithstanding the effeteness of the genre and the tenuity of the matter. The theme is the punishment of an over-jealous lover, and the over-jealous lover is Goethe himself. The effect of his literary disillusion at Leipzig had been to put him out of humour with ambitious projects, and to convince him that he would do best at first with little things growing out of his own experience. This conviction guided him aright into his foreordained path of " confession." This first little play, to be sure, was laboriously filed and polished, but that and its successor, the *Fellow Culprits,* were the last of his poetic " efforts." After that the things welled up of themselves from that living spring which Lessing ruefully admitted that he could not find in himself. Goethe wrote henceforth to relieve emotional tension by stating the case in imaginary form. His characteristic process was to be rapid, unconscious, at times even somnambulistic; yet always a faithful rendering of the inner agitation. And of the outward fact, too. His sketching and drawing, which he worked at industriously under Oeser at Leipzig, and practised for many years thereafter, helped to make him a keen observer of things in general; and when reflection had shown him that all things, whether men like them or not, have their place in nature's scheme, and hence some possible value in the artistic expression of life, he was fitted to be the prince of realists as well as the prince of dreamers.

In the fall of 1768 Goethe returned to his Frankfort home desperateiy ill. For a year and a half he led the secluded life of an invalid, occupied with brooding thoughts, with curious studies in magic and alchemy, and with musings and debates on the subject of religion. While at the time the blessing was hardly visible beneath its deep disguise, it was really no misfortune for him to have heard, at the age of twenty, the winnowing wings of Death. His saintly friend, Fräulein von Klettenberg, who was eager to have him make his peace with God in her way, was unable to make him see that he had been a very great sinner; but he envied her her calm and went with her to the meetings of the local pietists. He learned to speak their language and to be very devout in their way. Erelong the current of a larger life swept him away from them, but it had become for ever impossible for him to think otherwise than nobly and tenderly of genuine religious feeling. He had been deeply touched by its mystic appeal, and henceforth religion was one of the great and revered facts of human existence. In time men called him a pagan and an enemy of Christianity; but modern literature owes to him some of its most exquisite and sympathetic portrayals of the religious life.

In deciding to continue his law studies at Strassburg, Goethe was actuated principally by a desire to perfect his command of French. He had hitherto felt himself half a Frenchman, and was wont to write many of his familiar letters in French, with copious sprinklings of verse.

But in Strassburg, on French soil, it was fated that he should draw nearer to the fatherland. He fell in with a group of young countrymen whose Teutonic French was derided by those to the manner born—with the result that they decided to drop the foreign tongue and stand on their dignity as Germans. This anti-Gallic feeling was then stimulated by intercourse with Herder into a fervid enthusiasm for things German, and especially for the national element in poetry. The famous names appeared to him in a new light. He began to think of Homer, Shakespeare, and Ossian as mighty voices of nature—the nature in which they had severally been rooted. The great criteria of merit—so the new gospel seemed to say—were genuineness, force, native vigour, the smell of the soil; the signs of degeneracy were imitation, artificiality, over-refinement, solicitude about conventional rules. It was a corollary of this doctrine that the songs of the rude forefathers and of unlettered folk in the present were actually better than the imitative productions of learning and culture. In his *Fragments* Herder had admonished the ambitious German poet to " study the superstitions and sagas of the forefathers and adapt them to the poetic spirit of the present." " Let him don the goatskins of the prophet," said Herder, " and wander through the mythologies of the old skalds and bards, as well as those of his own honest countrymen." Herder was already making, for the private delectation of himself and his betrothed, Karoline Flachsland, a collection of German poems which seemed to him the " true expression of feeling and of the whole soul." " Do not be surprised," he wrote to her, " that a young Lapp who does not know his letters, has never been to school, and hardly has a God, sings better than Major Kleist. For the Lapp sang his song on the wing, as he was gliding over the snow with his reindeer, impatient to see Lake Orra, where his sweetheart lived; but Major Kleist made his song by imitation from a book."

Under the influence of such ideas Goethe became a collector—the first real collector in Germany, since Herder was getting his gems from books—of folksongs. On a tour through Alsatia he gathered a dozen, catching them, as he said, from the throats of ancient grandams, and sent them to Herder as a priceless treasure. "All girls who wish to find favour with me," he declared, "shall learn them and sing them. My sister shall copy the music for you. N. B., the old tunes as God made them."

But literary theories and enthusiasms do not make a poet, else Herder should have been one. It was love, again, that gave the lyric impulse; and how different from the *New Songs* of Leipzig are the really new songs that were inspired by the country maid Friederike Brion! We no longer hear clever conceits or echoes of conventional sentiment, but genuine bird-notes that sing themselves and have no need of any cunning derived from reflection. Take the *May Festival* and note how perfectly true it rings:

> *Wie herrlich leuchtet*
> *Mir die Natur!*
> *Wie glänzt die Sonne,*
> *Wie lacht die Flur!*

O Lieb', o Liebe,
So golden schön,
Wie Morgenwolken
Auf jenen Höhn.

The songs which were written by Goethe during the next few years of his life, after he had thus found himself as poet, opened a new era in German lyrism. His art is seen at its best in such poems as the *May Festival, Welcome and Parting, On the Lake, New Love, New Life, Restless Love, Comfort in Tears, To the Moon,* the *King in Thule.* It is no doubt a simple art; compared with the wonderful word-craft of Keats or the imaginative splendours of Shelley, it seems almost tame. But in its simplicity its power resides. It is based on absolute fidelity to the truth: nowhere is there anything scintillant or exaggerated. In these songs the love of woman seems to blend with a deep joy in the visible forms of the outer world, and a suggestion of feeling too deep for words is conveyed by means of descriptive touches that are copied exactly from nature. The famous little " Wanderer's Night-song," beginning *Über allen Gipfeln ist Ruh*, is an example in point. It was Goethe's discovery that the finest poetic effects are producible by the simplest means, through the power of suggestion. The great lyrists of the romantic epoch—Eichendorff, Uhland, Heine, Mörike, Müller—all caught the trick from him, or caught it from the folksong, as he had done. It is a matter of waking responsive echoes by touching the right chord in the right way. The reader of Goethe has no difficulty in understanding Wagner's paradox that the greatness of a poet is to be measured by what he refrains from saying.

When Goethe returned to Frankfort as licentiate in law, in the summer of 1771, a world of new ideas and bitter-sweet memories were jostling one another in his inner being. His imagination, now drawn to masterful heroes with German blood in their veins, was already communing with two doughty figures of the sixteenth century: Götz von Berlichingen and Faust. In a few weeks he had turned the autobiography of Götz into a series of vivid dramatic pictures which so engrossed him that he " forgot Homer, Shakespeare, and everything." The rules were of course flung to the winds. On reading the manuscript, Herder wrote: " Shakespeare has spoiled you." In a docile spirit Goethe replied that the thing would have to be melted up and recast. In 1773 he made a revision and published it anonymously as *Götz von Berlichingen with the Iron Hand*. It caused a great and a very wholesome sensation. The young Frankfort lawyer had suddenly blazed out as the cynosure of the German firmament. To be sure, the " bewitching monster " did not fail, even in the first excitement, to draw the fire of the sober-minded. Lessing, who saw clearly enough that something remarkable had happened, made the oracular comment: " He fills intestines with sand and sells them for ropes. Who? The poet, peradventure, who turns a man's life-history into dialogue and proclaims it as a drama." Since then many and many a critic has complained that *Götz* is not a well-constructed play; yet there it stands, proof against the tooth of time, a monumental literary triumph. And, after all, when it is well acted it is highly effective on the stage.

The reason for its effectiveness in the theatre and for its literary classicity is the same: it is surcharged with life, and the life is genuine. From the tectonic point of view no doubt *Emilia Galotti* is the better play; but how much more there is in *Götz* to see, to think, and to feel! The whole sixteenth century is conjured back. We have fighting and love-making and negotiating; feudal foray, attáck, and defence; court intrigue, public affairs, the state of the law, the clash of opinion and prejudice, the administration of justice by the Veme. We have the domestic life of high and low, the wandering gipsy, the burning and marauding peasant. There is an almost bewildering variety of characters, each speaking his natural language and living himself out in his own way. Hardly a phase in the life of the time can be thought of that is not reflected sooner or later in *Götz von Berlichingen*. And through it all as a connecting thread runs the idealised life-history of Götz himself, conceived as a champion of freedom and self-help in an age of anarchy. No doubt certain parts are rather loosely connected with the central tragedy; others, perhaps, are unduly elaborated, because the eye of Goethe rested a little too fondly on this and that detail of his picture. By their great variety and their rapid changes the scenes made unprecedented demands on stage-craft, but the imagination is never baffled or seriously perplexed. It easily supplies the missing links of logic and history.

The author of *Götz* had not been spoiled by Shakespeare, nor did he imitate Shakespeare in the sense natu-

rally carried by that phrase. It is time *that* misconception
were laid to rest. Goethe did not belong to the order of
imitators. All his life long, it is true, he was a great
taker of what suited his purpose; just as Shakespeare had
been, and just as Homer would no doubt appear to have
been if we knew more of his antecedents. But whatever
he took he transmuted and vitalised with his own genius.
In writing *Götz* he was influenced not so much by Shakespeare as by the conception of Shakespeare that he had got
from Herder, who knew little and cared little about the
dramatic art. What Herder admired in Shakespeare was
the exuberant life, the mighty interaction of historical
and passional forces, that he found in him. He saw in
him the wonderful mirror of an epoch; but the artist,
the playwright, he hardly saw at all. Shakespeare, who
affected him so powerfully in the reading, was set down
as Nature's magician, who had done his wonders in a
spirit of sublime lawlessness. This notion of the great
Elizabethan was taken over by Goethe in the form of a
perfervid but utterly uncritical admiration. Naturally
enough, therefore, to Shakespearise was, for him, to be
original as Shakespeare had been; in other words, to lay
hold of German life in the fulness thereof and handle it in
a bold, free way, without inquiring at every step whether
this or that was permissible under the rules.

And then the subject-matter of the play was revolutionary. Götz was not presented as a pestilent robber
knight, warring against the forces that were making for
public order, but as the champion of a good cause—the
cause of individual freedom and self-reliance. He appeared as a pattern of sturdy German virtues, while

empire and church were made to play a rather shabby rôle of intrigue and oppression. *Götz* was thus in a double sense a manifesto of freedom, and it proved that Germany was all ready for just such a declaration of independence.

And then came, in 1774, the *Sufferings of Young Werther*—written in a month of such intense abstraction that it was likened by Goethe himself to the trance of a sleep-walker. From the point of view of common-sense, which happens to coincide in this case with that of science, *Werther* is a morbid book. The suicide of a young man because of a disappointment in love is not a subject on which a healthy imagination likes to dwell. Nevertheless, the melancholia of adolescence, as psychologists now call it, is a human fact. Goethe himself had suffered acutely from the malady, and in intercourse with sentimental friends had noted that feeling too much and doing nothing make a dangerous combination. In certain moods emotional excess struck him as a matter of mirth, in others as a tragic peril. The tragic peril is the theme of *Werther*. In writing the novel Goethe expelled the virus from his own system, never intending a contribution to the ethics of suicide, but only a faithful rendering of the melancholy vision that had possessed him. That the characters and incidents of the tale are a thinly veiled transcript of reality is well known.

Of all the sentimental novels of the eighteenth century, *Werther* is easily the best. Richardson, Rousseau, and Sterne give us the sentimental age in saturated solutions; Goethe proffers a concentrated extract. His hyperæsthetic, weak-willed, and toward the end rather maud-

lin hero no longer draws tears from mankind, because
the modern reader is rarely able or willing to receive the
pathetic tale naïvely and to suppress, for the time being,
his sense of humour. This, however, was what Goethe
did, who was himself richly endowed with humour.
In other works of his, both before and after *Werther,*
there is humour enough; but this particular tale was
to be a record of "sufferings" which the reader
was expected to take very seriously, regarding them
always from the sufferer's point of view. And how
fine the workmanship is! While his predecessors in
the epistolary novel are generally diffuse and often mawkish, Goethe is terse, rapid, natural. Never before had
the German language been made to do such work in the
rendering of temperamental subtleties. As the seasons
change, the moods of Werther conform to those of the
outer world, Nature being at one time a sympathetic
friend and the source of all high inspiration, at another
a cruel all-devouring monster. A new feeling for Nature
—something deeper, more mystic, more passionate, than
had been expressed before—comes into German literature
with *Werther.*

In his youth Goethe succeeded best with heroes of the
Werther type, that is, with sentimental weaklings who
are easily swayed by gusts of feeling, or perhaps by bad
advice. He wrote, indeed, part of a *Prometheus,* which
contains a fine soliloquy of the heaven-defying Titan, and
he planned a *Julius Cæsar;* but the strong man of steadfast mind was not in his line. His favourite form of
tragedy was the situation of a woman whom her lover
abandons, either from sheer fickleness of character or

from prudential considerations. So it is with Marie in *Götz von Berlichingen*. In *Clavigo*, again, we have a vacillating lover who, on the advice of a cold-blooded friend, deserts his inconvenient sweetheart, and is then done to death by her offended brother. The sickish Fernando in *Stella* first deserts his adorable wife Cecilia, and then his adorable mistress Stella—each time for no definable reason except the desire of a change. When the trio come together by accident, after a lapse of years, there is a conflux of tears and tender memories, in which womanly spunk plays no part. The distressed but magnanimous wife finally suggests to Stella that they share their recovered treasure together, and Fernando consents. In a later revision of the play, as is well known, Goethe rejected this bigamous solution of his dramatic problem and made Fernando shoot himself. This is no doubt better from a theatrical point of view; but the original solution is highly significant as showing how far he was willing to go, under the stress of youthful radicalism, in taking the side of the afflicted heart against the conventional usage of society.

Finally, there is a tragedy of desertion in *Faust*.

When Goethe began to dramatise the Faust-saga, it is probable that he had no thought of carrying his dramatic action beyond the grave. In a sense, to be sure, the fate of Faust after death was the crux of the whole problem. The legend had presented him as a bold bad man damned for deliberate sin. But his sin, at least the root of it, was intellectual curiosity, which, for the age of enlightenment, was no sin at all. Nor could intelligent folk of the new era be expected to take much interest in the witless

Mephostophiles of the legend. Neither the easily deluded Faust nor the easily triumphant devil would do. On the other hand, the league with the devil, conceived as in some sense or other a spirit of evil, was a fundamental datum without which there could be no *Faust* at all. It is clear that from the first Goethe thought of the old magician who had sold his soul for a mess of pottage as a man better than his reputation; as a titanic truth-seeker, in whose nature there were the very largest potentialities of good as well as of evil. He began to think of him as an academic polyhistor who had been driven by acute disgust with the futility and narrowness of book-learning to league himself with an evil spirit, in order that he might really live. And then, following a meagre hint of the story, he caught a vision of this transformed Faust as falling in love with a beautiful girl, making havoc of her life, deserting her in her shame and remorse, and finally witnessing her pitiful death in prison. The tragedy of Faust and Margaret was written, substantially as the world knows it from the final version of 1808, in 1774 and 1775. In those early scenes Faust appears as a rakish man who cannot resist the pull of carnal desire, yet has a conscience that puts him on the rack for his sins. Mephistopheles, with hardly a trace of the legendary devil, is a cynical abettor of Faust's lust—a personification of that particular evil spirit which prompts a man to obey impulse and passion rather than conscience and will.

One inevitably asks what was to come after the death of Margaret, and how it was all to end. That something more was to come is not in the least open to doubt. Fol-

lowing the lines of the puppet-play legend in a general
way, the play was to represent, like *Götz von Berlichingen,* a whole life-history in a succession of scenes and pictures. Faust was to appear in the great world, that is,
at the court of a prince. He was to marry the phantom
Helena and become by her the father of a wonderful
clairvoyant son. At last, in all probability, he was to
find some occupation which would make life seem seriously worth while, and to die unsatisfied yet glad of having lived. The final details were to be so managed that
the reader or the spectator would feel that such a man
as Faust, notwithstanding all his sins and errors, would
be safe in the hands of the Eternal Pardoner. But there
is no reason to suppose that the judgment of heaven was
to be anticipated on the stage. Faust was to be left at
death, as all men are left, in the hands of his Maker.
That Goethe ever planned a mere repetition of the old
tragedy of sin and damnation is very improbable, for
the reason that he all along identified Faust with himself
and made him the mouthpiece of his own most intimate
feelings. A young poet does not plan to send his own
soul to perdition.

In November, 1775, Goethe paid the young Duke of
Weimar the memorable visit which resulted in linking
the rest of his life to the little Thuringian city on the
Ilm. For some time previous to this momentous change
in his life he had been occupied with the tragedy of
Egmont, which thus really belongs to his pre-Weimarian
youth, though it was not entirely finished until 1787. It
is a superb character-study, but somewhat lacking in
dramatic movement and tension. Egmont is a pendant

19

to *Götz von Berlichingen,* in that he too regards himself as a martyr to liberty. In order to make Egmont " free," Goethe converted him from an elderly man with a large family into a young cavalier who solaces his leisure hours with the low-born but bewitching Clärchen. A strange fascination goes out from him on account of his amiable personality. But the buoyancy of temper which trusts and laughs and declines to worry, blinds him to the obvious dangers which other men can see; thus it becomes the tragic weakness that carries him to his doom. Goethe had come to believe that some men are impelled through life by a mysterious power which is neither reason nor instinct nor volition. He called it " the demonic," and had much to say, first and last, about the matter. What he meant by the demonic would seem to be the unexplained residuum of personality, as manifested in men of an impetuous but at the same time self-reliant disposition. Egmont is done to death by the demonic power of his happy-go-lucky temperament.

After his settlement in Weimar as a member of the ducal council of state, Goethe devoted himself strenuously to the public service, in various branches, and allowed his unfinished literary projects to remain unfinished. Gradually his mind underwent a momentous change; and when, presently, the poetic impulse reasserted itself, it was to seek expression for a new order of emotions and ideas. Meanwhile, a group of young writers—for the most part friends of his who had caught something of his spirit—were actively furthering the literary revolution. The most important of them were Klinger, Leisewitz, Wagner, Lenz, and Müller. A wild play of Klinger,

called *Sturm und Drang,* or *Storm and Stress,* has furnished a convenient name for the period and the movement; and the phrase has become a part of the general
vocabulary, both in German and English, for denoting
the impetuous radicalism of youth. Of the group in
general it may be said that the genre they most affected
was the prose tragedy of passionate error; but they also
expressed themselves in lyric verse, in sentimental tales,
and satiric pasquinades. MAXIMILIAN KLINGER (1752–
1831), the most productive and the most extravagant of
them all, is best known for his plays *Storm and Stress*
and the *Twins,* and for his tumultuous *Life of Faust,*
which is a narrative with interspersed dialogues.
JOHANN ANTON LEISEWITZ (1752–1806) wrote the
tragedy *Julius of Tarentum,* dealing, like Klinger's
Twins, with the subject of two contrasted and mutually
hostile brothers. JAKOB MICHAEL REINHOLD LENZ
(1751–92) was a gifted lyrist, who became insane and
died in abject misery. He wrote plays of a more or less
revolutionary tendency (the *Tutor,* the *Soldiers*), and
left an unfinished epistolary novel, the *Hermit,* which
shows the influence of *Werther.* HEINRICH LEOPOLD
WAGNER (1747–79), best known for his play the *Infan-
ticide,* had a notable talent for the drama, but his realism
is sometimes all too repulsive. FRIEDRICH MÜLLER
(1749–1825), better known as Maler Müller, is at his
best in the play *Golo and Genevieve.*

The animating spirit of the " Storm and Stress " was
the spirit of passionate revolt against the conventional
standards of life and of literature. The battle-cries were
freedom, genius, power, nature; genius meaning lawless-

ness, and nature being conceived in the spirit of Rousseau as the antithesis of civilised convention. Shakespeare was ignorantly worshipped as the archetypal genius. There was a disposition to attack social arrangements, or at least to put them on trial before the tribunal of feeling. The passionate soul at war with society, or caught some- how in the meshes of a galling social bondage, was the favourite form of tragic pathos. Feeling, instinct, and passion were regarded as the only noble elements of human nature. As a German writer puts it tersely, *Urnatur* was appealed to against *Unnatur*. As for style, the worst of shortcomings was tameness, the greatest of merits an unbridled energy of expression. Hence an appetence for hyperbolic diction, wild comparisons, repe- titions, broken sentences, perfervid exclamations. Curi- ously enough, it became the custom to speak of the amor- phous prose play, in which the creative ego ran riot through the principles of dramatic construction, as " Eng- lish." England was regarded as the land of freedom.

In the year 1781 a play appeared which made all previous manifestoes of the literary revolution seem tame enough. It was the *Robbers*, by FRIEDRICH SCHILLER (1759–1805), who was then twenty-two years old and had just left the ducal academy at Stuttgart, where he had taken a course in medicine.

The legend that Schiller was moved to revolt by the asperities of his student life—the strict military disci- pline, the petty official surveillance, and all that—rests on no very solid foundation. The radicalism of a young poet is not so rare a thing as to call for special explana- tion. Enough that, in spite of the official prohibition of all dangerous books, Schiller found opportunity to read what other Germans were just then reading, and the literature of insurrection set him on fire. In his Plutarch he read of great, strong men, of splendid self-assertion : what had become of the greatness and the strength? The age seemed to him a pusillanimous, servile, cringing, babbling, ink-spattering age; the social order a conspiracy against all towering manhood. Such thoughts, lodged in the mind of a youth given to passionate dreaming, and convinced of his call to the tragic drama, lead naturally enough to the idealisation of a criminal. So it was with the young Ibsen who, being at war with society, found his first hero in Catiline. Taking a hint from a story by Schubart, Schiller wrote, while still in the academy, his sanguinary and thunderous drama of the contrasted brothers : the one an abysmal villain of the cold and calculating order, the other a fiery sentimentalist, who, in a fury over personal wrong, breaks with the social order and wages war against it at the head of a band of outlaws. In the end the " sublime criminal " comes to a realisation of his folly and returns to the track of the law by giving himself up to justice.

The *Robbers* first appeared in print as a book for the reader, the preface disclaiming all thought of the stage. A copy fell under the eye of Dalberg, director of the flourishing theatre at Mannheim, and he saw that the production was playable. At his suggestion Schiller undertook a revision for the stage and was rewarded by seeing the Mannheim public go wild over his band of dissolute students metamorphosed by stage fiat into bloody and blustering outlaws. To-day one naturally judges

Schiller's first play in the light of what he afterward became, and one shrinks accordingly from the fatuity of dwelling on faults which he himself was the first to point out, and which, after all, were full of high promise. When he wrote the *Robbers,* he had seen very little of men, almost nothing of women. His ideas of human nature had come to him from books. In his contempt of tameness he fell into the vice of over-emphasis : as if the furious tirade were the natural expression of strong will and strong emotion. And then the plot is so very audacious, and the conduct of the leading characters so very unhuman, as to invest the whole play with a certain air of absurdity. On the other hand, the power of the born playwright is there—full fledged at the first flight. And the essentials of all great tragedy—the clash of wills made visible in action, the suspense, the pity and the fear, the disburdening catharsis—these are also there.

In September, 1782, Schiller took clandestine leave of Stuttgart, where he had been employed as army doctor, in order to escape the personal tyranny of the Duke of Würtemberg. He first went to Mannheim, hoping to prosper there as a playwright ; but Dalberg could see no merit in his second play, *Fiesco,* and was not at once eager to befriend a man who had compromised himself with a neighbouring prince. So Schiller hid himself for several months at the village of Bauerbach, where he worked upon a third play, which was afterward called *Cabal and Love.* In the summer of 1783 he emerged from his seclusion and made a contract with Dalberg for a year's service as theatre poet at Mannheim. Here his new plays were performed, his stage-craft was subjected to the discipline of more or less expert discussion, and higher ideals of the dramatic art began to possess his mind.

The *Conspiracy of Fiesco at Genoa* was published, before it had been played, with the sub-title " a republican tragedy." There is good reason to think that Schiller's initial conception of Fiesco, which he had got indirectly from Rousseau, was that of a high-minded patriot conspiring to deliver his country from the clutches of a tyrant —in short, that of a modern Italian Brutus. But as he read the historians he found in Fiesco rather more of Catiline than of Brutus. The completed work shows a certain vacillation between these two conceptions of the hero. Fiesco appears now as a political idealist, again as a selfish conspirator; and the dramatic interest is made to turn largely on the conflict in his mind between the better and the baser motive. In the book-version the Catiline conception was finally allowed to prevail: when the conspiracy has succeeded and Fiesco has donned the purple robe of sovereignty, the disgusted patriot Verrina pushes him into the sea. This gives a tragedy of republican idealism corrupted by selfish ambition and ending in disaster. But in the stage version the tragic catastrophe was changed to a happy ending. When hard pressed by the fanatic Verrina, Fiesco declares that his heart has been right all along; only he desired to effect the liberation of his country and to be responsible for it all alone. So he breaks his sceptre and bids the people embrace him as their " happiest fellow-citizen."

It is evident that a play whose essential import could

be thus radically altered by a few strokes of the pen at the end had not been clearly and consistently thought out. Schiller was not yet ripe for historical tragedy in the grand style. Nevertheless there are fine scenes in *Fiesco*. It is dramatically alive from beginning to end. While in substance the least weighty of Schiller's plays, it is theatrically effective in virtue of its picturesque details and its imaginative daring.

Cabal and Love is much more vitally related than either of its predecessors to German life. It belongs to the family of *Sara Sampson* and *Emilia Galotti* in that its principal figure is a sentimental girl whose course of true love runs unhappily to a tragic end. Several other plays from which Schiller took hints present the same situation. But it was not in his nature to write a merely personal or domestic tragedy: in some way or other he always connects the calamity of the individual with the larger life of society. *Cabal and Love* is a drastic comment on class feeling as a factor in the social order, and on the infamies that might flourish, and often did flourish, beneath the glamour of court life in the eighteenth century. The heroine Luise is a poor fiddler's daughter, while her lover Ferdinand is a nobleman. His bent of love is entirely honourable: he is ready to marry his plebeian sweetheart and jump the consequences. Her mother favours, the father strenuously opposes, the aristocratic connection, and the girl herself is timid and irresolute. A court intrigue of Ferdinand's father, who has risen by crime to the premiership and wishes his son to marry the duke's mistress, succeeds in making Ferdinand mad with jealousy. He poisons Luise and himself, whereat the wicked statesman repents and gives himself up to the law.

In writing *Cabal and Love* Schiller drew copiously on ugly facts in the recent history of Würtemberg. At the same time he spared the prince with whom he had quarrelled, taking pains to avoid everything that might smack of caricature or personal bitterness. He let the tragic nemesis overtake *bourgeoisie* and aristocracy alike. In the main, notwithstanding his passion for sharp contrast and rhetorical vehemence, the play is a true presentation of what might have occurred at a German court. The lovers, indeed, are not drawn with perfectly convincing art, and their tragedy lacks the effect of inevitableness. But this is relatively of small moment. The play lives, on the boards and as literature, by virtue of its fearless and virile treatment of the relations existing between the plain people and the so-called nobility. Like the *Robbers,* it belongs emphatically to the literature of revolt, but its criticism of the social order is much more temperate than in the earlier play. This time Schiller had his eye on the facts, and not on a madman's dream.

CHAPTER XV

THE BIRTH OF THE NEW POETIC DRAMA

THE most valuable part of what the Germans call their classical literature is unquestionably that which took the form of the drama in verse. Other genres flourished and good things were achieved in them; but just as in the Athens of Pericles, the England of Elizabeth, and the France of Louis XIV, it is in the poetic drama that we find the form and pressure of the time most richly bodied forth. Lessing led the way with *Nathan the Wise* in 1779. Soon afterward Goethe and Schiller began, each in his own way, to evolve a blank verse drama which, in each case, subordinated the requirements of the contemporary stage to the inner need of artistic self-expression. *Iphigenia* and *Don Carlos* were finished in the same year (1787), the one in Rome, the other in Dresden. Then came Goethe's *Torquato Tasso*. In the subsequent years of their memorable friendship and co-operation Goethe wrote nothing of great importance in the dramatic form except the completion of the *First Part of Faust* and the *Natural Daughter*, which remained a splendid torso. On the other hand, the best energies of Schiller were devoted to play-writing, and he it was who first gave the German drama its European prestige. It is largely due to his influence that, throughout the nineteenth century, there was a continuous current of creditable production in the line of poetic tragedy, and that to this day nearly every German poet regards success in that genre as the highest kind of success.

Three years before his death Lessing delivered his weightiest message in the form of a noble drama of religious tolerance and humane aspiration. *Nathan the Wise* is a good stage-play in its kind, but that is not its most important aspect. This time the great critic was not so much concerned to exemplify sound principles of dramatic construction as to preach an effective and durable sermon on human brotherhood.

Soon after the fiasco of the Hamburg National Theatre Lessing accepted from the Duke of Brunswick the post of librarian at Wolfenbüttel. In the bookish seclusion of this office he presently became involved in a religious controversy which absorbed a large part of his mental energy during the remainder of his life. He had come into possession of a bulky manuscript which attacked the credibility of Scripture. The author was a recently deceased scholar, H. S. Reimarus by name, who had devoted years to the treatise, but had not cared to publish it because he had reached conclusions which would shake the foundations of Lutheran orthodoxy. Albeit he could not agree with Reimarus at every point, Lessing was impressed by the gravity and acumen of his argument; and being of the opinion that the pursuit of truth is better than an assured conviction that one has it already, he began to publish extracts from the manuscript under the title of " Anonymous Fragments." The result was a memorable fluttering in the dove-cotes of orthodoxy. A Hamburg pastor by the name of Goeze attacked Lessing, over the head of the " Great Anonymous," as an enemy of religion. Lessing replied in a series of pamphlets which, taken together, constitute a brilliant vindication of what is now called the higher criticism. In particular, he argued that religion is older than the Bible, and hence cannot be made to rest solely on the Bible; and that the truth of religion must be proved, not by historical argument, but by its effect on the character of its votaries. The war was progressing hotly, and Lessing had just finished the eleventh chapter of his withering *Anti-Goeze*, when the orthodox party succeeded in persuading the Duke of Brunswick to silence his dangerous librarian by official decree. It was then— in the summer of 1778—that Lessing conceived the idea of stating his case in a dramatic poem. " I must see," he wrote, " whether they will at least let me preach on undisturbed in my old pulpit, the theatre." In the following May *Nathan the Wise* was given to the world.

The nucleus of the play was the tale of the three rings as told by Boccaccio. According to this Italian version Saladin was once in sore need of money and set a trap for the rich Jew Melchisedec by asking him which was the best of the three religions. The Jew extricates himself by telling the ring story, which was already old when the *Decameron* was written. Boccaccio's ring is only an unusually valuable jewel, which the head of the house regularly bequeaths to the favourite son who is to succeed him in the headship. At last it comes to a father with three sons who are equally obedient, equally beloved. Unwilling to choose among them, he has two new rings made, so exactly like the original that he himself can scarcely distinguish them. He gives to each son a ring and dies. Each son claims to be the head of the house, but there is no way of deciding which has the genuine ring. " The question which was the father's very heir abode pending and yet pendeth." Thus the story ends in the *Decameron*, where the main stress falls on the shrewdness of the Jew.

By means of two happy inventions Lessing so changes the story as to give it an infinite depth of symbolic sug- gestion and to make it body forth his whole philosophy of religion. In the first place, he ascribes to the genuine ring the magic power to render its possessor beloved of God and man, *provided it be worn with faith in its effi- cacy*. Secondly, he makes the quarreling sons appear be- fore a wise judge, who first rebukes them for their conten- tiousness, declaring that he is no solver of riddles, and then points forward to a time, after a thousand thousand years, when a wiser Judge may be able to render a decision.

Thus *Nathan the Wise* regards religion under the aspect of evolution. Its doctrine is much finer than the ordinary eighteenth-century doctrine of tolerance, which was quite compatible with a cynical contempt for all religions. Lessing preaches a tolerance born not of the rationalist's contempt, or the statesman's indifference, but of love and emulation. He makes his judge say:

> Let each of you vie with the other twain
> To manifest the magic of the gem
> In his own ring.

Every religion—so the teaching runs—is to be judged by its fruits rather than by its proofs; only it is to be remembered that the fruits are not yet all garnered, nor will be for a million years to come. The value of the mystic appeal in religion is not overlooked by Lessing, as some have charged, but it is undoubtedly subordinated to the great end of producing good men on earth. The quarrelling brothers are admonished, each believing that he has the genuine ring, to come to the aid of its magic, not only with virtuous deeds and mere morality, but

Mit innigster Ergebenheit in Gott.

Thus religion is presented as an instrument in the long education of the human race.

The two most important characters of the play are found in the parable. The magnanimous Saladin was a fixed datum of literary tradition, and Lessing took him very much as he found him. The cunning Jew Melchisedec became the wise Nathan, bearer of Lessing's main message of love and good works, his representative *humanus*. The plot is purely romantic. Saladin is provided with a lost brother, who had a son and daughter by a German wife. The girl appears in the play as Nathan's adopted daughter, her brother as a hot-headed Templar, who falls in love with the supposed Jewess. The end is a happy family reunion, in which Mussulmans and Christians embrace one another as kin, while the high-minded Jew who has brought it all about receives the general benediction. There is no dramatic conflict anywhere, no clash of strong wills. At one time, indeed, Nathan seems to be in danger from the machinations of the fanatical patriarch, whom Lessing drew from the historical Heraclius, with here and there a touch suggested by Goeze. But the patriarch's malignity turns out to be only a passing cloud; nothing comes of it, and the peaceful drama moves on serenely to a happy end. Serenely, but never tamely; for the lack of a dramatic conflict is compensated by the superb skill with which the characters are drawn.

Nathan the Wise expresses the best thought of the Age of Enlightenment on the subject of religion. While the actual writing of it was the work of a few months, its substance of doctrine had matured slowly in Lessing's mind during many years. It has depths and far-reaching implications which make it one of the most fascinating of all dramas that have a specific religious tendency. A German proverb has it that many a pretty pathway leads between Either and Or. Lessing found a pathway between the Either of orthodoxy and the Or of rationalism. His thesis is, in effect, that all religions are provisionally true, so far as they make for goodness in human relations. He treats the great theme nobly and sympathetically; and as if in full prescience that he was creating a literary masterpiece that would occupy the minds of men for ages to come, he gave it a metrical form and called it a " dramatic poem."

In his use of blank verse for *Nathan* Lessing was virtually, though not in the strictest sense, a pioneer. It had become patent to all progressive minds that the alexandrine, which had held the field for serious drama a century or more, must go; it was ill adapted to the genius of the German language, and especially ill adapted, with its rigid structure and monotonous cadence, to brisk or impassioned dramatic dialogue. But what was to take its place? The increasing vogue of Shakespeare seemed to offer an answer to this question. In his *Fragments* Herder came out strongly in favour of blank verse as a form that would combine strength with freedom. Such a form was just what Lessing needed for his trenchant dialectic. His verse is poor in all the elements of poetry: it does not glow, it does not flow. On the other hand, it talks admirably. The line as a rhythmic unit counts for but little. Lessing breaks it up in various ways, is lavish of *enjambement* and often disregards the iambic cadence. His nervous, incisive style, with its rather frequent cacophonies, is very different from the smooth and soulful verse-melody of Goethe or the billowy sonorousness of Schiller.

The year in which *Nathan the Wise* was published saw the completion of *Iphigenia* in the rhythmic prose which, for the time being, Goethe thought best adapted to the requirements of an idealising style. The change that had taken place in him, since the days of *Werther* and the beginning of *Faust*, was in part only the normal change that follows adolescence; but there were also certain personal and local factors involved. Hard work, such as left little time for poetic somnambulism, had somewhat tamed his imagination. Court life at Weimar, simple as it was in the main, had begotten a kindlier feeling for the conventional, both in human relations and in art. The moods of revolt and pessimism had passed, and in their place had come a steady resolve to make as much of life as possible. In the creative frenzies of the earlier time he had delighted in the bizarre and the incommensurable; but now he felt that beauty was the worthiest aim, and that this was an effect producible only under rules and restrictions. After all, conformity seemed to be a larger and wiser doctrine than insurrection. In the ethical sphere the study of Spinoza had done its work by producing a conviction that God is in all things, and that the great wisdom is acquiescence in the will of God. This meant the acceptance of life and the recognition of self-control as the fundamental, character-building virtue. We understand what Wieland meant when he spoke, in 1780, of Goethe's increasing σωφροσύνη.

However, the muse of *Iphigenia* was not Sophrosyne, but Charlotte von Stein. Goethe had made her acquaintance soon after settling in Weimar, and found in her the precise embodiment of the Eternal Womanly that his present stage of progress needed. She was a wife, a mother, and belonged to the nobility—in the higher as well as in the conventional sense. Goethe made her the confidante of his soul and the object of a devotion that was much more than Platonic in its forms of expression. His letters address her as dearest lady, noblest lady, golden lady, dear angel. He credits her with " knowing every trait of his being," with " guiding his wild, erring course," with " quieting his tumultuous blood." He avers poetically that in ages past she must have been his sister or his wife. It is this relation which we find transfigured in *Iphigenia,* the theme of which is the saving, clarifying, ennobling power of womanhood. The German Iphigenia is womanhood at its heavenly best; and yet, so delicately

20

was her character studied that there is no point in the
play at which she can be said to transcend such human
goodness as is easily thinkable. The heroine of Euripides
has her fair allotment of Greek shiftiness. When she has
recognised her brother Orestes and has heard that he can
be released from the pursuing Eumenides only by carrying away the image of the goddess, she herself takes the
lead in devising the ruse by which King Thoas is to be
eluded. This being so, there is no possible rescue for the
three Greeks, after their plot has miscarried and they have
fallen into the hands of the king, except the Euripidean
dea ex machina. Athena appears and bids Thoas let them
go. But Goethe's heroine cannot stain her soul with
falsehood. She throws herself on the power of truth and
prevails by the sheer winsomeness of her appeal to the
king's better nature. Conquering his love and his anger,
and rising to the heights of Goethean renunciation, the
much-tried barbarian speaks the word " farewell."

Still more closely connected with Goethe's private
experience is the relation of Iphigenia to Orestes. He
comes to her desperate, sick at heart, pursued by the
Furies, haunted by gloomy hallucinations ; he is saved and
restored to the joy of living, when he knows that he has
found his sister. The magic of her presence, the assurance of her love, suffice. It is this intensely subjective
character of the play, together with its exquisite poetry,
that gives it its perennial interest. The Greek element—
the names and all that was taken over from the ancient
legend—is mere setting. There is really nothing Greek
about the play, least of all an attempt to imitate the style
of the Greek tragedy. Unlike *Nathan the Wise* and

Don Carlos, Goethe's drama is not concerned with ideas which were then agitating mankind at large, but with crises of the individual soul. It was really written for the little circle of Goethe's friends at Weimar; and when they played it at their amateur theatre, the part of Orestes fell naturally to him. He *was* Orestes; or better, he *had been* Orestes.

The final form of *Iphigenia* was the result of infinite filing. There are three phases of the text in prose, and a fourth in irregular verses. In despatching the completed manuscript from Rome in 1787, Goethe wrote to Herder that he had worked on the verses till he was weary. He asked that the play be read at first in the Weimar circle as "something quite new, without comparison." And something new it certainly was. So far, indeed, as the small question of genre was concerned, it was like the Greek *Iphigenia* in threatening a tragic conclusion and then avoiding it. But here, for the seeing eye, the resemblance to anything Greek ended. In its fewness of characters, its simplicity of structure, its dignity of style, its observance of the unities, it suggested a reversion to the classic French tragedy. But it differed from this in its absence of pomp, its profounder thought, its greater delicacy of analysis and phrasing. In short, it was a poetic drama of the soul. The German public, expecting something like *Götz von Berlichingen*, received it indifferently. They thought it an imitation of the Greek; that it was cold, statuesque, undramatic. But it is the reverse of all these things. To be sure its "action" is not of the kind to captivate Philistia. But given actors and an audience equal to its demand on their culture and intelligence, and Goethe's *Iphigenia* is a fascinating play, as well as a beautiful poem. This is now no longer a matter of debatable theory, but a fact of oft-proved experience.

Torquato Tasso sprang from the same soil as *Iphigenia* and belongs to the same order of art. Its theme, to quote Goethe's own formula, is the disparity between talent and life. Of course there is autobiography in it. With all his assiduous devotion to the public business, Goethe sometimes felt that he was out of his element— was like a bird caught in a snare, as he puts it in a letter of 1780. His inmost being was faithful to poetry, and he would often have preferred to muse by himself rather than to bother with council meetings or to run on errands of state. At the same time another side of his nature asserted that the prosaic labour was good for his soul. So he held steadily to his course, until the conflict between the poet and the man of affairs reached the stage of an acute malady—a " terrible disease," he afterward called it. Then he escaped to Italy to recover his equanimity and his joy in living. For ten years, therefore, he had had the best of opportunities to study the collision of the artistic temperament with practical affairs and practical men. Add to this his love for a " golden lady " with whom marriage was out of the question, and who sometimes had occasion to check the ardour of his devotion, and his interest in the situation of Tasso at Ferrara is fully accounted for.

Goethe conceived his *Tasso* as a kind of tragedy, though he chose to entitle it a *Schauspiel* instead of a *Trauerspiel*. " The essential thing in all tragic situa-

tions," he wrote afterward in *Kunst und Alterthum,*
" is separation, for which we need neither poison nor dagger, neither fire nor sword. Departure from a familiar
and beloved situation, through more or less of com-
pulsion, is a variation of the same theme."   The catastrophe would thus be the parting of Tasso from his familiar and beloved Ferrara. To account for this Goethe
had recourse to the apocryphal legend of the kiss, which
the passionate Torquato had one day bestowed on the
Princess Leonora in the very presence of her brother the
duke. The story ran that, on witnessing this shocking
transgression, Duke Alphonso had ordered the arrest of
Tasso, exclaiming, for the benefit of those present:
" Behold the melancholy situation of a man so great who
has thus far lost his wits! "   The kiss is made the cul-
mination of Tasso's troubles, which go back to his quarrel with the cool and accomplished man of affairs,
Antonio. We see that the framework of action is very
slight. A poetic dreamer at court is in love with a high-
born lady whom he cannot hope to possess, and whose
favour he can retain only by vigilant self-control. His
love involves him in difficulty with a courtier, and in
the mental agitation growing out of this affair he forgets
himself and gives the lady a passionate embrace. After
this he must, of course, go away, and can hardly be
expected to return. If one objects that a poet's enforced
change of residence in consequence of an amorous indis-
cretion is hardly an event of sufficient gravity to form
the catastrophe of a five-act play, the only answer is that
Tasso is depicted as a kind of adult child who lives
entirely in his feelings. For him the event is tragic

enough, and Goethe contrives that he never forfeits sympathy. And, after all, Tasso's calamity has its compensations; for out of what seems the wreck of his fortunes he saves the friendship of Antonio.

Work on *Tasso* was begun in 1781, but came to a standstill after two acts had been completed in rhythmic prose. In the spring of 1788 Goethe began to rewrite the drama in blank verse, his mind already oppressed by the thought of leaving the beloved Italy which had brought him a spiritual rebirth. Referring to the scenes written at this time, he afterward observed in the *Italian Journey* "that the painful emotion of a passionate soul which is drawn on irresistibly to an irrevocable banishment permeated the entire play." In the same connection he expressed the opinion that this subjective element had been written into the play with such fulness of detail as to render its representation on the stage virtually impossible. And, indeed, it can hardly be denied that much of *Tasso* is occupied with feelings a little too refined and delicate for human nature's daily food, or for the purposes of the acted drama. A. W. Schlegel thought, too, with all his admiration of Goethe, that the verse of *Tasso* and *Iphigenia* was not conversational enough for the stage; that it lacked *heurté;* that the periods "trail their slow length along through too many lines." This is no doubt defensible as an academic thesis. Nevertheless, the Germans have long since discovered that *Tasso* as well as *Iphigenia* can be played with excellent dramatic effect.

We turn now to *Don Carlos*, which was originally conceived by Schiller as a tragedy of love and intrigue in a royal household. As he first thought of it, in the summer of 1783, it was to be very much the same sort of play as *Cabal and Love;* only there would be no class conflict, and the lovers would be separated by the law of the church, not by barriers of social prejudice. St. Réal's historical novel *Dom Carlos*, which was Schiller's main source, told of a Spanish prince in love with his French stepmother and communicating with her at court through a loyal friend, the Marquis of Posa; of a court intrigue that had excited King Philip's jealousy and led him to murder Posa; of a charge of rebellion trumped up against Don Carlos and leading to his arrest and execution; of the subsequent poisoning of the virtuous queen. There is an early outline of the proposed play, which shows that Schiller intended to follow St. Réal rather closely in the main, but to deviate from him in three important points: first, the ambition of Carlos was to waken and prevail over his selfish love; second, Posa was to sacrifice himself deliberately for his friend; third, the lovers were to renounce each other. But the sketch contains no suggestion of interest in large political ideas. Posa, a quite subordinate figure, is a supremely loyal friend, but not yet the " ambassador of all mankind."

For various reasons Schiller did not fulfil expectations as salaried playwright of the Mannheim theatre; wherefore his contract was not renewed at the end of the stipulated year. He had by this time begun work on *Don Carlos*, and had decided to write it in verse. This decision was due primarily to the fact that of late the aspiration of the poet had begun to prevail over the ambition of the playwright. Schiller had begun to dream of a lasting fame. With true insight he felt that his proper field was historical tragedy, but could any prose tragedy endure? On this subject a weighty word had lately been uttered by Wieland, then the most influential man of letters in Germany. In a *Letter to a Young Poet,* published in the *Teutscher Merkur* for October, 1782, Wieland had said, after commenting on the painful lack of German tragedies comparable to the works of Racine and Corneille: "A tragedy in prose is like a heroic poem in prose. Verse is essential to poetry. So the ancients thought, and so the greatest of the moderns have thought; and one who is able to write a tragedy or a comedy in beautiful verse will hardly ever be so careless of his fame as to prefer prose." Such words from such a quarter can hardly have been written in vain. Wieland even declared that rhyme was indispensable. On this point, however, Schiller was of another mind. He preferred to follow the example of Lessing.

In the early stages of his work on *Don Carlos* Schiller was much enamoured of his hero. He even committed himself in a letter to the dubious theory that a dramatic poet ought to feel toward his hero as toward a sweetheart. One sees that artistic impartiality was no part of his creed. He freely wrote himself into the Spanish prince, especially his longing for friendship, his emotional warmth, his tendency to morbid melancholy. The essence of the tragic idea was to be that the love-sick prince should first be made a man by the saving power of friendship, by the altruistic dream of a noble service to mankind, and by the renunciation of his hopeless love; and then, when he had thus grown to heroic stature, that he should meet his fate in the moment of his inner triumph. A very good scheme, certainly. But, as time passed, Schiller gradually grew cool toward Don Carlos and transferred his affections to the noble friend who was to work the prince's regeneration. This change is attributable in part to the influence of Körner, in whom Schiller found his dream of saving and inspiring friendship realised. His letters to Körner tell in glowing language of a relation very like that of Carlos to Posa in the play. In the spring of 1785 he left Mannheim, which had by this time become hateful to him, and went to live at Leipzig, in order to be near his new-found friend. Here life opened before him as a thing of grand and joyous possibilities. The mood of the time is expressed in the *Song to Joy*, a jubilant pæan of universal brotherhood. In the society of Körner he slowly brought *Don Carlos* to completion. The first edition, of 1787, contains more than 6,000 lines—evidence enough that the stage had not been kept in view.

As Schiller himself admitted, the long and slow genesis of *Don Carlos* left its mark in the form of a certain incongruity between the first three acts and the last two. That which had begun as a love-tragedy, with Don Carlos for a hero, shaded little by little into a tragedy of political idealism, with Posa for a hero. Yet the death of Posa is not due to his amiable enthusiasm for liberty, which is taken in very good part by the king, but to the mad self-sufficiency with which, after he has won the king's confidence, he enters on a desperate course of intrigue and deception. This he does, not because it is at all necessary, but because the more quixotic and

dangerous mode of procedure appears to him the more
" heroic." Toward the end the intrigue becomes so very
complicated that the spectator, or even the reader, can
hardly keep track of it. The play lacks the simplicity and
the concentration that are necessary to a harmonious
tragic effect. There is material in it for two tragedies,
and they interfere with each other. In a later redaction
Schiller left out nearly a thousand verses of the first
edition, but without attempting a radical revision in the
interest of organic unity.

In its literary aspect the dominant note of *Don Carlos*
is its enthusiasm for certain ideas—an enthusiasm that
expresses itself in stately rhythm and magniloquent
phrase. The iambic cadence is very regular, there is
usually a pause at the end of a line. In the *Letter to a
Young Poet* which was lately cited, Wieland demands of
the poet, among other things, a native bent for imaginative soaring in the realm of ideas—*einen angeborenen
Hang zum Schwärmen in der Ideenwelt*. This is exactly Schiller's gift, as evinced conspicuously in *Don
Carlos*. Feeling is expressed in a glowing diction that
is very different from speech. Schiller is aflame with
ideas of love, friendship, renunciation, ambition, humanity; and there are fine phrases about all these things.
Writing in early manhood and on the eve of the Revolution, he was possessed by the beatific vision of a glorious future for mankind, to be realised by liberty and wise
kingship. Since then the world has grown a little cold
toward all such supernal idealisms, wherefore Schiller
now seems to many rather hollow and rhetorical. But he
was intensely in earnest, as were the other progressive

spirits of the epoch. Humanity was their word of power, and their imagination invested the name and the future of humanity with a sort of golden halo. What Posa says in his famous colloquy with King Philip, in the third act, came from the heart of Schiller and of his time. The scene is thus an interesting pendant to the fable of the rings in *Nathan the Wise*. It is worth noting, finally, that patriotism plays no part in *Don Carlos*. Posa is a cosmopolitan, and his humane idealism is quite compatible in his own mind with treasonable designs against his own country.

CHAPTER XVI

THE GREAT DAYS OF WEIMAR

O Weimar! dir fiel ein besonder Los;
Wie Bethlehem in Juda, klein und gross.

THUS Goethe in a poem of the year 1782. The greatness of Weimar consisted at that time—it was a place of some 6,000 inhabitants—in its having a prince who had chosen to surround himself with eminent writers, and had made one of them his intimate friend and counsellor. Besides this, the court circle took a keen interest in certain forms of art, more especially in poetry and play-acting. The outside world often spoke cynically of the unconventional proceedings in Weimar, the serious and lasting import of which was not at once apparent. This is particularly true of Goethe himself. During his first ten years in Weimar he published nothing of prime importance. Of the larger matters that were occupying him the public got no tidings. *Faust* lay untouched. He worked at *Egmont* now and then, but was unable to finish it. The new poetic dramas in which he undertook to embody present experience soon came to a standstill. He began a novel, *Wilhelm Meister,* but that also had to wait. To an outside observer it may well have seemed that the high promise of his youth had come to nothing, and that he was wasting himself on bagatelles for the Weimar court.

In the public opinion of that time, and indeed for many years thereafter, the real strength and ornament of literary Weimar was not Goethe but Wieland. The fecundity and versatility of Wieland were amazing, while his interests, much more than Goethe's, were those of the public at large. He always wrote entertainingly, though with an increasing bent for diffuse expatiation. To his *Teutscher Merkur* (1773–1810) he contributed a large number of imaginative works in prose and verse—lyric dramas, cantatas, Greek and Oriental tales, allegories, burlesque romantic poems, translations and imaginary conversations. Of all these the most important are the tale called the *Abderites* (1774) and the romantic poem *Oberon* (1780). The spirit of both is the spirit of humorous persiflage. The annals of the dull-witted people of Abdera, with their parochial narrowness and contentious stupidity, as evinced in their management of their own affairs and their treatment of the philosopher Democritus and the poet Euripides, are a veiled account of what Wieland himself had seen and suffered in various small places.

In *Oberon* he retold the story of Huon de Bordeaux, blending with the French romance certain features of the Oberon-Titania story as known to him from Shakespeare. The good knight Huon is required by Charlemagne to go to Bagdad, enter the banquet hall of the Kalif, kill his chief counsellor, kiss his daughter, and bring away some of his teeth and hair. He succeeds by the aid of

the friendly Oberon's magic. Having captured the fair
Saracen Rezia, he is bidden by Oberon, who is in search
of a pair of ideally faithful lovers, to go with her to the
Pope and marry her in the proper Christian way; until
which time she is to remain a virgin. This command
the lovers violate—whence come terrible trials, until
Oberon is appeased and convinced, and all ends happily.
The form is an eight-line stanza with the rhymes variously linked, and the lines varying in length from eight
to thirteen syllables. It was Goethe's opinion that " as
long as poetry should remain poetry, gold gold, and crystal crystal, Wieland's *Oberon* would be loved and admired
as a masterpiece of poetic art." If this be set down as the
too partial verdict of a friend, it may at least be said
that in *Oberon* we have the poet Wieland at his very
best. But he was a man of letters rather than a poet.
The novelist should be read in *Agathon* and the *Abderites,* the publicist in the articles he contributed to the
Merkur after the outbreak of the revolution in France.

The third member of the Weimar triad (from 1776
on) was Herder, in whose far-gazing mind the critical
intellect wrestled continually with the mysticism of the
poet and the seer. His study of ancient lore, and his
constant search for the national or ethnic element in
every manifestation of the artistic spirit, had brought
him little by little to the evolutionary point of view. In
the *Spirit of Hebrew Poetry* (1782–83) he pointed the
way to a new science of the Bible. The orthodox held
that the miraculous tales of the Old Testament were literally true, the rationalists that they were frauds of sacerdotalism. Lessing regarded them as parts of a never-

ending revelation, whereby the divine Teacher had given to men from time to time such glimpses of truth as their stage of progress permitted them to understand and use. Herder taught that they belonged to a body of national poetry, the value of which lay in its prevailing spirit. The sagas of the Hebrews were to be studied historically, with the aid of archæology, for the purpose of elucidating the *spirit* of Hebrew poetry—even as Montesquieu had sought to elucidate the *spirit* of the laws.

Such inquiries led up naturally to the great question of the meaning of history. What was the essential import of the human drama on earth? Was the progress of man an illusion, as Rousseau had thought? If not, what was the goal of evolution? This is the problem which Herder attacked in his *Ideas for a History of Mankind* (1784–91), the weightiest and most lucid of all his writings. The treatise begins far back with a description of the earth—man's dwelling-place—as a planet among planets, and of man as an animal among animals. The characters and aptitudes of the *genus homo* are explained in accordance with the scientific conceptions of the time, but with much intermixture of poetic ideas and fanciful speculation. All is made to lead up to the doctrine that what we see in the devious historic process is the " training of mankind for humanity "—*die Heranbildung der Menschheit zur Humanität*. Then follow a series of chapters on the more important nations of antiquity, the object being to show what each contributed, by its character and achievements, to the advancement of mankind. The work breaks off unfinished with the Middle Ages, which are here viewed less favourably than in the aforementioned booklet of 1775 (page 261). The tone of the *Ideas* is literary rather than scientific. The book interests the reader of to-day by its evolutionism, its largeness of outlook, its warmth of feeling. While its science is long since antiquated, and its logic often vulnerable, it is still readable for the sake of the fine idealism that permeates it. The perfectibility of man—of which Lessing was dreaming in *Nathan*, Goethe in his poem the *Mysteries*, and Schiller in *Don Carlos* and the *Artists*—is here reduced to a system and explained with persuasive eloquence.

In the summer of 1787 Schiller joined the Weimar coterie and settled down to those historical studies which presently led to a professorship at the University of Jena. For a whole year he was fated to listen, wherever he turned, to idolatrous praise of the absent Goethe. He made up his mind that he could never like the great man, however much he might admire his genius. From afar Goethe seemed to him a self-sufficient son of fortune, who showered his gifts like a god, giving everything but himself. Nor did their first meeting, after Goethe's return from Italy, effect any immediate change in their personal relations. Schiller persisted in his prejudice, and Goethe thought of Schiller only as the author of violent plays which had been debauching the public taste. So each went his own way. Goethe was just then somewhat out of humour with the German public. His heart was still in Italy, which had cured him of his mental troubles. Weimar was the place where he had been caught in a net and had suffered: it seemed to him cold, foggy, and withal parochial. He was minded henceforth to lead a freer life. A poet he would continue to be, of course, but no longer the poet of soul-sick self-tormentors. He took Christiane Vulpius to his bed and board, and celebrated the emancipation of the sensuous man in his *Roman Elegies*. His friends did not know what to make of the new Goethe, and he began to feel isolated. The public at large showed little interest in his new poetic dramas, or even in the published fragment of his *Faust* (1790). So he turned his attention to botany and other scientific studies, and for several years he wrote nothing of more than third-rate literary importance. Two or three prose plays, dealing with ephemeral aspects of the Revolution, and a hexameter version of the old poem of *Reynard the Fox*, were the most notable.

Meanwhile Schiller had travelled far on his separate way. In the first place he had discovered the Greeks and found them very sanative, very clarifying. The idea of Beauty began to bulk large in his thinking. He wrote the *Gods of Greece*, an elegy on the vanished loveliness of the Greek religion, and the *Artists,* a glorification of the artistic sense as the chief factor in man's upward progress. In his historical work, on the other hand, his lodestar was the idea of Freedom. His *Defection of the Netherlands* and his *History of the Thirty Years' War* were rather hastily written, with but little examination of the sources; but their eloquent dignity of style, their philosophic temper, and their vivid portraiture of scenes and persons set upon them the stamp of literary classics. From history Schiller turned to æsthetic philosophy. He determined to fathom the laws of beauty, believing that sound theoretic knowledge would aid him as a poet. So

21

he plunged deep into Kant and wrote the series of studies which have given him a place in the history of æsthetic theorising. The most important of them, so far as literary influence is concerned, is the famous essay on *Naïve and Sentimental Poetry*, a masterpiece of penetrating thought and lucid exposition.

This essay was published in 1795 in the *Horen*, a new magazine which had already brought Schiller and Goethe together in friendly co-operation. Three years before that time Schiller's health had broken down; for months he lay at the point of death, and his recovery brought him only to a condition of precarious invalidism. Compelled to give up his lectures in Jena, he undertook, with the financial support of the enterprising publisher Cotta, of Stuttgart, to edit a literary journal which should eschew politics and seek to divert the minds of men from the fierce excitement of the Revolution into the serener fields of art. The request for contributions, which he sent to all the most eminent writers in Germany, met with a politely favourable response from Goethe, who was glad to see—so he wrote in July, 1794—that Schiller was becoming more friendly. A happy accident brought the two men together after six years of neighbourly estrangement; interchanges of opinion followed, and they soon found that by different routes they had reached the same general outlook upon life and art. They decided to travel the rest of the way together. They became friends, allies; and the decade of their intimacy is by far the most memorable decade in the whole history of German letters.

They began with a broadside of epigrams, the so-

called *Xenia*. At first they hardly thought further than
to amuse themselves at the expense of the literary old
fogies and other unenlightened folk who had declined
to support the *Horen* and doomed it to an early death.
But the idea of the *Xenia* grew apace. Targets for satire,
genial or caustic, objects of epigrammatic blame or praise,
were visible in countless numbers. So the stinging and
stingless distichs multiplied until there were nearly a
thousand of them. A selection, comprising about half
the total number they had written, was published in
Schiller's *Musenalmanach* for 1797 and caused great
excitement. The victims retorted in kind, or with scurrilous abuse, and there was much angry vociferation.
But Goethe and Schiller had the wisdom not to continue
the rasping warfare. They had cleared the air, defined
their position, and shown themselves to the world as
allies.

In the intervals of the more important work to be
considered presently, both wrote numerous ballads and
other short poems. Schiller had some difficulty in effect-
ing a return from philosophy to poetry. He had discovered that poets were either naïve or sentimental, and
that he himself belonged to the latter order; that is, he
was a poet of the infinite longing, a searcher after the
lost harmony between feeling and thought. His problem,
then, was to express his ideals of culture in language of
emotional warmth and rhythmic distinction. This is
what he undertook in his philosophic poems—most happily in the *Ideal and Life*, the *Walk*, and the *Song of the
Bell*. As for the ballad, he had never cared greatly for
the folksong, and in any case its style was not at his

command. His early narrative poems show a mastery of dramatic vigour and rhetorical pathos, but not of naïve simplicity or symbolic suggestion. Under the influence of Goethe he tried to school himself in the "naïve" way, and with some success. But meanwhile Goethe himself had lost somewhat of his earlier lyric wizardry. He, too, had become reflective, and had his ideals of life and art. Thus it resulted that the new ballads of 1797 and the ensuing years—among the best are the *Bride of Corinth* and the *God and the Bayadere* by Goethe, and the *Pledge* and the *Cranes of Ibycus* by Schiller—have little resemblance to anything previously known by that name. They are more artistic, more thoughtful, more elevated in style. The story always seems to be told for its own sake, it is true, but one never forgets that it is being told by a highly refined minstrel for highly refined men and women.

The prestige of Goethe was enormously increased by the publication, in 1796, of *Wilhelm Meister's Apprenticeship*. This nutritious but not very exciting novel had been twenty years in the making, and had developed with its author. It is probable that Goethe first conceived it as a sort of antidote to *Werther*. It was to tell the story of a very impressible young man much like Werther in all respects but one, that one being his possession of a saving quality in the form of an artistic passion. Goethe felt that he himself had continually been saved from the perils of hyperæsthesia by his poetic gift. To *tell* a trouble in song or play or tale, was to get rid of it and render it innocuous. It is worth noting that Werther is an artist who does not paint. For his new and saner hero Goethe chose the name Meister, and for his redeeming pursuit the histrionic art. But at Weimar his experience was such, for a while, as to cast doubt on the sanative value of artistic self-expression, and to exalt in his mind the saving efficacy of practical business. So the centre of gravity of the proposed novel gradually shifted, *Wilhelm Meister's Theatrical Mission* becoming *Wilhelm Meister's Apprenticeship* in the school of life. By large and varied experience a volatile youth was to find a needed anchor for his being in socially helpful labour. This is the scheme of the novel as we have it, but the idea does not emerge very clearly at the end. When Wilhelm, after many fleeting affairs of the heart, has found an ideal wife in the faultless Natalie, and has decided to go to work in earnest, he does not do it, after all, but sets out with his son for a tour in Italy. This is because Goethe saw possibilities in a continuation of the tale—one can see that it is indefinitely continuable— under the name of *Wanderjahre*.

As a gallery of portraits and a repository of wise observation by a very wise observer, *Meister's Apprenticeship* is wellnigh incomparable. Its details—some of them at least—are a source of perennial delight. On the other hand, the modern taste in fiction is apt to be displeased with its extreme discursiveness. Episode follows episode in a leisurely flow of narrative and ratiocination, but their bearing on the story is not made evident. Such discursiveness, however, belongs to eighteenth-century fiction (*Werther* being a conspicuous exception), and the public of that day did not find it tiresome. Just as the older romancers presupposed an inexhaustible interest in adventures of a certain sort, so Goethe presupposes an inexhaustible interest in human nature. It was a theory of his that the novel should concern itself with events and modes of thought, the drama with characters and deeds. This is a dubious theory, so far as it relates to prose fiction, and it explains perhaps why no healthy boy of normal literary appetite was ever heard to praise *Wilhelm Meister*. Its author wrote as a psychologist; he was interested in modes of thought and their natural history. He makes a free use of direct description. His topography is quite vague; one never knows where one is. With all his realism he is fond of mysterious and romantic complications.

Goethe's next work of importance was *Hermann and Dorothea*, in which he undertook to wed the ancient hexameter to a tale of humble German life. The associations of the form were mainly with high epic themes; still, the ancients had their eclogues, and Voss and others had employed the hexameter for idyls of German country life, which they had thus invested with a certain air of quaint and dignified simplicity. Goethe greatly admired the *Luise* of Voss, but it seemed to him that idyllic description would gain very much in interest if connected with an epic element of some dignity. Of late he had given himself much practice in the writing of hexameters, both pure, as in *Reynard the Fox*, and mixed, as in the *Roman Elegies*, the *Metamorphosis of the Plant*, and the *Xenia*. As for the subject-matter, the suggestion came from a published story relating to the expatriation of the Salzburg Protestants in 1732. The story told of an emigrant girl who, on the way to a new home under distressing circumstances, had won the love of a well-to-do youth and married him. Goethe changed the time and place. The Salzburg Protestants became Alsatian Germans who had been uprooted from their homes by the Revolution and driven to seek refuge on the east side of the Rhine. Thus we get a picture of German still life, painted against the background of the great revolutionary upheaval. This impingement of the great world on the small makes the characteristic charm of the poem. We hear of the terrible doings in France as they affect the lives of common folk in the immediate present. But the folk of the poem are not so common after all. In the young Hermann and his parents one quickly recognises the young Goethe and *his* parents; while in the wise judge who discourses so ably of the Revolution we hear the maturer Goethe, who had come to look with aversion on the course of events in France. And just as in *Wilhelm Meister* all the characters speak the choicest German, and often exhibit a mental subtlety hardly to be expected of their kind, so in *Hermann and Dorothea* they reel off their philosophy of life in stately hexameters, with many a reminiscence of Homeric phrase. In both the common reality is invested with a stylistic veil that idealises everything.

In the *Natural Daughter* this idealising veil was made still thicker. Here Goethe's purpose was to deal in a large and serious way with the Revolution, which he had treated with satiric levity in the *Grand Cophta* and the *Citizen General*, and with cryptic symbolism in his *Märchen*. The memoirs of Stephanie de Bourbon-Conti, which fell under his eye in 1799, suggested the outline

of a plot. He began to write, the matter pleased him, he
decided to make a trilogy of it. After the completion of
the first part, however, his interest waned and he dropped
the whole enterprise. It is clear that his pursuit of a
fact-transfiguring style had here carried him a little too
far. He wished to get rid of everything quotidian and
leave a pure artistic essence. So he laid his scene
nowhere and nowhen, gave his characters no names, and
made them speak in blank verse of exquisite melody and
preternatural delicacy of feeling. The desire to avoid
everything commonplace led to a terse and pregnant diction that sometimes does violence to German idiom. The
character of the heroine is superbly drawn, but the whole
is undramatic, unlifelike—mere poetry in the best and
the worst sense of the phrase. As for the French Revolution, it is simply not there at all. Goethe was out of
his element in trying to write plays on that subject. His
strength lay in depicting the aspirations and struggles
of the individual toward peace, light, and inward harmony. And the pre-eminently right theme for his genius
was at hand in his symbolic drama of the magician who
had mortgaged his soul to the devil.

In 1790 Goethe had published *Faust, a Fragment.*
The publication did not include all the Faust scenes that
he had written before settling in Weimar, and it did
include some recent additions written in Italy. There
was enough of it to excite curiosity and whet the appetite
for more, but there was not enough of it to show the drift
of the whole. It ended with Gretchen's swoon in the cathedral. The nature of the tie between Faust and Mephistopheles was left in the dark. Knowing the saga, the pub-

lic was justified in surmising that Faust was to be damned
for the seduction of Gretchen. This, however, was very
far from Goethe's purpose. In 1797 he resumed work on
the long-neglected play, which he now looked on with
a degree of cynicism as a " barbarous composition "; and
one of the first things he did was to write the Prologue,
which hinted that the comrade of the devil, the rake, the
seducer, the murderer, was after all a confused " servant
of the Lord," and might be expected to bring up in
heaven. He then proceeded to fill in and round out, so
as to make a coherent and intelligible action up to the
time of Gretchen's death, and also to sketch and in part
to write out that which was to come afterward. Like
Wilhelm Meister, Faust was to learn wisdom from experience, and in the end to find satisfaction in altruistic
effort. His " striving " was to be, in the eyes of the
Eternal Pardoner, his redeeming quality. And the most
important single agency in the uplifting of his character
was to be his contact with the Greek ideal of beauty as
symbolised in Helena. As the vast subject thus expanded
before him, Goethe decided, just as he had done in the
case of *Wilhelm Meister*, to publish a *First Part of Faust*
provisionally, and to let the completion of the poem bide
its time. When the *First Part* was given to the world,
in 1808, discerning minds began to see that Goethe's
design was something vast, stupendous, incommensurable; but just what it was in detail, they could not even
now make out. They could see, however, that the part
already completed contained some of the noblest imaginative poetry, the profoundest criticism of life, the most
engaging realism, the most exquisite humour, and the

most pathetic tragedy of woman's love, that had ever found expression in the German language.

In the *Elective Affinities,* published in 1809, the novelist Goethe gathered himself together once more, as he had done long before in *Werther.* The tale is told with masterful technic and with only a little of that straggling discursiveness which characterises *Wilhelm Meister.* The book was indirectly a contribution to the ethics of marriage. There was a growing disposition, in certain circles of German society, to treat the marriage tie as a bond to be lightly broken under the attraction of a new " affinity." Goethe, who had lately legalised his own conscience-marriage to Christiane Vulpius, saw the tragic peril of a doctrine which seemed to regard human beings as if they were non-moral chemical atoms. The novel shows the working of the doctrine in a particular case. The wife and her affinity save themselves by moral self-control. The husband weakly indulges his vagrant passion for his step-daughter, and the remorse and pathetic death of the girl Ottilie by self-starvation are the consequence.

We now return to Schiller, whose invalid body had succumbed to its ever-impending fate in the year 1805, but not until his five great plays had made Weimar the centre of the world for matters of dramatic art. A permanent court theatre had been established in 1791 under Goethe's directorship. It was a modest affair in point of material resources, but it provided the necessary touchstone of dramatic effectiveness. In securing plays and endeavouring to educate the public taste to his own artistic standard, Goethe leaned heavily on Schiller, who was thus brought back, after an interval of ten years, to the " boards that signify the world." He wrote again for the stage, but never for the evening merely, or for the groundlings. A certain high seriousness permeates all his work. Humour has no part in it. His men and women, even the humblest of them, seem to dwell on the heights, and to think and feel in the terms of Schiller's own idealism.

He began with *Wallenstein*, and found the subject at first intractable, because it had to do with repellent passions and an unheroic hero. For the historical Wallenstein, while he had terrorised Germany at the head of an army, had not been a great soldier, still less a great statesman. The fact of chief interest in connection with him was the question of his treason to the empire. And however that question might be decided, his assassination had really nothing to do with it, but was an act of private vengeance. To arouse sympathy for such a man and invest his miserable fate with the impressiveness of tragedy, and to do this without falsifying history or taking sides in a partisan controversy, was indeed a difficult problem; and Schiller's solution of it is perhaps his very best title to the fame of a great dramatic poet. By the honesty of his dialectic, that is, by bringing out the good and the excusable in Wallenstein's character, as well as the bad and the dubious; by contrasting him with lesser men; by showing him as a man of mystery and of deep feeling, and giving him a cold, calculating adversary; above all, by contriving that the spectator see him through the partial yet searching eyes of the young idealist, Max Piccolomini,—Schiller makes his hero's taking off appear like the tragic nemesis of a great man's error.

Of course history is idealised in *Wallenstein*. Schiller held with Goethe that art consists in showing the essential truth of human nature through a veil of poetry. The drama for him was always a conflict of emotion and will, and he felt that the cold passions—hate, ambition, envy, vindictiveness, and so forth—would make a dull play. So he invented the romantic lovers, Max and Thekla. Their sentimental idealism, like the occasional lyric passages, and indeed the sonorous verse itself, are but a part of the poetic veil by which he sought to give warmth and colour to a historical picture. Underneath all that, however, the play of real historical forces is justly and luminously denoted. In this aspect of it Schiller's art has been aptly likened to monumental fresco-painting. From a theatrical point of view it is perhaps regrettable that he chose so large a canvas. His real theme at the outset was Wallenstein's death; but as he worked at the exposition and the historical setting, the matter expanded until there was enough of it for two five-act plays. So he wrote a dramatic overture called *Wallenstein's Camp*, which was played at the opening of the theatre in 1799, and then completed the drama proper in two parts entitled the *Piccolomini* and *Wallenstein's Death*. The whole is in no sense a trilogy, but a colossal drama in ten acts, with a poetic prelude in a different meter and a lighter vein. The necessity of dividing the representation between two evenings detracts somewhat from its effect. But for all that, Wallenstein remains the most impressive tragic figure in the German classical drama.

In *Mary Stuart* (1800), even more than in *Wallen-stein,* the central personage was an object of controversy. According to the point of view, the Scottish queen had either suffered condignly on the scaffold, or she had been the victim of an atrocious outrage. To write a Catholic or a Protestant play about her would have been comparatively easy—the thing has been done many times in many languages—but Schiller wished to make a human drama, the interest of which would not depend on any possible conclusion as to the legal and political merits of Queen Mary's case. The great difficulty was that, if the action was to end with her death, her long-past misdeeds could not be represented, but only narrated. Thus she would appear all along as a doomed prisoner awaiting her fate—a pathetic rather than a tragic situation. In some way it was necessary to make her fate seem the consequence, not of acts done long ago, but of acts seen by the spectator. To attain this end Schiller had recourse to two inventions: first, Mary's attempt to escape with the amorous fanatic Mortimer, involving her co-responsibility for his attempt on the life of Queen Elizabeth; secondly, a personal encounter of the two queens, resulting in a mortal insult to Elizabeth. By these devices, and by making Mary a beautiful young woman still capable of engaging the chivalrous but unsteady devotion of Leicester, Schiller shifted the issue, so to speak, from the sphere of politics and religion to that of love and jealousy. And he succeeded perfectly in making Mary's death appear as the consequence of her own passionate error. To have left the matter there, however, would have been to stamp the Scottish queen's character as essentially ignoble; and this, at any rate, was not Schiller's conception of her. He accordingly converted the intricate political drama into a simple psychological drama of inward purification. The climax is reached when Queen Mary rises to the height of accepting her doom, with all its ignominy and injustice, as the expiation divinely required of her for the real sins of long ago.

In the *Maid of Orleans,* just as in *Mary Stuart,* Schiller undertook to portray a Catholic heroine whose character was one thing in the house of her friends, something very different in that of her enemies. According to the loyal Catholic tradition, she appeared as a divinely appointed rescuer of France. The voices, the miracles, were a genuine manifestation of divine power, her death a holy martyrdom. For Shakespeare she had been a vulgar witch, for Voltaire a pious fraud of the mediæval church. What had she been in reality? For a proper appreciation of Schiller's dramatic answer to this question, it is well to bear in mind two facts. In the first place, the mighty work accomplished by the Maid in the rekindling of French patriotism was in no sense matter of doubt; and Schiller, as a student of history, was not the man to believe that great effects could proceed from mean and trivial causes. In the second place, he was by nature a lover of womanhood, always prone to idealise it, and especially to see in women a capacity for heroic conduct. It was thus quite natural that he should conclude, in the then state of historical and psychological knowledge, that the essential truth regarding the Maid of Orleans was to be found rather in the house of her friends than among the rationalists.

So he threw himself boldly on the Catholic tradition, even adding to it some dubious supernaturalism of his own invention, and called his play a " romantic tragedy." In his hands the rustic maid became a divine amazon, fighting in the ranks with men, slaying Englishmen with a magic sword; but all the while invincible, under the terms of her mandate from the Holy Virgin, only on condition of resisting all earthly love.   An instantaneous glimpse of the face of Lionel, as she is doing battle with him, causes her to forget, to her own way of thinking, the Virgin's command.   Thence follow remorse, helplessness, humiliation; until at last, her expiation completed, she receives back her supernatural power and dies in glory on the field of battle.   The play is replete with Schiller's finest dramatic effects.   Any one not constitutionally hostile to his methods will come away from a good performance of the *Maid of Orleans* saying: It is magnificent, even if it is not Jeanne d'Arc.

The anti-naturalism of Schiller reached a culminating point in the *Bride of Messina*, just as did that of Goethe at the very same time in the *Natural Daughter*. Having now become a zealous student of Sophocles, and knowing how important a factor the chorus was in the total effect of Greek tragedy, he wished to find a modern equivalent for the ancient chorus. A real chorus, with song and dance, would have meant simply an unthinkable mixture of drama, opera, and ballet. So he hit on the expedient of providing each of his hostile brothers, Don Manuel and Don Cesar, with a band of retainers, and allowing these to function both as persons of the drama and as semi-choruses; the choral parts not to be sung, but spoken by designated leaders. At the same time he endeavoured to find, in his subject-matter, a substitute for the fate-idea as it appears in *King Œdipus*. A pregnant queen of mediæval Messina is widowed by the death of a husband who has committed a crime. She has an ominous dream, which is interpreted by a soothsayer to mean that the child to be born will cause the death of the two princes who are co-heirs to the throne. To defeat the dream-oracle she conceals the birth of a daughter, and has the child brought up in secret at a distance from the court. So much is presupposition. The play gives the fulfilment of the dream. Schiller's lofty poetic diction is at its very best in the *Bride of Messina,* but his innovation in the matter of the chorus met with little favour. On the other hand, his use of the curse-idea—the extinction of a family conceived as the foredoomed expiation of ancestral guilt—was as a seed dropped on fertile soil.

The *Bride of Messina*, an experiment in pseudo-Hellenism, is the least available for the stage among Schiller's plays. It was followed by *William Tell*, the most popular of them all, and the only one which is not a tragedy. Like the *Maid of Orleans*, it is a drama of patriotism; but the Swiss farmers follow no celestial banner, and no miracles come to their aid. They rely on their own united strength. They are not actuated by any enthusiasm for freedom in the abstract, but by a sturdy determination to get rid of their tyrannical satraps. They do not preach revolution, save as the inherent right to throw off intolerable oppression. They do not preach democracy at all, their aim being to restore the old system of home rule under the empire. Nevertheless, when the disunited German people began to chafe under the tyranny of their own reactionary princes, it was natural enough to see in Schiller's *Tell* a gospel of union, self-help, and popular rights. It is this play, pre-eminently, to which he owes his name of poet of freedom. And what an intensely human drama it is! Young and old, learned and simple, alike find their account in its picturesque setting, its dramatic energy, its strong appeal to the love of country. The modern drama can show no better exposition anywhere than the exposition of *William Tell*—unless it be that of the *Maid of Orleans*. One must suppose that the critics who have sometimes taxed it—the play as a whole—with a lack of unity and concentration, can never have seen a German audience hang on it with delight from first to last, without ever becoming aware of any such defects. The fact is that Schiller here undertook something essentially new; namely, a play with an entire people for a hero. The theme is the liberation of a people by their own efforts. All the scenes converge, all the characters contribute, to that end. *William Tell* is a *Volksdrama* in the best sense of the word.

CHAPTER XVII

THE RISE OF THE ROMANTIC SCHOOL AND THE WAR
AGAINST NAPOLEON

It was a long time before the work of Goethe and
Schiller at Weimar took on the glamour of classicity.
They had made enemies by the *Xenia*, and in other ways.
The cause for which they stood—ideal art as the expression of a large, free, and harmonious life—was not
exactly a popular cause, and that part of the public which
was absorbed in politics and practical affairs found little
nutriment in them. The death of Schiller attracted no
attention in comparison with the ostentatious mourning
for Klopstock two years before. The popularity of Wieland had hardly begun to abate. The favourite playwright of the epoch was Kotzebue, whose taking stage-
craft and skill in catering to the average appetite gave
him, for a short time, a European reputation. He had,
however, neither ideas nor ideals; wherefore his multitudinous plays contain nothing for the historian of literature. In prose fiction the man of the hour was Jean
Paul Friedrich Richter (1763–1825).

In his lifetime Jean Paul enjoyed the vogue of a great
writer and a wonderful searcher of hearts. Women
idolised him, and good critics regarded him as a peer of

the best. His fame spread abroad, Carlyle wrote a brilliant essay about him, several of his books were translated
into English. When he died Ludwig Börne said of him
in the course of a glowing eulogy: " He has not lived
for all men, but the time will come when he will be born
for all, and all will mourn his loss. He stands patiently
at the gate of the twentieth century, waiting with a smile
for his crawling countrymen to come up with him." The
prediction has not been fulfilled, and only illustrates the
difficulty that besets the vocation of prophet. To-day
Richter is hardly read at all. In an age of revivals there
is no sign of a reviving interest in him. The neglect of
him may be ascribed first and foremost to his style—
to what Carlyle called his " fantastic, many-coloured,
far-grasping, every way perplexed and extraordinary
mode of writing." The effect of his method is that his
characters do not stand out clearly in the mind's eye, but
seem to move about dimly in a welter of baffling details.
He was unable to tell a story straightforwardly. Withal,
notwithstanding his sobriquet, the Unique, he lacked
real originality. He was indeed a unique note-taker.
Among his effects were found nearly two hundred manuscript volumes in quarto, together with a multitude of
separate portfolios, containing excerpts from his reading;
and these excerpts he worked into his stories quite as the
whim took him. Anything was in order at any time.

The style of Richter is that of *Tristram Shandy*, with
the discursiveness and irrelevancy raised to a higher
power. He is a disciple of Sterne, too, in his fondness
for the eccentric sentimental hero. The most of Jean
Paul's characters are odd fish with strange names and

strange habitudes. Humour he has in abundance, but it is the humour of a freakish fancy rather than of sane observation. His people shed the smiling tear on occasions—so has the fashion changed—that do not now seem to call for it. Still, if we take him at his best—say in *Quintus Fixlein* or *Siebenkäs*—and forget the futility of the story as such, it is not hard to find the charm which his contemporaries felt in the play of his humour about the prosaic facts of life, and in his sympathetic portraiture of small folk and small things. In respect of literary affinity Richter was a child of the sentimental age; he owed but little to the new romanticism which began to make a stir as a militant doctrine just as his popularity was culminating.

The history of the so-called Romantic School may be said to begin when the Schlegels and Tieck and Novalis began to be conscious of a certain community of ideas, and to use the word " romantic " as a name for what they believed in. This happened about 1798. But the ideas of these men were not new, or were new only in part, the way having been prepared by earlier writers. Of these earlier writers the most important were Herder and Goethe. But there were other influences at work. Bodmer's exhumations of mediæval romance and minnesong; Lessing's attack on the classical French canon and his use of romantic elements in *Nathan the Wise;* the unbridled individualism of the " storm and stress " period; the work of the Göttingen poets; the new feeling for nature as a source of mystic suggestion—all these must be taken into account in studying that romanticism which is older than the Romantic School.

One of the best contributions that appeared in Schiller's short-lived *Horen* was an appreciation of Dante, with some specimens of very good translation from the *Divine Comedy*. The drift of the essay was to explain Dante from his mediæval environment. " One must dream one's self back into that heroic monkish confusion, must become Guelf or Ghibelline, else one will throw aside the book in disgust." " Full of barbarism, excesses, and horrors as was the century in which he (Dante) lived, I do not hesitate to prefer it to this." These sentences indicate the writer's point of view. His name was AUGUST WILHELM SCHLEGEL (1769–1844). He had studied at Göttingen, enjoyed the friendship of Bürger, and got the reputation, by his facility in the making of smoothly vacuous verse, of being a poet. In 1796 he settled at Jena to make his way as a contributor to the journals. Here he was presently joined by his younger brother FRIEDRICH SCHLEGEL (1772–1829), who was then thinking of an academic career. Both the brothers were fervid admirers of Goethe, and at first of Schiller also. The younger, a student of Greek philosophy, had caught the fever of Fichte's idealism. Fichte was then a professor at Jena, and in the morning of his immense influence as a teacher; and the essence of his doctrine was that the ego is the only reality. To his youthful disciples this discovery seemed to promise a wonderful rejuvenation of life and letters. Feeling the need of an organ to disseminate their views, the brothers started the *Athenæum*, which ran for three years (1798–1801) and then died an easy and unregretted death.

The *Athenæum* is usually regarded as the starting-point of German romanticism, so far as the word denotes anything like the concerted effort of a school. The leading spirit of the journal was the younger Schlegel, who assumed the air of an inerrant law-giver, though himself painfully lacking in creative power. He was fond of paradox, regarded obscurity as rather meritorious, and preferred to express himself dogmatically in oracular fragments. His enthusiasm for Goethe was very genuine. He averred that Goethe's poetry and Fichte's philosophy were the two centres of German art and culture. But Goethe's " poetry," he thought, was best represented by *Wilhelm Meister*, which formed one of the three " greatest tendencies of the century," the other two being Fichte's philosophy and the French Revolution. He declared in the *Athenæum* that *Wilhelm Meister* was " an absolutely new and unique book," in which " everything was thought and expressed as might be expected from one who was at once a divine poet and a perfect artist." The wonderful novel was an all-in-one—prose, poetry, philosophy, criticism, self-revelation. In short, it was the perfection of *Romanpoesie*, or poetry of the novel. Then, by a juggle of words, *Romanpoesie* became *romantische Poesie*, and Schlegel proceeded to define " romantic " as an ideal of perfection, having really abstracted it from the unromantic *Wilhelm Meister*. Romantic poetry was explained as " progressive universal poetry." Its mission was to fuse all the different genres in one, and this one with philosophy and rhetoric. In this wider sense, Schlegel thought, all poetry ought to be romantic. " The more popular an author is, the more romantic." Finally the word-intoxicated man wrote to his brother: "I cannot send you my explanation of 'romantic,' because it is 125 pages long."

The significance of all this is not that the jargon has any bearing on intelligible literary criticism, but that it brought into use, as the shibboleth of a school, a word whose meaning was hopelessly vague. And this vagueness has adhered to the word ever since—more especially, perhaps, in the usage of German writers, who are prone to label as "romantic" any poetic, literary, religious, philosophic, artistic, scientific, musical, or political tendency that can be shown to have been favoured by one or more members of the so-called Romantic School. But really there never was a school, except in the very loosest sense of the word. There was simply a coterie of friends who were very differently endowed, and were driving at very different things. For five or six years they continued in close personal relations, oscillating between Jena and Berlin, praising one another's writings inordinately, and regarding themselves as the apostles of a new gospel that was to revolutionise the whole of life. Then they separated and went their several ways. In the immediate circle of the Schlegels there was a deal of talk about the principles of romantic art; about irony, and subjectivity and universality, that is, completeness of self-revelation; about the autocracy of the creative artist, and other such matters. There is no evidence that the lingo ever really influenced a man of genius (how could it?), but it gave a sort of sanction to authorial caprice and literary amorphousness. As for the two brothers, the younger did good work as a philosophic essayist, as the pioneer historian of literature, and as the author of the first German book on the language and wisdom of the Hindus. But he achieved nothing very memorable in criticism, and his attempts at poetry, drama, and fiction were futile beyond description. The elder brother's service consists in his admirable translation of seventeen of Shakespeare's plays, his well-known lectures on dramatic literature, and his less-known early essays on the works of Goethe, which had much to do with the rapid increase of Goethe's prestige in the era of romanticism. As an appreciator, Wilhelm Schlegel is one of the three or four greatest names in German history; as a translator, the very first, with the exception, perhaps, of Luther. But his original verse could easily be spared. There is no substance in it.

One of the best contributions to the *Athenæum* was a collection of aphoristic sayings called *Pollen*. The author was Friedrich von Hardenberg, an amiable dreamer who took the name NOVALIS (1772–1801). The *Fragments* of Novalis, which form the larger part of his extant work, are broken lights flashed from the mind of a man who had become enamoured of Fichte's idealism, and took delight in tracing out its consequences in religion, art, mathematics, physics, geology, and other lines of thought. He was of Protestant lineage, and did not, like Friedrich Schlegel, go over formally to the Catholic Church, though he probably would have done so if he had lived longer. At any rate he loved Catholicism for its æsthetic appeal, and gradually came to see in the Middle Ages, when the undivided church had dominated life and enwrapt it with poetry, the excellent home of the soul. Naturally, therefore, he found *Wilhelm Meister*, with all his admiration of it, too banal and prosaic

—not romantic enough. So he undertook to vie with Goethe by writing a romance of culture which should carry its hero through the school of life in the Middle Ages. He took the legendary minnesinger, Heinrich von Ofterdingen, for his hero and sketched a vast plan. After searching experience of love and sorrow, Heinrich was to catch a glimpse of a wonderful blue flower, which would then become the symbolic goal of his spiritual longing. He was to wander over the known world, learning the import of art, religion, and statecraft, and at last in the fulness of wisdom to achieve the blue flower. Only a little of the singular romance was ever completed. The fragment begins well, with charming pictures of mediæval life, but the symbolism soon becomes rather unintelligible. The pages exhale, if they do not succinctly express, the idea that the present is mean and prosaic, hence unavailable for art; that all poetry and all higher satisfaction of the soul must be sought in a faraway time when men had lived passionately and imaginatively amid strange happenings.

Unlike Novalis, his friend LUDWIG TIECK (1772–1852) lived to a ripe age and wrote voluminously in all the genres. He is perhaps more completely representative of the German romantic movement than any other writer. He began, if we ignore a few quite minor things, with a gloomy novel, *William Lovell*,—an expression of the black despair that he himself had sometimes felt in his youth. Then, as if cured by confession, and convinced that he had taken life too seriously, he turned his hand to light satiric skits, using nursery tales as a setting and poking fun at the rationalistic tendencies of the day. In this vein he wrote *Bluebeard* and *Puss in Boots*. As one who had recoiled in disgust from the pain of thought, he was fascinated by the old folk-tales, which set reason at naught and knew no such thing as a riddle of life. They were entertaining and soothing—like a children's game to a sad philosopher. He began to revise and publish folk-tales, and presently to attempt things of his own in the spirit of the good old times. His so-called dramas were not meant to be played, but to shed a rosy light on the age of superstition by making it appear as the age of passion, faith, and poetry. The reader of the *Life and Death of Saint Genevieve,* of *Fortunatus,* or *Octavianus,* is expected to take the legend at its face value and not to play the rationalist. The miraculous is treated as a matter of course. The characters are not clearly limned, but seem to float in a mist of vague emotion. They are legendary and historical personages, also ghosts and allegorical figures, such as Church, Faith, Love, Romanza. They speak in all the varieties of cunning and mellifluous verse, including sonnets and *terza rima*. The best effects are musical and poetic, never dramatic. Tieck introduces Romanza as a child of Faith and Love and makes her say:

> *Moon-illumined summer night,*
> *That holds in thrall the fantasy,*
> *Fair wonder-world of faerie,*
> *Arise in all thy ancient might.*

This note of longing for a beauty that once was but no longer is—the feeling that there have been better

times and better men than those that now are—may be
called the *Leitmotif* of romanticism. In Tieck's dramas,
as in his contemporary poems and plays, one may notice
a predilection for sights and sounds that suggest or
accord with a vague and dreamy longing—the moonlit
night, the dim woods, the distant sound of hunter's horn
or shepherd's shawm, the rose as symbol of desire. In
his case the romantic impulse took the form of an æsthetic
fondness for the wonder-world of mediæval legend. He
found in its mystery and symbolism and mental *chiar-
oscuro* a source of poetic inspiration, but his mediævalism
never became a practical matter. It did not lead him into
the Catholic communion or cause him to take an active
interest in politics, either as a reactionary or as a patriotic
poet. It did lead him, however, in the direction of what
was afterward to be known as pre-Raphaelitism. While
a student he wandered about South Germany with his
bosom friend Wackenroder, and the two Berliners were
fascinated by early German art. It appealed to them by
its warmth of religious and patriotic feeling. For Wackenroder early Christian art became a sort of religion. He
poured out his feelings on the subject in a little book
entitled *Heart-effusions of an Art-loving Lay Brother*—
the beginning of the " Nazarene " movement which annoyed Goethe as a lover of Raphael and the Greeks, but
was thought well of by Friedrich Schlegel and other
romanticists. Tieck made his contribution to the subject in *Franz Sternbald's Wanderings* (1798), which is
another romanticised *Wilhelm Meister*. Sternbald is a
pupil of Albrecht Dürer, a prayerful and poetic youth.
He leaves his beloved master in Nürnberg and goes to

pursue his education first in the Netherlands, then in Italy, where he finds a sweetheart. There is much talk about art and the religion of art, and there is an immense number of interspersed songs. The coldness of the Protestant churches is touched on.

The feeling that there have been better times and better men than those of the present may work out different results, according as the mind in which it finds lodgment is more or less practical, more or less virile. So it was with the romanticists. Tieck and Novalis were led to a poetic idealisation of mediæval life, and such poetic idealisation is one of the most important aspects of the romantic movement. But this same mediævalism might also take the form of a dreamy philosophy, a leaning toward the Catholic Church and pre-Raphaelite art, a joy in the lustihood of chivalry, a patriotic desire to bring back the brave days of old—the days of German union and strength and glory,—a quickened intellectual interest in mediæval matters, including all folk-lore, or the exploitation of mystery and superstition in novel, poem, and play. Again, while one man might find in his romantic vision of the Middle Ages a spring of poetry or a spur to practical effort, another might dream himself into a quarrel with life; into inefficiency, helplessness, pessimism, insanity. Finally, a man of essentially romantic temper might find his soul's account in a dream, not of the Middle Ages at all, but, say, of the glory that was Greece.

This last was the case of FRIEDRICH HÖLDERLIN (1770–1843), whose fine lyric gift and passion for Greek beauty mark him as a spiritual congener of John Keats. His poems continually suggest the condition of exile from the land of beauty. Many of them betoken an ardent love of the fatherland, but along with the patriotism we hear the elegiac note of mourning for a vanished splendour. And when it is a question of denoting this vanished splendour, that is, the higher life in beauty and for beauty, from which the modern man has fallen away, Hölderlin resorts to the symbols of Greek religion. This philhellenism of his was profoundly sincere. His romance *Hyperion* (1799) is the story of a modern Greek who joins an uprising of his countrymen against the Turks. His idealism is sorely tried by the miserable conduct of the patriot army, he loses his beloved Diotima, all his hopes are wrecked. Then he takes refuge for a while in Germany, only to find himself wretched among the cold and dull barbarians. At last he returns to Greece to seek nepenthe in nature. Hölderlin's idealism proved unable to make terms with common reality. Before half his days were numbered his passionate unrest carried him over the line which separates genius from insanity.

The activities of Tieck, Novalis, and the Schlegels between 1796 and 1804 constitute the first phase of the German romantic movement. The second followed immediately in the work of Arnim, Brentano, and their friends at Heidelberg. Clemens Brentano (1778–1842), the son of a Frankfort merchant, was of half-Italian Catholic stock, while his friend Achim von Arnim (1781–1831) was a Prussian squire of the Protestant connection. In his youth Brentano studied at Jena, came into contact with the Schlegels and their circle, led a rather wild life on " romantic " lines, and recorded his early experience of life and love in *Godwi,*

which he called a " romance run wild." He was of an
extremely volatile temper, steady in nothing but his tendency to emotional excess. *Godwi* is a formless and
frivolous book, written on the pattern of Friedrich
Schlegel's maudlin *Lucinde*. Like the latter, it made a
scandal by its frank preaching of free love, self-indul-
gence, and social pococurantism. In after years Brentano became ashamed of it and declared that he dared
not mention its name for fear of being turned into a pillar
of salt. But it did contain some very good songs. The
young Arnim, in every way a more solid character than
Brentano, also began with autobiographic fiction. Both
men had early taken to collecting folksongs, and when
they became friends they decided to join forces and work
together. In 1805 they published the first volume of
their collection, calling it by the rather odd name *Des
Knaben Wunderhorn,* or the *Boy's Magic Horn.* In
1808 two more volumes followed, with an excellent essay
on the folksong by Arnim. The whole collection was
dedicated to Goethe, who reviewed it with warm appreciation, expressly declining to go into the question of the
genuineness of the texts.

As a matter of fact, the texts were not genuine in
the strict modern sense, but had been edited and embellished in very much the same way as the English texts
of the Percy collection. In no other way, probably, could
the old songs, with their frequent coarseness and ca-
cophony, have been made acceptable to the public of that
time. As it was, they were highly acceptable. The *Wunderhorn* came as a revelation of unsuspected national
wealth. Herder's *Folksongs* of 1778 had roused gen-

eral interest in the subject, but Germany had not been very well represented in his cosmopolitan undertaking. In the three volumes of the *Wunderhorn*, however, there were riches undreamed of—a vast body of song revealing the soul of the German people for ages past in all its intimate concerns. Here were passion and pathos, homely vigour, and grim force; now and then there was haunting beauty or a mysterious depth of suggestion. Naturally, the common folk who had created all this began to appear in a new light. The plain man had suddenly become as the hero of a long-neglected romance. Men began to feel that the irrational element of life, that which the Age of Reason had tried to get rid of as outworn superstition, was much more deeply rooted than had been supposed. Tradition took the place of Reason as the word of power. The *Wunderhorn* pointed the way to a new science as well as a new lyrism, both grounded on national feeling and permeated with respect for the plain people. Closely connected with Arnim and Brentano were the Grimm brothers, who in 1812 published the first volume of their *Kinder- und Hausmärchen,* or *Children's and Household Stories*. These now world-famous tales, taken down from the lips of story-tellers who had received them from an age-long tradition, are an interesting by-product of the new romanticism.

Aside from his work on the *Wunderhorn* Arnim did little that is very memorable, though he wrote voluminously in the lines of prose fiction and closet drama. As a novelist he proved unable to control his riotous imagination and execute a plan as conceived : he often began well only to end badly or not at all. Brentano succeeded best with songs of romantic vagabondage or ballads of traditionary lore. Of his most readable prose tales, *Kasperl and Annerl* is only an elaborated folksong, while the *Chronicle of a Wandering Student* is a story of romantic vagabondage in the Middle Ages. He himself was a vagabond of the spirit—restless, impulsive, erratic, without a definite purpose in life—until his " conversion " in 1817. After that he abjured his former works and ways and became a Catholic zealot. Lost to his former friends and to secular literature, he devoted some years to taking down the outgivings of a stigmatised nun whom he thought divinely inspired.

Shortly before Brentano, another romantic vagabond of the spirit had likewise come to anchor in the supposedly calm waters of Catholic dogma. This was ZACHARIAS WERNER (1776–1823), a Prussian of Protestant family. In his profligate youth he oscillated between debauchery and religious mysticism. After writing two rather ineffective semi-historical plays, the *Sons of the Vale* and the *Cross on the Baltic*, the one dealing with the collapse of the order of Knights Templar, the other with the conversion of the heathen Prussians, he scored a modest stage triumph with his *Martin Luther* (1807). The play contains some good scenes of homely realism which made the title-rôle acceptable to the eminent actor Iffland. The great reformer is treated not unsympathetically, but without a clear and strong denotation of historic forces. When Werner appeared in Weimar, Goethe welcomed him as a good craftsman for the stage, and out of their intercourse grew the little play, the *Twentyfourth of February*—the seed of an abundant crop of so-called fate-tragedies. Werner had lost his mother and a dear friend on the same day—February 24, 1804—and was temperamentally inclined to occult fatalism. The presupposition of his play is this. A Swiss youth named Kunz Kuruth quarrels with his father over the wife whom the son has chosen. Kunz hurls at his father a dagger which misses its mark, but nevertheless causes the old man's death. In dying he imprecates a curse. Kunz and his wife have a son who, in playing with the fatal dagger, accidentally kills his little sister and is in consequence driven away under *his* father's curse. In the play Kunz and his wife appear as an aged couple living alone in their Alpine hut, abjectly poor. A stranger comes and asks for shelter. In the night Kunz murders him for his money, and finds out too late that he has killed his own son. All the crimes are committed on February 24th and with the same tool.

Werner's gruesome one-act tragedy of crime, which was first played at Weimar in 1808, is poetically and dramatically a very good piece of work in a not very noble or important but still perfectly legitimate genre. It drew after it, however, in the coming era of romanticism, a pretty large number of plays in which the idea of a fatal destiny resting on a family because of some long-past crime was very much overworked. They became ridiculous at last because the fate-idea was not treated as having anything to do with the central rightness of things, but was made to attach mechanically to a particular time or place or instrument. They were grounded in superstition, though hardly in that kind of superstition which Goethe had in mind when he spoke of

23

it as the " poetry of life." They were grounded, namely, in the superstition which causes people of low intelligence to feel that there is a peculiar retributive fitness in meting out punishment to a wrong-doer in the very place, or with the very instrument, or perhaps on the anniversary, of his own wrong-doing.

Among the co-workers on the short-lived *Zeitung für Einsiedler* or *Journal for Hermits,* which was started in 1808 as an organ of the Heidelberg romanticists, were Uhland, Kerner, Fouqué, and both the Schlegels, as well as Arnim, Brentano, and the brothers Grimm. The spirit of the coterie was intensely patriotic, but the reverse of practical. When the mood was propitious Brentano could make a good song in praise of the fatherland, but he was only a jongleur whom no one could take very seriously. He and his friends had come to feel that the love of country was not an ignoble emotion, and that they themselves had, or ought to have, a country worth loving. But where was this ideal Germany ? What were its boundaries ? What was its religion and form of government ? Was it in sympathy with or opposed to the ideas of liberty and democracy which the Revolution had spread abroad ? On these questions the literary patriots of the *Journal for Hermits* were as divided as the rest of Germany. Meanwhile Napoleon had made himself master of Vienna as well as Berlin, and was parcelling out German territory, and in other ways riding rough-shod over German national feeling. To be sure, he had his allies among the minor princes, and some of the intellectuals regarded him favourably as a liberator from the hoary abuses of feudalism. But whatever might be the value of particular ideas of government, and however men might differ about religion, the opinion rapidly prevailed that there could be no good future for Germany under a régime of foreign domination. The internal questions could wait. The duty of the hour was to get rid of Napoleon. From this conviction came the life-and-death struggle of 1813, with its frenzy of patriotic devotion, affecting high and low alike, its appalling sacrifices, and its final triumph at Waterloo. Germany was not yet united—far from it—but the War of Liberation was essentially the result of a national uprising. Saxons and South Germans, whose rulers were or had been in alliance with Napoleon, flocked to the Prussian or the Austrian standard.

Among those who thus fought for the national cause was the Saxon THEODOR KÖRNER (1791–1813). When the campaign of 1813 began he was prospering at Vienna as a playwright. The future was bright, so far as his personal fortune and happiness were concerned. An exalted sense of duty led him to enlist as a soldier, and ere long he was killed by a French bullet. As a chivalrous soldier-poet who gave his all for the Germany of his dreams, Körner won a kind of renown which asks no favour from literary critics, and is perhaps a little out of proportion to the permanent value of his work. And yet it would be difficult to name any German poet who had behind him a better record at the age of twenty-two. His lyric collection *Lyre and Sword*—many of the poems written in camp or on the march, and one fine sonnet while he was lying in the woods near Leipzig and suffering from what he believed to be a mortal wound—

is a thrilling expression of the blended religious and patriotic feeling which inspired him to the supreme sacrifice. His tragedy *Zriny*, while too ethereal and monochromatic for a good drama—all the characters being doomed to certain death from the first, and having nothing to do but to express their emotions and sell their lives as dearly as possible—is instinct with the stern joy and the blessed hope of dying for the fatherland.

Another poetic champion of the national cause was ERNST MORITZ ARNDT (1769–1860), author of many a stirring song on the duty of hating Frenchmen, fighting hard and trusting devoutly in the God of Battles. In his series of fiery pamphlets called *Spirit of the Time,* Arndt denounced Napoleon as a growing menace to Germany and used strong language in describing the abject condition of German public opinion. The short-sighted princes, he said, were occupied with their personal and dynastic interests; the intellectuals, as if they had no German blood in their veins, were arguing over futile abstractions, and the people at large were an inert mass. After the Battle of Jena, Arndt retired for safety to Sweden, but presently returned under an assumed name and pursued his anti-Gallic campaign with song and pamphlet. As secretary of Stein and associate of other leaders, he was able to work effectively in the final struggle. The " fatherland " meant for him, as lyrically proclaimed in a well-known poem, all the lands where the German language was spoken and the forms of life were German. The great thought that inspired him was the idea of union on the basis of identity in language and ethnic traditions.

But the important literary figure of the Napoleonic age—let Goethe for the moment be left out of account —was neither Körner nor Arndt nor Schenkendorf, nor any of the other lyrists who voiced the passion of the hour in song. Nor was it Fichte, whose stirring *Addresses to the German People* had much to do with the regeneration of prostrate Prussia after the disaster of Jena. It was rather a man whose genius found little recognition at the time—the gifted dramatist Heinrich von Kleist. In general the earlier romanticists proved incapable of real drama, though they all affected the dramatic form. Wilhelm Schlegel's *Ion* is a Pygmalion statue without the breath of life, and Friedrich's *Alarcos* was laughed off the stage at Weimar, where Goethe benevolently undertook to see if anything could be done with it. Brentano's would-be comic *Ponce de Leon* was received with derision at Vienna, and his long-winded *Founding of Prague* is as unplayable as the dramas of Arnim and Tieck. Werner had talent, but gradually lost touch with human nature and with the necessary temperance of the dramatic art. In 1811 he was received into the Catholic Church at Rome; then he became a priest and propagandist, recanted his former praise of Luther in a fanatical poem, and took no further interest in secular things. In short, from all the efforts of the earlier romanticists there never emerged a single romantic drama which took and held a place on the stage; not one that can now be enjoyed as a play by virtue of its human interest and dramatic excellence. To find that, one must turn to *Katie of Heilbronn*.

HEINRICH VON KLEIST (1777–1811) was a poor

Prussian nobleman who set out in early life to be a soldier, but gave up the military career in order to pursue a strenuous ideal of personal culture. But study soon palled on him; he fell into a Faustian despair and suffered terribly from *Weltschmerz*. "For an hour of forgetfulness," he declared, "I could turn Catholic." Restless, moody, eccentric, but possessed all at once by a vaulting poetic ambition, he began to wander about Europe in search of peace. Thoughts of suicide haunted him. At one time he dreamed of finding what seemed to him an "infinitely glorious grave" in England by joining Napoleon's contemplated invasion. In Switzerland, whither he had gone with the idea of leading the simple life as a farmer, he found congenial society and completed his first work, the *Schroffenstein Family*. It is a romantic verse-tragedy in which two lovers are done to death, like Romeo and Juliet, by a bitter feud of their families. The plot is wildly extravagant, moving the reader now to horror and now to laughter, and is pervaded by a dark fatalism. But the characters are firmly drawn and make an illusion of reality.

An engraving which Kleist saw at the house of one of his friends in Switzerland suggested the idea of the play which was afterward completed under the name of the *Broken Jug*. A lecherous country justice enters a young woman's room at night, and in making a hurried exit breaks a jug. The wrong person is arrested on suspicion and brought before the justice, who conducts the trial in such a way as to entangle himself. The *Broken Jug* is only a bagatelle, though it contains some very effective satire on social conditions, but is, on the whole, the liveliest and most amusing verse-comedy in German literature. In *Penthesilea* Kleist undertook to romanticise an ancient Greek subject; and so completely did the matter possess him that he thought, when the play was finished, that he had laid bare in it " all the pain and all the splendour of his soul." His Amazon queen is an impossible being, whose fierce passion for her lover-foe Achilles turns to insane frenzy when she sees that he vilipends her fighting prowess. She kills him with an arrow, rends his dead body with her teeth, and then recovers her queenly poise and wills her own death. There is fine poetry in *Penthesilea*, but it is only a character study, not a dramatic masterpiece; and in depicting the reckless egoism of passion, Kleist certainly overstepped the line which separates the terrible from the horrible.

When the Battle of Jena occurred Kleist was holding a humble government clerkship at Königsberg. The great Prussian disaster, with its bitter discipline of suffering, roused in him a holy ire against Napoleon, and he wondered why some one did not " put a bullet through the head of this evil genius of the world." He, too, began to feel that the only hope for Germany lay in a union of all the German states, and in the development, among princes and people, of a self-denying patriotism. Nevertheless, he did not at once turn his hand to plays bearing directly on present conditions. Giving up his position he went to Dresden, and there, in friendly intercourse with Tieck, he devoted himself to literary work which, for the most part, either remained unknown to his contemporaries, or met with little favour. *Katie of Heilbronn*, now the popular favourite among his plays, was published in 1810, but not played in his lifetime. Indeed, he never saw one of his own productions on the stage. Katie is the polar opposite of Penthesilea—a type of the womanly devotion which beareth all things in patient submissiveness. Like a faithful dog she attaches herself to the knight Wetter von Strahl, and no harshness of his can drive her away. At last it turns out that she is the natural daughter of the emperor, hence a fit bride for his knightship. This concession to caste feeling is generally and rightly regarded as a blemish; but the dreamy indomitable Käthchen is a delightful creation, and the play is full of romantic charm.

Hermann's Battle, which was not published till 1821, is a dramatic apologue of German political conditions in 1808. Hermann unites the contentious German chieftains for a victorious assault on the Roman tyrant. This he effects by his eloquent appeals, and by sinking his personal and dynastic interests for the common good. He even counsels union under his rival Marbod. Hermann is Prussia, Marbod is Austria; the selfish and lukewarm tribesmen are the South German princes, and the Roman is Napoleon. The play is an impassioned plea for self-abnegating union, a demonstration of its possibility, a forecast of its results. But the very fact of its being an apologue, addressed to transitory conditions and making its appeal more by virtue of what it symbolised than by virtue of what it represented, detracts a little from its permanent interest. As a work of art it is inferior to the *Prince of Homburg,* in which romance is made to temper the stern demands of military law and public duty in such a way as to scatter the ominous clouds of impending tragedy. What must happen when a military officer, disregarding the express order of his commander, leads a charge in battle and wins an important victory? This was the crux which was suggested to Kleist by an anecdote of the Great Elector. What actually did happen, according to the story, was that the Great Elector remarked, after the Battle of Fehrbellin in 1675, that strictly speaking the Prince of Homburg had forfeited his life by disobeying orders; nevertheless, he, the Elector, thanked God for such a bringer of victory. What happens in the play is that the Elector imposes the death-sentence; and then, after the mind of Homburg has passed through all the stages from angry revolt and pitiful dread of death to resignation and calm acceptance of his fate as just and necessary for the general good, pardons the offender. This he does because he has learned that the prince did not really hear the order, having been at the critical moment lost in a trancelike dream of his lady-love, though apparently awake and attentive.

The *Prince of Homburg* is a masterpiece of such fine and satisfying texture as to suggest almost limitless possibilities for the young dramatist who wrote it at the age of thirty-two. His tale of *Michael Kohlhaas*, too, the story of an upright citizen who, under the smart of outrages for which he can obtain no legal redress, becomes an anarchist—is one of the very best novelettes in the German language. But Kleist's course was run. In 1809 he went to Berlin and tried without success to have his *Prince of Homburg* put on the stage. He was in dire poverty. The works on which he had expended the finest dramatic genius thus far vouchsafed to any Prussian found no recognition anywhere. Personal distress and the woes of the fatherland so darkened his life that it seemed worthless. In November, 1811, he made an end of all the misery with a pistol-shot.

CHAPTER XVIII

THE ERA OF ROMANTICISM

THE period to be traversed in this chapter extends from the Battle of Waterloo to about the middle of the thirties. Frightened by the atrocities of the Paris Terror, and mistaking these for the real French Revolution, the German princes entered on a reactionary policy, the aim of which was to repress all democratic tendencies. Their instruments were close censorship of the press, espionage, arbitrary arrests, and strict police enactments. It began to look as if the tremendous effort of the war of liberation had gone simply for the stronger intrenchment of the privileged classes in their old position. Thus the tempest of patriotic feeling which had swept Napoleon into banishment was followed by a calm which soon became oppressive to all who had ever felt the inspiration of the eighteenth-century ideal of progress. That century, on the whole the most important in human history, had taught a large part of mankind to locate their golden age in the future, and to make social progress the highest, the all-embracing criterion. On the other hand, there had always been those who believed that human affairs—conduct, art, manners, religion, language, everything— tended to the bad, and that the only way to make matters

better was to return in imagination, or perhaps in practice, to the past. There was thus a cleavage between the
men who looked forward and outward, and those who
looked backward and inward; between the men of Reason
and the men of Tradition. That the romanticists were
found mainly in the last-named camp goes without saying. But the classification must not be pressed too hard:
there were divers interaffiliations. In general the literary spirit of the time was opposed to what we now call
realism. Almost without exception the men of poetic impulse found their inspiration in the far-away past, in distant lands, or in the realm of superstition. The present
fact was felt to be vulgar and depressing, poetry to be
a relief from it. Said Börne, in that same eulogy of Jean
Paul which was cited above:

" Centuries pass down, seasons roll by, the weather
of fortune changes, the steps of age mount and descend.
Nothing is permanent but change, nothing constant but
death. Every beat of the heart inflicts a wound, and life
would be an eternal bleeding-to-death if it were not for
poetry. That gives what the world denies; a Golden Age
that does not rust, a spring that never fades, cloudless
happiness, and eternal youth. The poet is the comforter
of mankind."

It was partly his feeling that the present was worthless, and partly his indomitable eagerness to explore and
appropriate, that turned Goethe to the poetry of the
Orient. If we leave the Old Testament out of the account, the Oriental current in eighteenth-century literature derives mainly from the *Arabian Nights* and other
fantastic tales. Accurate knowledge of the real Hindus

and Persians and Arabs had not been easily obtainable. Now, however, it was becoming obtainable. The labours of Jones, Burnouf, Grotefend, Hammer-Purgstall and other Orientalists were opening the treasures of Eastern poetry to the Occident, and the saying *ex oriente lux* was acquiring a new and fascinating import. Both the Schlegels learned Sanskrit, and their example was followed by many eager young scholars. The dreamy mysticism, ingenious fancifulness, and didactic profundity of some of the Orientals harmonised well with the romantic spirit and led naturally to imitations of them. Goethe set an example in his *West-Easterly Divan* (1819), which is Persian in the same sense that his *Iphigenia* is Greek. That is, it is not Persian at all, either in form or spirit. The songs of the *Divan* are instinct with the Western poet's delight in having found a new kinsman in Hafiz, and in pretending to look out on life through his eyes. But it is all a masquerade. Goethe only plays with the Persian apparatus of names and tropes and fancies, while giving expression to his own thoughts and emotions. The muse of the collection was Marianne Willemer, who actually wrote some of the songs included in it.

Among the younger men who took the infection from the East were Rückert and Platen. FRIEDRICH RÜCKERT (1788–1866) was a Bavarian who would gladly have joined the patriot army in 1813, but being physically unfit contented himself with fighting the Corsican in a series of *Sonnets in Harness*. They have all the belligerency of Arndt and Körner, but less religiosity. In the course of a long life spent partly as professor of Oriental languages and partly as a quiet recluse, Rückert wrote more verses, probably, than any other German of his century. A collection of ghazals published in 1821 was followed by divers translations from the Sanskrit, Persian, Chinese, Arabic, Hebrew, and other languages. He tried his hand at the imitation of almost every exotic form, both ancient and modern. Withal he was wont to versify his daily experience, even its trivial phases. With the lapse of time his sense of poetic values deteriorated and he wrote quantities of rubbish. But in his earlier years his not yet overworked muse occasionally vouchsafed him a pearl. Read in a small anthology of his best work, Rückert will be seen to deserve a permanent though modest place among the lyrists of his time.

Not long after Rückert, COUNT PLATEN (1796–1835) also came out with a collection of ghazals, which exhibited an amazing virtuosity in the handling of the difficult form. He had a very serious faith in the poetic value of the ghazal, and his work was mildly commended by Goethe. Other less benevolent critics, however, saw in it nothing but hollow metrical ingenuity. Heine published a sharp epigram by Immermann about eating too much from the fruit of the Garden of Shiraz and then vomiting up ghazals. This led to personal ridicule of Immermann and Heine in Platen's *Romantic Œdipus,* and this in turn to an atrocious attack on Platen in Heine's *Pictures of Travel,* and to a somewhat less venomous retaliation by Immermann. It is partly due to this ugly feud that Platen's real worth as a poet has often been underestimated. Critics have taken him at Heine's estimate and set him down as a cunning master of form without substance. And true it is that he is not popular, not singable; and that he had a fondness for difficult foreign forms such as wake no echoes of association. But there is always room in the world for exquisite verse of the pensive type, and in that Platen was a master. There are no better sonnets in German than his Venetian sonnets. And speaking generally, his verse is sincere, noble, and deeply felt, as well as delicately chiselled. One may read him long without coming on a cold or a vacuous line, any more than on a false rhyme, a harsh cadence, or a concession to dialect. This is more than can be said of Goethe, Schiller, or Heine. On the other hand, it must be allowed that he had no important message, unless it were the dignity and responsibility of the poet's calling. The last nine years of his life he spent in Italy, where he developed a liking for ancient rhyme-less metres. In his early plays he attempted, like Tieck, to utilise fairy-tales for satiric purposes. In his *Fatal Fork* and *Romantic Œdipus* he paid his respects, with laughable parody and polished Aristophanic parabasis, to the horrors and inanities of the fate-tragedy.

But it is not in the Orientalising tendency, and not in the clever adaptation of alien forms, that romantic lyrism is at its best; it is rather in the trail of the *Wun-derhorn*—in the work of Eichendorff, Uhland, Heine, and Müller. JOSEPH VON EICHENDORFF (1788–1857), scion of a noble Catholic family of Silesia, and in later life distinguished as a Catholic publicist, was happily endowed for a winsome poet of nature. In his boyhood a lover of folk-lore as well as of the hills and woods, in his youth familiar with country toil, he became an

intimate of nature in all her moods. To surrender himself to these moods as reflected in his own dreamy temperament, to hear the voices, to feel the thrill of the sensitive lover, and then to express it all in simple, truthful,
always singable verse—that was Eichendorff. He resembles Goethe in what may be called the sanity of his feeling
for nature, being a mystic only so far as the sensitive
modern soul is a mystic. He found poetry only in seclusion from the haunts of men, but there he found it abundantly in the things of common experience: in the wistful
suggestion of morning and evening; in whispering wood
and babbling brook and flitting cloud; in the pain of
parting and the joy of meeting again; in the subtle associations of memory with particular places; in the changing emotions of the care-free wayfarer. He has a special
fondness for the moon and the evening hush. While
Eichendorff was not a poet to shake the world or draw
men after him in passionate allegiance, he was a most
lovable interpreter of nature's placid, dreamy moods, and
of ordinary human joys and pains. One gets the purest
essence of romanticism from his tale of a *Good-for-
Nothing* (1826), which has been called a lyric novelette.
Of all the sensitive progeny of the peripatetic Wilhelm
Meister, Eichendorff's happy-go-lucky fiddler is the most
humanly captivating.

So far as poetic endowment is concerned, the Swabian
democrat LUDWIG UHLAND (1787–1862) was a congener of the Silesian Baron von Eichendorff. The son
of a Tübingen professor, a Swabian to the core, possessed
by a strong racial instinct and a devoutness which felt
no need of breaking away from traditionary religion,

Uhland early came under the spell of the *Wunderhorn* and found it, as poet and as scholar, the pointer of the way through life. " I never had," he said of himself, " any leaning toward poetry as something dissociated from the life of the people and expressing only individual sentiments; whatever attracted me had its root in the people, their customs and religion." This evidently is not the confession of faith of a poet destined to conquer new realms; and Uhland was no innovator, but the apostle and perfecter of the old. In his youth he took no passionate interest in the national uprising against Napoleon, but when the war was over he entered earnestly into the local fight of the Würtemberg liberals for the " good old law." But his political verse is of small moment. His fame rests, apart from his valuable work as a scholar, on his ballads and on the songs in which he voiced the feelings he shared, or believed himself to share, with the common man. He cared little for the theories of the romanticists, though at heart altogether one of them, and metrical artificialities were an offence to him. Poetry for him was the simple voice of the heart, expressing itself in old familiar cadences; or else it was the sympathetic rendering of some stirring vision from the brave days of old. He rewrote and corrected with infinite pains, and his poetic aggregate is small; but it includes a pretty large number of songs that have endeared themselves to all Germany. Among the best contributions of Uhland to romantic balladry are *Taillefer*, the *Minstrel's Curse*, and the *Luck of Edenhall*.

The spirit but seldom the power of Uhland is discernible in a number of minor singers whom German

24

writers are wont to group together as the Swabian School
—Karl Mayer, Gustav Schwab, Justinus Kerner, and
others. It is, however, rather difficult to find the Swabian
hall-mark, since romantic dilettanteism was now at home
everywhere. The disposition to seek relief from actuality
in dream-fancies and melodious ditties of the simple life
was not confined to any one region. Even prosaic Berlin
became a centre of thorough-going romanticism. The
leading lyrist of the Berlin group was WILHELM MÜL-
LER (1794–1827), the son of a Dessau shoemaker, and
the father of the famous Orientalist, Max Müller. None
succeeded better than he in reproducing the flavour of
the folksong. He is at his best where he identifies himself with the miller, the shepherd, the postilion, the wandering bugler, and sings their characteristic joys and
woes. He is especially charming in his love-songs which,
wedded to Schubert's music, have become a familiar
household joy in Germany. On his contemporaries Müller made a deep impression by his Tyrtæan songs of sympathy with the Greek Revolution. Muzzled and kept
down at home, the Germans kindled all the more easily
over any foreign struggle for liberty. It was Müller who
first aroused that spirit of philhellenism to which Goethe
paid so noble a tribute in his Euphorion.

The verse of Eichendroff, Uhland, and Müller shows
little trace of a serious quarrel with life or of revolt
against established ideas. All had an abiding belief that
tradition was not only full of poetry, but good enough
to live by, if only the heart were right. It was different
with the Jew HEINRICH HEINE (1797–1856), who was
a romantic poet on the side of his emotions and instincts,

but intellectually a rationalist and an heir of the Revolution. In his first collection of poems, published in 1822 while he was still a student, he appeared as one suffering the pangs of despised love, and hence prone to take a sombre or a bitter view of life in general. His melancholia had assumed the form of a passionate addiction to poetry, which brought a certain relief from overtension of feeling. The pose of the sufferer—the sensitive, misunderstood, buffeted, yet in virtue of genius self-sufficient poet—became him well and proved an excellent stock-in-trade at a time when Byron was looming large in the European outlook. The word " pose " is not here meant to imply that Heine was radically insincere, but only that he continued to exploit his pangs of despised love long after they had ceased to be a poignant fact of experience. He wrote two plays, *Almansor* and *William Ratcliff*, in both of which disappointment in love leads to criminal desperation. Presently his lyric art took the form of a poetic diary, in which, without giving a name to the separate effusions, he registered the moods and fancies that possessed him. Sometimes it was a gruesome dream of death and the grave; again a romantic legend of mysterious suggestiveness; a fleeting vision of far-away happiness on the banks of the Ganges; a reminiscence of love's ecstasy turned to gall by woman's heartlessness; a bit of nature-symbolism, in which human yearnings were ascribed to the snow-laden pine or the glittering stars. Withal, Heine had a Mephistophelean eye for the ridiculous side of all his visionary brooding, and even for the personal woes which he transmuted into such appealing melodies. In wit and cynical humour he was rich, and in his romantic years he often turned his shafts back on himself. It is not a very lovable character that is unveiled in Heine's poems; but the sense of lyric beauty, and the gift of simple, suggestive, and melodious expression were combined in him with an unerring instinct for poetic values. His *Book of Songs* (1826) contained a larger number of unforgetable gems than any other collection of German lyric verse of the century.

And then came the *Travel Pictures* (1826–31), which almost rose to the dignity of a new literary genre. There had been books of travel freighted with solid information, and there had been sentimental journeys in the would-be manner of Sterne. The romance of wandering, too, in which an unattached, usually mediæval, youth of artistic bent had ranged about among men and cities in pursuit of experience, was a familiar type. Heine took himself for his hero, introduced songs, amours, and other well-tried romantic witcheries, and incidentally let his wit play with unheard-of audacity. In particular he poked fun at the bigwigs and solemnities, at old-fogyism in all its manifestations, at the parochial mind intrenched in routine and prejudice. Nothing so wicked, and at the same time so brilliant and amusing, had before been written in the German language.

Heine's quarrel with life was not a matter of temperament, still less of conviction, but of moods superinduced partly by poetic brooding and partly by the incipient nervous disease which finally stretched him on his mattress grave at Paris. In happier moments he could always lay the spirits of gloom with ironic laughter or mirth-provoking jest. Normally he found the human

drama interesting, believed in progress, and thought it
worth while to fight in humanity's war of liberation.
In the great Austrian lyrist, on the other hand, the melancholy note is pervasive and temperamental.   Nikolaus
Niembsch (1802–50), better known as LENAU, was of
German stock, but had a strain of Slavic and a strain of
Hungarian blood in his veins.   A sceptic from boyhood,
early acquainted with intellectual despair and embittered
by disappointment, he turned for solace to Nature and the
lyric rendering of her message.   And the message that
he heard on all hands was one of gentle melancholy.
Everywhere a suggestion of sadness, mourning, dissolu-
tion; voices whispering of decay and death.   That which
appealed most to him was the autumnal scene of fading
beauty, falling leaves, silescent birds.   " I love this gentle
dying," he said, and the words give the key-note of his
verse.   For joy he had no affinity, and humour was
denied him.   One may read him through without being
moved to smile.   But the pensive melancholy which led
him to go in search of sadness was paired with an almost
Goethean gift of accurate observation.   It is due perhaps to the delicacy and subtlety of his phrasing that he
is not singable.   The great composers have passed him
by as intractable, though he was a master of verbal
melody.

Let us turn now from the lyric poets to take note of
the main currents of prose fiction.   The most voluminous
and for a while the most popular story-teller of the period
was DE LA MOTTE FOUQUÉ (1777–1843).   His interest
in mediæval chivalry and Norse saga was genuine, and
he was very diligent in exhuming and revamping.   Had

he been granted a modicum of humour, a keener historical sense, and a livelier feeling for the plain, homely fact, he might have become the German Walter Scott. As it was, his creations were so very supernal and unlifelike, and so mixed up with futile irrationality, that the public soon tired of them, even as it tired of the dissimilar unrealities of Jean Paul. Of all the immense mass of Fouqué's writings in prose and verse, only *Undine* (1811) can be said to have survived. In this little tale of the soulless nixie who gets a soul by experience of grief, and then plays out her brief tragedy as the sweetheart of a flesh-and-blood knight, there is certainly something of the savour of genuine romantic folk-lore. But even *Undine* has been overpraised. It is not free from literary sophistication. At best it was a thing for the very young, and the very young were better provided for by the brothers Grimm.

About 1820 Tieck struck out on a new path and began to publish quasi-realistic novelettes. In these stories, of which he ultimately wrote more than thirty, he relied for interest not so much on the strangeness of the occurrences or the ingenuity of the plot as on the discursive sapience of the conversations. They are novelettes of discussion. Tieck's scheme was to bring together a pair or a group of persons, each having a tolerably definite character of his own, and then to let them talk themselves out about things in general—most often about art, literature, poetry, music, philosophy. He had a keen interest in human nature, but his concern was with what his people thought rather than with what they did and suffered as individuals. His conversations do

not consist of lively give-and-take in short sentences, but
of leisurely exposition in long speeches. Thus the
tales lack movement, and the real *Geschichte* sometimes
reduces to almost zero; but taken in the aggregate they
are a very good index to the intellectual life of the time.

On the whole, Tieck made but sparing use, in his novelettes, of the supernaturalism which figures so promi-
nently in the literary fashion of the period. If it is not
quite exhaustive to speak of the romantic movement as
a renascence of mystery or a rehabilitation of superstition, it is still true that either of these phrases aptly
describes one important phase of the matter. The starting-point was a love of traditionary folk-lore, in which
much supernaturalism was found embedded. But from
a love of ancient mysteries grounded in popular tradition
it was only a step to the invention of new mysteries
grounded only in dreams of the imagination; and when
that step had been taken the way was open for fantastic
tales of the incredible. In this domain ADELBERT VON
CHAMISSO (1781–1838) led the way with his *Peter
Schlemihl* (1814). By birth a Frenchman, by vocation
a man of science, Chamisso achieved genuine popularity
as a German poet—especially with his lusty and satiric
songs of freedom in the style of Béranger. His " marvellous tale " of Peter Schlemihl, a poor youth who sells
his shadow to the devil for boundless wealth and finds
out that he has made a bad bargain, carried its author's
name all over Europe. Apart from the elusive symbolism
of the story, which is suggestive without being tantalis-
ing, the charm of Chamisso's little masterpiece lies in
his easy and natural approach to the impossible. And

it is just this plausible realism of detail, gradually leading up to and at last inextricably blent with the spooky, chimerical and gruesome, that constitutes the literary knack of ERNST THEODOR AMADEUS HOFFMANN (1776–1822).

Skilled in music and drawing, an acute observer with a keen eye for the grotesque, extremely sensitive to æsthetic impressions of every kind, Hoffmann began with *Fantasy Pieces in the Manner of Callot*, for which Jean Paul wrote an introduction. They marked the advent of a new specialist in Jean Paul's own field of the whimsical-profound. Then came *Murr the Tomcat*, the *Night Pieces*, the *Elixirs of the Devil*, and the multitudinous Serapion stories, with the frame narrative of the story-telling club in Berlin, where Hoffmann spent the last six years of his life as judge of a criminal court. Although he could dispense with the atmosphere of spookiness and horror if he chose, his imagination gravitated more and more in that direction. He chose for his province the dim border-land which separates positive knowledge from superstitious belief, writing of ghosts and doubles and haunted houses; of mesmerism, clairvoyance, and sleep-walking; of hallucination, diabolic influence, and eccentric criminal impulse; of strange metamorphoses and the corrosion of character by mental disease. And all this haunting uncanniness he was able to make vividly real by mixing it with realistic narrative and description. This gift he shared with Poe, whose tales of terror were to some extent influenced by Hoffmann. But the German differs from the American virtuoso of the spooky in that the former was no poet at all. Hoffmann wrote no verse, and his prose is devoid of rhythm or other stylistic charm.

"Teufels Hoffmann," as they called him, is the pre-eminent German artist in his specialty. He has had a large vogue in France and has left his mark on three literatures. Historical romance he did not attempt, except in the form of short stories with a historical setting. In romantic fiction of the Waverley pattern the most important production of the time was Hauff's *Lichtenstein*. WILHELM HAUFF (1802–27), the short-lived author of the fine lyric *Morgenrot,* of sprightly satiric sketches, and of several novelettes that are still in favour, was moved by the popularity of the Waverley novels to attempt for his native Würtemberg what Sir Walter had done for Scotland. His *Lichtenstein,* a historical romance of the sixteenth century, evinces no great original power, but it is pleasantly written and shows, especially in its scenes and characters from humble life, that its author had read Scott to advantage.

Just at the end of the period now under consideration (1835) appeared a peculiar masterpiece of romantic fiction called *Goethe's Correspondence with a Child*, a book which so fascinated Emerson that he thought for a while never to need other reading. Its author was BETTINA VON ARNIM (1785–1859), the sister of Clemens Brentano. Within a space of ten months Bettina was fated to lose by death the husband whom she had devotedly loved, and the poet whom she had idolised from girlhood. Behind her lay a momentous epoch through which she had "lived" in the deepest sense of the word—her sensitive nature responding in poignant joy and pain to each new experience. She had known all the eminent men of the day. She had met Goethe several times, had a few

kindly letters from him. She had also the notes she had
taken, the stories she had heard, from the lips of his
mother at Frankfort. On the basis of these, but treating the written word only as a suggestion for the reminiscent imagination—somewhat as he himself had done in
his *Poetry and Truth*—she undertook to build a monument to the Goethe of her girlish dreams. She did not
fail to foresee the misconstruction that would be put on
her unusual procedure, but comforted herself with the
thought that her memoir was intended for " the good,"
and not for " the bad." And the good have always understood her, recognising in her imaginary correspondence,
not a memoir of the real Goethe, but the romance of a
gifted woman-soul dreaming of what might have been.
She might have called her book " a poet's correspondence
with a woman "; for the " child " of the title means only
that she felt herself the child of Goethe's spirit; that she
worshipped him as a lover, a man who lived in his feelings and impulses and dared to follow them, as she herself had done. This is but a fraction of the truth about
Goethe; but when one recalls the defamations with which
ignorance and partisanship were now beginning to assail
his character, Bettina's glowing pages become as the
white light of pure science.

In the drama of the romantic era the commanding
figure is FRANZ GRILLPARZER (1791–1872), the most
illustrious name in the literary annals of Austria. There
was that in Grillparzer's nature which stamps him as a
congener of the passionate souls who were born to agonise
and end in insanity or suicide, like Kleist and Hölderlin,
or in ascetic zealotry, like Brentano and Werner. A

neuropathic strain was in his blood: his mother and one of his brothers committed suicide, another brother came near to insanity. On the other hand, he inherited from his father a tough common sense and philistine stoicism, which made a virtue of holding on and knuckling under. "There live in me," he said of himself, "two entirely distinct beings: a poet of exuberant, even extravagant fancy, and a rationalist of the coldest and toughest kind." Hence it was that he could spend his days in the treadmill work of a government office in Vienna, and find in the commonplace a needed counterpoise to his poetic hyperæsthesia.

A large number of dramatic plans and beginnings, dating from Grillparzer's early youth, bear witness to the strength and persistence of his poetic impulse. It was not so much ambition as sheer necessity of self-expression. But he could not satisfy himself and was often in despair. In the stress of his young enthusiasm for Schiller he finally completed a Spanish tragedy in blank verse, *Blanca of Castile*, but the theatres would not have it, and it was not published during his lifetime. Then in 1817 he won fame at a bound with his *Ancestress,* a spook-tragedy that met with great success on the stage. It is replete with artificial horrors very similar in kind to those of the fashionable fate-plays. A carnal sin of long ago must work itself out horribly in the lives of a tainted and doomed progeny. The guilty ancestress must haunt the house as a restless ghost until the last of her descendants is dead. The play was written at fever heat in about three weeks of the most intense absorption. It is a kind of delirium, but the delirium of a poet and a dramatist.

The romantic and gruesome *Ancestress,* written in
the tripping trochaic measure of the Spanish drama, of
which Grillparzer was an earnest student, was followed
by two Greek plays in blank verse, *Sappho* and the
Golden Fleece. In the former there is no romanticism
whatever, save as the legend of the leap from the Leu-
cadian rock is itself romantic. Grillparzer conceived
Sappho as a gifted and idolised woman-artist who is
lonely on her heights of renown, and longs for the ordinary lot of love. When she finds through passionate
error that this one boon has been denied her, she conse-
crates herself to the gods, who have given her all things
else, and plunges into the sea. In the fine trilogy of the
Golden Fleece the supernatural again plays a part, the
fleece itself being the dark symbol of a fatal curse. But
this is rather incidental; essentially the play is grounded
in human nature. Just as in the case of Sappho, the
problem was to translate an ancient saga into the terms
of modern feeling; for with all his love of Greek literature Grillparzer was not the man to attempt a mere
imitation of Greek tragedy. What kind of woman could
that Medea have been who had murdered her own children? How could her character, her sufferings, the circumstances of her life, be so portrayed as to win and
hold sympathy, and make her final frenzy appear tragic
and not merely horrible? This is the problem to which
Grillparzer's dramatic imagination addressed itself. The
result is a convincing tragedy, though its poetic effect
is somewhat marred by the heroine's sorcery and the dark
fatalism of the fleece.

Next in order came two plays from Austro-Hungarian history, *King Ottokar* (1825), and *A Faithful Servant* (1828). They are dramatically effective character studies, but present no clear and sharp conflict of great historic forces. The issues involved are dynastic and personal, the point of view is that of a loyal Austrian monarchist. King Ottokar of Bohemia is depicted—the portrait being somewhat indebted to Napoleon—as a recklessly ambitious despot who goes down before the rising power of the more benignant Rudolf of Hapsburg. The theme of *A Faithful Servant* is loyalty to the throne. During a short absence the King of Hungary leaves the elderly statesman Bancban in charge of the public business. Bancban has a charming young wife, who is persecuted and finally driven to suicide by the queen's profligate brother. To save the miscreant the queen takes the murder on herself. Smothering his own grief and anger, Bancban risks his life to rescue the queen from the angry people, but succeeds only in bringing away the little crown prince. Then the king returns, and Bancban delivers the boy to him, claiming to have been a faithful servant of his master. It was inevitable that a play constructed on such lines should be criticised as an idealisation of servility.

Notwithstanding the intense loyalty of these historical plays they involved their author in rasping experiences connected with the censorship and the exigencies of court politics. He returned, therefore, to the safer fields of antique saga and romantic legend. The *Waves of the Sea and of Love* (1831) is a dramatisation of the Hero and Leander story, while the *Dream a Life* (1835) was suggested by Voltaire's Oriental tale *Le Blanc et le Noir*.

Both are prime favourites of the German stage. The former is one of the most exquisite of modern love-trag-edies—a play instinct with the pure poetry of passion and needing no other romantic lures. Hero in particu-lar is an altogether charming creation, who belongs in the select company of Shakespeare's Juliet and Goethe's Mar-garet. In the *Dream a Life* we have a young Persian of humble station who is ambitious to play a part in the great world. On the eve of setting out for a life of stir-ring adventure he falls asleep and dreams. By means of a bit of transparent symbolism the events of the dream are passed before the spectator as a part of the dramatic action, and the whole is so managed that when the dreamer wakes he is cured of his illusion.

Aside from the work of Grillparzer and the comple-tion of Goethe's *Faust,* presently to be considered, not much of importance for posterity was written in the dramatic form during the two decades that followed the Battle of Waterloo. The would-be titanic CHRISTIAN DIETRICH GRABBE (1801–36), who finally drank him-self to death, began furiously with the *Duke of Goth-land* (1826), which is a reek of loathsome horrors, with sporadic signs of dramatic genius. His *Don Juan and Faust* (1829) is a lurid extravaganza of two typical monsters on the road to hell. After these loud blasts of pessimism Grabbe calmed down and wrote a number of historical plays which have solid merit, though the stage has rejected them. His strength lay in the strong deno-tation of passional conflicts, but he had a bent for real-istic details which light up with grim humour the tragi-comedy of great men's lives. Another voluminous

dramatist of the period was KARL LEBERECHT IMMER-
MANN (1796–1840), a Düsseldorf magistrate whose
more solid fame rests on his novels. In his early plays
Immermann merely swam with the current of romanticism, taking hints from a wide range of reading, and
imitating Tieck and others. In his effort to be all in one,
according to the romantic doctrine, that is, to combine
poetry and prose, tender sentiment and satiric humour,
mysticism and rationalism, pathos and irony, and withal
to evince a mastery of all the possible verse-forms—he
always fell short of real dramatic excellence. He is a
plane mirror which reflects the rays of suggestion from
many sources, but never focuses them so that they really
burn. He came nearest to a masterpiece in his *Merlin,*
a dramatic poem which contains splendid passages, but
as a whole is abstruse and bewildering.

It now remains to speak of the closing years of
Goethe, of whose spirit the whole romantic movement
was in one sense but the wayward offspring. His brief
excursion to the Orient was only an episode in his life's
serene afternoon : it left no deep mark on his philosophy,
least of all did it impel him in the direction of quietism,
pessimism, or any other ism which implies a weakening
faith in the goodness of life. He took no active part in
the national uprising against Napoleon, because, as he
said, he was not a good hater, and felt that inflaming the
war spirit was not his affair. After the Congress of
Vienna he continued to hold aloof from politics, dis-
trusting alike the shibboleths of democracy and the re-
pressive tyranny of princes. Yet he loved his country,
and had a buoyant confidence in its future. As an evolu-

tionist he was the natural enemy of reaction, obscurantism, and despair. That which lay nearest his heart was the healthy progress of society through the spread of intelligence, the well-directed labour of individuals, and the drawing together of the nations in mutual understanding and goodwill. At the same time he believed that more would depend on the individual's general attitude toward life than on forms or machinery of any kind. The really important things were the eager acceptance of life, the large outlook, the honest effort, the free play of intelligence.[1]

And so the monarch of European letters, as Byron called him, devoted his later years to those works which have become the world's classical expression of the " calm, free, and onward " spirit. He wrote his *Poetry and Truth,* describing the *redlich Streben* of his youth, and the influences that had made him what he was. He continued *Wilhelm Meister,* making of the *Wanderjahre* a book which is amorphous and haphazard as a novel, but full of ripe wisdom and suggestive discussion of social ethics. And then, between 1825 and 1831, he completed his great life-work, the incommensurable dramatic poem which he had begun sixty years before, little dreaming whither the enterprise would lead him. First he

---

[1] The following passage from a letter to Zelter, written in May, 1820, will serve better than much description to put the reader in touch with the spirit of the septuagenarian Goethe: "Unbedingtes Ergeben in den unergründlichen Willen Gottes, heiterer Überblick des beweglichen, immer kreis- und spiralartig wiederkehrenden Erdetreibens, Liebe, Neigung zwischen zwei Welten schwebend, alles Reale geläutert, sich symbolisch auflösend. Was will der Grosspapa weiter?"

disburdened his Faust of all the old sensuality and pessimism; then carried him through divers wonderful experiences in the great world; made him end his earthly career
in an ecstasy of altruistic joy over the draining of a pes-
tilential swamp, and took final leave of him as a purified
soul mounting heavenward among the saints under the
mystic guidance of the Eternal Womanly.

The time is past when one may say, as Matthew
Arnold once said, that the *Second Part of Faust* does not
count. One who wishes to express his preference for
the *First Part* should at any rate find some happier
formula than that. For it is perfectly certain that the
essential content of the *Second Part*, though not indeed
its details, lay clear in the mind of Goethe long before
the *First Part* was published. All along the vital question had been simply this: Shall a man hate life and work
havoc with it for himself and others, or shall he love and
honour life and make the best of it as a social being?
For the understanding of Goethe nothing can possibly
be of greater importance than his answer to that question; and his answer is given in the *Second Part*. It
emerges at the end of a highly imaginative symbolic
poem, which is at once deeply religious and strictly scientific. True, the pivotal idea is not kept to the fore
all the time, for *Faust* is no metaphysical treatise. Its
fantastic character is given in the nature of the saga.
Perhaps some portions of the *Second Part* are spun out
to excessive length. The folk-lore, mythology, and
science are sometimes a little recondite, providing hard
nuts for the commentator to crack. But they were all
cracked rather easily as soon as the Germans got a firm

25

hold of the idea that *Faust* was poetry, humour, and vision—not cryptic philosophy or veiled biography. Goethe was before all things a poet, who saw visions and thought in symbols; and such he remained to the end of his days. And how interesting his mighty swan-song is, in its sovereign sweep of imagination, its delicious humour, its infinite suggestiveness, its penetrating criticism of life! It is Goethe's antidote for the pessimism which was settling over German life, chilling and corroding the very heart of it; the pessimism which could lead such a sane thinker as Alexander von Humboldt to declare that " the whole of life is the greatest insanity," and that " after striving and inquiring for eighty years one is obliged to confess that he has striven for nothing and has found out nothing." Not so, says Goethe, for the purpose of life is to live; and he who lives on a high plane of aspiration and endeavour, seeking to realize the good for his fellow-mortals and to make the territory about him a better place for better men and women to come,—such a man shall not miss his reward from the Central Rightness of the world.

CHAPTER XIX

THE literary reflex of the stormy period which began with the revolutionary excitement of the thirties and ended with the establishment of the new empire in 1871 is extremely chaotic. The motley facts reveal nothing like a common trend or a pervading spirit. In literature, as in politics, it was an era of rampant dogma and confused striving toward different goals. There is a stream of tendency toward realism, but one must take account of divers cross currents and refluent eddies. The age of Keller and Reuter is also the age of Wagner and Schopenhauer. The primacy among the genres, which on the whole had rested with lyric poetry during the era of romanticism, now went over to the novel. The drama, while worthily represented in the work of Hebbel, Ludwig, and the aging Grillparzer, is of quite secondary importance as a mirror of the time.

The literature of political and social agitation can here receive but scant attention. In the year 1835 a dull-witted decree of the Federal Diet forbade " the publication and sale of the writings of the literary school known as Young Germany," and named, as constituting the school, Heinrich Heine, Karl Gutzkow, Ludolf Wien-

barg, Theodor Mundt, and Heinrich Laube. All these
men had lately published radical opinions of one kind
or another, but apart from that simple fact they did not
constitute a literary school in any sense whatever. Wien-
barg and Mundt may be passed by entirely. GUTZKOW
(1811–78) and LAUBE (1806–84), who afterward won
distinction in ways not connected with Young Germany,
were at this time just becoming known as radical writers
who used the form of the novel, or that of the travel-
sketch in the manner of Heine, for the ventilation of
their opinions on church, state, and conventional morality. Gutzkow had published a novel, *Wally the Doubter*
(1835), which for that time was rather shocking in its
free treatment of Christianity, marriage, and sexual love.
He had also published Georg Büchner's *Death of Dan-
ton,* a play which its fiery young author had written in
fear of the police, and which was in effect a glorification
of the Terror. The spirit of religious radicalism was in
the air : Strauss's *Life of Jesus* was also a product of the
year 1835. As for Heine, he was now in Paris, whither
he had been drawn by the July Revolution, and was busy
as an apostle of St. Simonism and of democracy *à la
française.* Among his friends, for a time at least, was
LUDWIG BÖRNE (1786–1837), also a Jew, a brilliant
journalist and a gallingly witty critic of German political conditions. For some mysterious reason Börne was
not officially included in Young Germany.

The astounding decree of the Diet, which actually
undertook to suppress books not yet written, had the
natural effect of advertising Young Germany and giving
it a factitious importance. Its history is in reality little

more than a chapter in the history of German journalism. A laudable agitation for wholesome reforms was more or less mixed up with hatred of Goethe, advocacy of free love, irreligion, and emancipation of the flesh, and with the idea of enlisting literature in the service of political and social warfare. About these incidental matters, to be sure, the writers of the group disagreed; but their enemies, naturally enough, inclined to lump all the radicalisms together and proclaim them all as the logical outcome of French democracy. Thus the issues were wofully confused; and this confusion was not the least part of the mischief for which the régime Metternich was responsible. Undertaking to gag the German liberals altogether, it drove the hottest of them to Paris, where they attracted more attention than they could have done at home; for they readily found means to evade the censorship or to turn it to strategic advantage. But their miscellaneous radicalism, their constant praise of France, their campaign of pin-pricks and satire, actually hurt the cause of practical democracy. While it amused a portion of the reading public, it compromised the good cause by leading many honest folk to believe that a German democrat was a man who loved France better than his own country, and did not believe in God or in monogamous marriage.

All this has a bearing on the appreciation of the later Heine. What wonder is it if the Germans of to-day decline, on the whole, to concede to him that towering importance commonly ascribed to him in English books? He was a great lyric poet, they say, but what else? A witty journalist, an entertaining but not a profound or just critic, a radical agitator, who, to a great extent, misread the signs of the times and embittered the very people whom he professed to love and serve. Where are the great imaginative works which entitle him to be regarded as the inheritor of Goethe's mantle, and as the most important German writer of the nineteenth century? They simply do not exist. Heine's fame must rest on his verse, and not on what he chose to call his service in humanity's war of liberation. He was not one of the great liberators, for in the long run men are set free only by the truth and by high sincerity; but he cared less for truth than for piquancy, and high sincerity was not in him, though he knew how to counterfeit it effectively. His assaults on Platen, Wilhelm Schlegel, Prussia, the Catholic church, are not the work of a deliverer, but of a man who himself needed to be delivered from malice.

But the verse of Heine remains a precious possession, however far it may fall short of proving that talent can dispense with character. In his gibes at the men whom he regarded as bunglers he was often shockingly unjust; but his wit, his verbal drolleries, and the odd rhymes in which he fairly outdid Byron, are irresistible. *Germany, a Winter's Tale* (1844), with its wonderful blend of genuine tenderness, bitter irony, and cynical wit, is a thing so entertaining that even Prussian grenadiers and Westfalian Catholics can at last afford to forgive and forget, and laugh with the rest of the world. The mock-romantic *Atta Troll* (1847), in which Heine tried to conjure back the dream he had once dreamed with Chamisso, Fouqué, and Brentano, and at the same time to mix in some "modern trills," is extremely amusing when read in the light of an intimate knowledge of those forgotten literary squabbles. And then what fascination there is in *Romancero* and the *Last Poems* (1851–53), in which the doomed sufferer " set his pain to music." It is, indeed, a discordant music, altogether poor in what Wordsworth called the joy of elevated thoughts. But there is surely some reason on the side of those who find in those jangled chords of pessimism and disillusion, of pathos, laughter, and sensual frivolity, the strongest and most characteristic expression of Heine's genius.

The singers of political discontent were numerous, ranging all the way from mild liberalism to red republican fury. One of the earliest voices was that of Count Auersperg, an Austrian gentleman who wrote under the name of ANASTASIUS GRÜN (1806–76). In his *Saunterings of a Vienna Poet* (1831) he drew a telling contrast between the régime Metternich and the kindly people-trusting rule of earlier monarchs. One of the poems represented the loyal Austrian people as appearing before the mighty Man of State—so gay, so affable and debonair—and humbly praying: Might I take the liberty, sir, to be free? A few years later the democratic strain was taken up less cautiously by HOFFMANN VON FALLERS-LEBEN (1798–1874), a scholar eminent in Germanic studies, and a very fecund song-writer. He was at home in all the specialties of romanticism, turning out songs of love, wine, vagabondage, good fellowship, and especially of the fatherland. His *Non-political Songs* (1840) were political enough in their humorous castigation of existing abuses, but not technically revolutionary. Hoffmann's famous *Deutschland, Deutschland über Alles*

came out in the year 1841, the year after Schnecken-
burger's *Die Wacht am Rhein.*

These were songs of German solidarity and patriotic
pride; the slogan of internal war—war of the democracy against the princes—was first sounded by GEORG
HERWEGH (1817–75), in his rattling and incendiary
Poems of a Live Man (1841). He was followed a little later by FERDINAND FREILIGRATH (1810–76), a far
more important literary personage. Freiligrath first attracted attention by hot and plangent poems in which
he pictured the ways of rude men and fierce animals in
far-away lands. This perfervid poetry of the desert and
the jungle, of lions, giraffes, negroes, and Arab sheiks,
was a new form of protest against tameness and conventionality. It took the fancy of the public, but is not
at all comparable to the more personal love-songs that
came a little later. In haunting melody and the effect
of tense, vibrant passion, Freiligrath's *With Weeds* and
Rest in the Beloved have hardly been surpassed in the
German language. For some time it was his creed that
a poet should stand aloof from party strife. This doctrine was fiercely attacked by Herwegh, others took
part in the debate, and Freiligrath presently became convinced that the duty of the hour for him was to " go
with the people." It was the great crisis of his life and
his art. That rugged reality and fierce excitement which
he had sought far away among lions and tigers seemed
to lie right at hand in the impending revolution. For
he thought the Germans wanted and were going to have
a republic. Beginning with the collection *Confession of
Faith* (1844), his verse is a crescendo of republican radi-

calism, until the collapse of the revolutionary excitement
of 1848 sent him into exile—with many another disgusted patriot of that stormy epoch. In London, where
he lived until the amnesty of 1866, he wrote occasional
poems and a large number of excellent translations of
French, English, and American poets. But the marrow
of his poetic energy had been consumed in his hot fight
for a cause that failed.

The chief literary apostle of the cause that triumphed
was EMANUEL GEIBEL (1815–84), by far the most popular lyrist of the mid-century epoch. In recent years
his star has declined, the word having gone forth that
he is "too beautiful." He was a Prussian (native of
Lübeck) and a late-born romanticist. His earliest poems
(1841), published just after a two-years' sojourn in
Greece, were eagerly read as a voice of good cheer from
the old-fashioned serene heights of art; for there were
many who resented the prostitution of poetry to factional
ends. He besought his countrymen to love one another
and purify themselves with prayer, and he warbled pret-
tily in the old way—all of which drew on him the ridicule
of the poetic belligerents. Later he concluded that Germany was ill with the disease of Hamlet and needed
blood-letting. He won the name of *Kaiserherold*. But
his political verse has not the clangorous momentum of
Freiligrath's. After his *June Songs* (1848) there was
no one to dispute his lordship of the German Parnassus.
The King of Bavaria called him to Munich, where he
lived many years as the comrade of royalty, and the
leading figure in the local school of art for art's sake.
He lectured on poetics at the university, and set great

store by formal perfection. And this was really his only
message. One reads the eight volumes of his verse,
including his poetic dramas, and finds it all exquisitely
chiselled, but lacking in rugged virility and weighty
import.

Among the other continuators of the romantic tradition in lyric verse, the most noteworthy are Mörike,
Storm, and Scheffel. EDUARD MÖRIKE (1804–75) was
a Swabian pastor who led a secluded life, taking little
note of the outward turmoil, and cleaving to the old
poetic creed. His first work, *Painter Nolten* (1832),
was a novel with an artist for hero—a book quite in
the romantic vein, admirable in parts, but rather badly
composed. His fame rests on his *Poems* (1838), which
charm by their sincerity and their delicacy of workmanship. The volume of his work is small, but the best of
it is so good as to give him a place with Eichendorff and
Uhland. His *Visit to Urach*, a reminiscent poem in
ottava rima, is as excellent in its kind as Wordsworth's
Tintern Abbey.

The savour of THEODOR STORM (1817–88) is very
like that of Mörike, but with the difference that his verse
is redolent of the north—of Schleswig-Holstein and the
sea. He was born at Husum, settled there as magistrate
in 1842, was presently driven into exile by his anti-
Danish proclivities, but returned after the war of 1864.
A few of his poems deal in strong language with the
Schleswig-Holstein question, but in the main they are
concerned with still life and the quiet aspects of Nature.
Many of them begin by picturing a definite situation,
such as a chilly day in October, with its invitation to

convivial pleasure within four walls; the hush of noon in midsummer; the evening fog floating in over the gray city by the sea. Others are lovers' reminiscences, or bits of sentiment suggested by the observation of plain folk and their ways. In all this there is nothing new, it being the familiar range of earlier romantic lyrists; but it is done so exquisitely, with such power of subtle suggestion, as to give Storm an assured place among the epigoni of romanticism.

The prime distinction of JOSEF VICTOR VON SCHEFFEL (1826–86) is his humour. The man behind the pen was a restless, nervous being with an almost morbid tendency to worriment; but the author whom we know from his books—all of them substantially were written between 1853 and 1860—is a genial soul with hardly a touch of acerbity or pessimism. Scheffel was before all things an entertaining writer, who put his reader in a pleasant mood, carried him along pleasantly through grave and gay, and left him satisfied, if not edified. This is the secret of his immense popularity. His *Trumpeter of Säkkingen*, probably the most widely read narrative poem of the century, was built on familiar romantic lines. It is a romance of artistic vagabondage, with interspersed songs and serious reflections, and the story told in slovenly, easy-going verse, instead of the poetic prose of Eichendorff. His famous collection *Gaudeamus* is only excellent fooling at the expense of scientific and historical solemnities, but excellent the fooling really is. There is good fun in his potatory tragedy of the *Black Whale in Ascalon*, as also in his pathetic visions of the ichthyosaurus and the guano-fowl.

In *Ekkehard*, the most popular of German historical novels, Scheffel undertook to account imaginatively for the writing of the Latin *Waltharius Manu Fortis* (above, page 34). To this end he invented a love-affair between its author and the historical Hadwig, Duchess of Swabia, conceiving her as a modern emancipated lady. He made Ekkehard a lusty monk, with a quite modern capacity for *Weltschmerz*, and a very Scheffel-like proneness to lonely brooding. In this frame he set a warm picture of full-blooded tenth-century life, warranting his verisimilitude with erudite notes, and devising for his narrative an artificial language which varies between crabbed archaism and colloquial modernity. The monstrous anachronism of the tale, as R. M. Meyer rightly calls it, disturbs the trained historical sense; but the reader who has no such scruples is delighted, and lays down the book with the comment: How very human, how very like ourselves, were those forebears of ours about the Lake of Constance a thousand years ago!

As for the other historical fiction of the time, let it suffice to mention the work of Häring, who wrote under the name of WILIBALD ALEXIS (1798–1871). The Germans are fond of calling him the Walter Scott of Brandenburg. Of his seven novels dealing with Prussian history, the best are *Roland of Berlin* (1840), the *Breeches of Lord Bredow* (1846), and *Keep Cool* (1852). The pervading idea is to exhibit the political and social evolution of the Prussian people. There is a patriotic drift, but not of the kind that leads to sentimentalism or rhetorical perversion. Alexis was not afraid of the facts, but respected them even in their ugliness; just as he

loved the sombre Brandenburg landscape, and the phlegmatic but masterful people whom he makes seem a part
of it. His novels grew out of a quickened interest in
national life as seen under the aspect of evolution. To
study the folk-soul at critical epochs, and try to disengage
the permanent identity from the accidents of time and
circumstance, was a fascinating problem. It was this
idea which inspired the excellent *Pictures of the German
Past* by Gustav Freytag. In a sense, too, the same idea
informed the work of the South German Riehl, whose
historical novelettes enjoyed great favour during the
third quarter of the century.

But the more important branch of fiction was that
which concerned itself with the living present. The
demand of Young Germany that literature come back
to life was in itself a wholesome demand. For more than
a generation fiction had consisted of fantastic tales, or
else of romantic variations on the scheme of *Wilhelm
Meister*. In either case there was unreality—characters
that wandered and dreamed and philosophised and became
entangled in strange adventures, but never led normal
working lives or seemed to be made of authentic human
stuff. The great illusion of the romantic era had been
that actuality, save as a foil to the marvellous and the
fantastic, was uninteresting. The first noteworthy attempt to make headway against this illusion was Immermann's *Epigoni* (1836). It was only a groping, half-
hearted attempt; for the tale is but an epigonal *Wilhelm
Meister,* with much of the old romanticism in its make-up.
But it did lay hold of actuality by giving a vigorous
picture of the sharpening conflict between the old social

order and the new epoch of the machine and the factory.
The invasion of modern industrialism in its effects on
squirearchy is also dealt with in Immermann's *Münchhausen* (1839), a romance of humbuggery. Each of the
important characters is the victim of a ruling illusion—
what Ibsen calls a life-lie. Immermann here came near
to making a great book, but the effect of his rugged
realism is marred by his satiric scheme, his fantastic plot,
and his extravagant humour.

Embedded in the bulky *Münchhausen* one finds an
episode called *Der Oberhof*—a charmingly realistic picture of Westfalian still life. When Immermann wrote
it he little thought, presumably, that this unpretending
story would become his most popular work. But the
time was now ripe for the village tale. The idea was
taken up by BERTHOLD AUERBACH (1812–82), who
began in 1843 to publish his *Village Tales of the Black
Forest*. They forthwith made him famous. Readers
were at first incurious whether the denizens of the Black
Forest were really as he depicted them. Enough that
the tales were interesting and seemed lifelike. To the
public they came as a welcome relief from the complicated
romance of high-toned society, and to the literary class
they opened a new vista. The country folk, who had
figured in polite literature chiefly as objects of super-
cilious satire, or else of idyllic eulogy at long range, now
came into it as naturalised citizens. The peasant was,
after all, a man and a brother; and a clown might be
as interesting as a prince or a mysterious adventurer.
As a matter of fact, Auerbach's people were somewhat
sophisticated by his own local patriotism (he was born

in the Black Forest), his very genial temperament, and his speculative bias. In his later and more pretentious works his didactic bent became so strong as to make him a special pleader. The author of *On the Heights* (1865) is clearly an apostle of pantheism, and an attorney in the case of country *versus* court.

No such partisanship can be attributed to GOTTFRIED KELLER (1819–90), the wizard story-teller of Zürich, whose books are on the whole the very best reading to be found in the whole range of nineteenth-century German fiction. The son of a Swiss mechanic, Keller was in his youth a sort of romantic ne'er-do-weel, who divided his time between painting, poetising, and waiting for something to turn up. Two years at the Munich art school left him still undecided about his vocation. He had already published a volume of not very remarkable verse when he received a public stipend which enabled him to study further in Germany. He spent two years at Heidelberg, five at Berlin; and there he finished his four-volume autobiographic novel *Green Henry* (1855), and also the first volume of the Swiss village tales called *Seldwyla Folk* (1856). Of his later writings, published during and after his long service as cantonal secretary at Zürich, the most important are *Seven Legends* (1872), *Zürich Novelettes* (1878), and *Martin Salander* (1878). Up to a dozen years before his death Keller had received little attention in Germany; to-day there is a library of books about him, and he is universally considered a fixed star of high magnitude. While he was an ardent Swiss republican, and while the life that he depicts is almost exclusively Swiss, the Germans of the empire have pretty

generally accepted him as their greatest master of prose
fiction since Goethe.

Keller was a romantic realist with the soul of a poet,
the eye of a man of science, and the temperament of an
artist who loves life in all its manifestations. But this
leaves his humour out of the account, and his humour
is precisely the best part of him. In a broad sense he is
didactic—like Goethe; that is, he felt that it was his
mission to comprehend and describe the character of his
Swiss countrymen, to the end of furthering them toward
higher ideals of communal life. But this attitude never
clouds his vision for the facts. He sees at every pore,
as Emerson said of Goethe. He does not select ugliness
for special or angry scrutiny, any more than he avoids
it through excess of daintiness, but takes all things as
they come. What he offers is not medicine but food—the
nourishment of sane and delightful art. But no one
should go to him for an exciting narrative. His spell is
not in his plot. In *Green Henry*, particularly, his pace
is so very leisurely that one sometimes wishes there were
not so many little things to be taken note of by the way.

Keller's realism did not extend to the use of dialect.
With all his Swiss patriotism he felt himself to be not
merely a local genre-painter in words, but a German
author of the line of Goethe and Schiller. It was different with the other great realistic humourist of the
time, FRITZ REUTER (1810–74), who with some justice
has been called the German Dickens. Reuter was over
forty, a victim of alcoholism, and almost a social wreck,
when a local success with a volume of humorous trifles
in his native Mecklenburg dialect started him on the road

to fame. He certainly had matter enough in his memory. For nine years he had led the hard life of a Prussian prisoner of state, being under commuted death-sentence for taking part while a student in a forbidden political demonstration. After his release he drifted, trying his hand at farm-stewardship, teaching, journalism. Nothing went well with him, but the result of his motley experience was an incomparable knowledge of the Mecklenburgers in all their types and social strata. In a series of books which took at first the form of rather loosely connected humorous sketches and anecdotes, later that of fictitious narrative, he portrayed the Mecklenburgers as he had known them. The best of them are *Ut mine Festungstid* (*From my Prison Life*, 1863) and *Ut mine Stromtid* (*From my Life as Farm Steward*, 1864). The latter in particular is a fine gallery of portraits drawn with bluff fidelity to the fact, and at the same time with delightful humour. Reuter wrote entirely in Low German, having been encouraged thereto by the success of Klaus Groth's dialect poetry. The merit of these attempts to rehabilitate Low German as a literary vehicle is a much debated question which cannot here be taken up.

By virtue of their sound realism and their engaging humour, Keller and Reuter are the two mid-century novelists whose work now seems likely to last the longest. But they were not the heroes of their own generation; these were rather Freytag and Spielhagen, and, in the domain of the short story, Heyse. GUSTAV FREYTAG (1816-95), in point of honours and emoluments one of the most successful German writers of the century, was a Silesian who set out in his youth to become a professional scholar,

26

but gave up that career for letters and journalism. He had already written a number of plays, including the very successful *Journalists* (1852), when he won the memorable triumph of *Debit and Credit* (1854). Weary of the windbags, agitators and idling reprobates of the current fiction that had sprung up in the wake of Young Germany, Freytag undertook to exhibit the German people at work. His aim was to dignify labour—or rather, business, for the novel is not concerned with the grinding toil of the proletariat. His message to the great middle class was, in effect: Away with the idea that work is dull or degrading; behold in your own daily routine a sufficient source of inspiration, a sufficient field for your energy, your idealism, your German *Tüchtig-keit*. In the *Lost Manuscript* (1864) he undertook to do for the university life of the day what the earlier novel had done for its commercial life. Neither book is unassailable. Freytag had little humour in him, could not depict great passion, was inclined to schematic didacticism. Nevertheless, the two famous novels are likely to hold a permanent place as pictures of German life in the middle of the nineteenth century.

While Freytag was an adversary of Young Germany, FRIEDRICH SPIELHAGEN (1829–), whose vogue was very great between 1860 and 1880, was essentially its disciple. That is, he was an ideologist, an opinionator, interested as novelist in the clash of doctrines. His characters are schematic embodiments of ideas and tendencies. To read him is like reading a parliamentary debate in which every speaker "represents" a pushing constituency. Withal there is much special didacticism. Instead of being given an æsthetic and intellectual treat, the reader feels that he is being put through a course of instruction. The mechanism of the exciting plot is usually very ingenious, but one soon comes to feel that it *is* mechanism. From the nature of the case such fiction loses a large part of its interest when the questions of the hour, with which it deals, have been forgotten. Spielhagen is at his best in the three novels, *In Rank and File* (1866), *Hammer and Anvil* (1869), and *Storm Flood* (1876).

The great distinction of PAUL HEYSE (1830–), perhaps the most versatile German writer of his century, is to have created a new standard of style and artistic finish for the novelette. An inheritor of the romantic tradition, trained as a specialist in romance languages, the friend of Geibel, he was in full sympathy with the Munich cult of art. His first collection of short stories was published in 1855, and contained the much-praised *L'Arrabbiata.* Since then Heyse has written voluminously in all the genres of prose and verse—unfailingly on a high level of craftsmanship, but without achieving anything indubitably epoch-making save his novelettes. In an excellent study of Heyse as a virtuoso of the short story, Georg Brandes has remarked of him that his fancy works like that of a painter or sculptor, always intent on " beautiful forms and movements, the pose of a graceful head, a charming peculiarity of posture or gait "; and that his art consists in fixing such plastic visions by means of language rhythmically attuned to the nature of the subject. In the fashioning of such literary pastels, especially of Italian life—pictures instinct with sensuous beauty and the poetry of conquering passion—Heyse has remained without a peer. But his very cosmopolitanism seems to have unfitted him to be a portrayer of German life in its humbler phases.

It remains to glance at the mid-century drama, which, as might be presumed from the militant temper of the age, was largely a drama of " tendency." The prominent playwright in that kind was Gutzkow, whose rise to fame and influence was not hindered in the least by the early prohibition of his writings. In fact, there is reason to think that the censorship proved the making of him. Speaking of the subject in 1871, long after the dawn of a better day, Gutzkow observed that the effect of the press censorship under the régime Metternich was to poison all the old springs of poetry. " As an antidote to that poison," he went on to say, " we invented *die Tendenz*." In other words, the drama now became an arena of discussion; an instrument in the warfare of liberalism against tradition and authority; a tribunal for the case of good people against bad. Gutzkow won his first success on the stage with the prose tragedy *Richard Savage* (1839), which now seems extremely turgid and unreal. This was followed by a long succession of tragedies and comedies, some in prose and others in blank verse, in all of which there is more or less of the spirit of the pamphleteer and the preacher. The best of them is *Uriel Acosta* (1847), a tragedy of religious liberalism among the Amsterdam Jews in the time of Spinoza. There is no poetry in Gutzkow's verse, and the play is gloomy to a degree; but it is effective in virtue of its sharply drawn conflict and its telling stage-craft. Some of Gutzkow's lighter prose plays, notably *Queue and Sword,* and the

Original of Tartuffe, have also proved to have vital stuff in them.

While Gutzkow attained a position of large authority and influence, his adversary, the man who is to-day regarded as the greatest dramatist of the epoch, won comparatively scant recognition from his contemporaries. FRIEDRICH HEBBEL (1813–63) was the son of a poor Dithmarsch mason. His early life was a hard struggle with seemingly untoward conditions, until his prose tragedy *Judith* (1839) attracted the attention of a Berlin actress, who made a success of the title-rôle. The Jewish widow of the Apocrypha, who murders her country's enemy from patriotic and religious motives, was converted by Hebbel into an erotic superwoman—a virgin wife who resolves to sacrifice her chastity for the public good, and murders Holofernes after having yielded herself to him in a paroxysm of mingled hate and love. This beginning was typical of much that was to come in Hebbel's work—fierce passional conflicts of an abnormal nature, situations trenching on the repulsive, tragic catastrophes growing out of exaggerated egoism.

Soon after his prosperity began, Hebbel received a Danish pension which enabled him to reside some time in France and Italy. Returning home he settled in Vienna, where he devoted himself mainly to play-writing. He took his vocation very seriously : in his diary and letters, as well as in more formal writings, we find him continually brooding over questions of dramatic art. The tendency-play was an offence to him, the Munich cult of formal " beauty " hardly less so. His creative work should be studied in the light of his philosophy, which was influenced by Hegel and by Schopenhauer. But that subject cannot be treated here. Suffice it to say that he is at his best where his theories are least obtrusive, and that he created a type of drama which anticipates Ibsen in its keen dialectic of passion, and suggests Nietzsche in its predilection for characters that live themselves out in a spirit of reckless and vehement self-assertion—supermen and superwomen. In *Mary Magdalen* (1844), the best of his early plays, he is the forerunner of the modern naturalistic drama. He here undertook to rehabilitate the domestic tragedy, which had languished since Schiller's *Cabal and Love*. The theme is the suicide of a girl of humble station after her ruin by a graceless scoundrel. The language is prose, but High German, the atmosphere otherwise thoroughly realistic. It is a sombre and depressing but powerful production, ending on a note of pessimism and despair. One is reminded of Ibsen's method of asking hard questions without undertaking to answer them.

In the two poetic tragedies *Genevieve* (1840) and *Herod and Mariamne* (1851) we have essentially the same theme, namely, the gradual conversion of an impetuous egoist, under the influence of erotic passion, into a loathsome monster. The later play is certainly a masterpiece of historical portraiture and psychological motivation, but there is little in its noisome atmosphere to warm the cockles of the heart. One pities Mariamne as one would pity a deer in the clutches of a tiger. To excite sympathy, as the older dramatists understood it, was not Hebbel's affair. There is on the whole most of poetic warmth in *Gyges and his Ring* (1853), which the general verdict rightly calls his masterpiece. But here, too, what a singular groundwork for a five-act tragedy! King Kandaules of Lydia is so proud of the beauty of his queen that he makes an opportunity for his guest-friend Gyges to see her loveliness unadorned. When the queen learns of the affront to her modesty, she demands of Gyges that he kill her husband and take her to wife. The deed done and the wedding celebrated, she commits suicide. The dramatic genius of Hebbel is nowhere more effectively shown than in his transformation of this singular story of Herodotus into a stately, chaste, and harmonious tragedy. Than *Gyges* there is nothing finer in the mid-century poetic drama—unless, indeed, one give the palm to *Libussa,* that subtle symbolic tragedy which was the last work of Grillparzer.

With the name of Hebbel, as a pioneer in the realistic drama, it is customary to connect that of OTTO LUDWIG (1813–65). He, too, was a strenuous theorist and an enemy of Young Germany, though friendly enough to the demand that literature come back to life. He first attracted attention with a play called the *Hereditary Forester* (1849), which was performed successfully and much discussed. It is a prose tragedy of family life, illustrating the peril of a choleric temperament. Two men who are good friends quarrel over a trifle, each insists on having his own way, and increasing exasperation leads to murderous madness. The forester shoots at his adversary's son, who is betrothed to the forester's own daughter, and kills the girl by accident. Better work than in this picture of a family vendetta was done by Ludwig in his poetic tragedy of the *Maccabees*

(1852), which has splendid scenes and characters, though as a whole it falls short of a harmonious effect. The high promise of the *Maccabees* was frustrated by failing health. As an invalid, cut off from the life of men, Ludwig worked on bravely, occupying himself partly with the study of Shakespeare, whom he idolised beyond reason, and partly with dramatic plans which he proved unable to execute. Fortunately, he did complete that admirable novel of Thuringian life *Between Heaven and Earth* (1856), which is, on the whole, his very best title to literary fame.

The last seven years of Hebbel's life were devoted mainly to his trilogy of the *Nibelungs* (1862), which won him the famous Schiller prize shortly before his death. Of all the numerous attempts to rehabilitate the old saga Hebbel's is the most faithful to its spirit and its details—the one which a scholar can read with the most satisfaction. It proved, however, that mediæval saga was to be effectively revitalised for the modern imagination not by Hebbel or Geibel or Jordan, or any other poet-scholar who attacked the problem with the aid of verse alone. That was to be the achievement of RICHARD WAGNER (1813–83), who accordingly bulks large in many recent histories of German literature. Max Koch delimits an important period of literary history as extending " from the death of Goethe to the Bayreuth festivals." We hear of Wagner as a great epoch-making poet, the creator of a new and wonderful art-form, of which poetry is the vital essence—a form which is specifically German and Germany's greatest contribution to modern art. Wagner's literary admirers repudiate the idea that he was merely a composer who modified the older opera by giving it a deeper emotional import, taking his subjects from mediæval saga-lore and writing his own libretti. On the other hand, his more savage enemies declare that his theory of a new art-form was chimerical and absurd from the first, and that his influence has been altogether pernicious.

The Wagner question cannot be debated here, still less decided without debate. Nor is it possible to separate the poet from the musician, and treat of the former only. For Wagner without his music is simply not Wagner at all. Read as literature, the great mass of his verse would have, for the public at large, but little interest. At any rate, it is not as literature that his works have won the popularity they enjoy. The multitudes who have come under the spell of the Wagnerian "art-drama" have always been chiefly attracted by his music. They have regarded him as belonging to the line of Mozart and Beethoven, not the line of Goethe and Schiller. The greatness of his genius and his achievement is not open to question; but he belongs to the history of music and opera rather than to the history of literature.

CHAPTER XX

This final chapter can attempt nothing more than to describe very briefly, with little discussion of individual authors, the general trend of literary activity under the new empire. It is a question of continuing tentatively a little farther the curve that we have been tracing through a thousand years of literary vicissitude. Beyond that, contemporary literature does not come into the scheme of this volume. It is a field for the appreciator, who may write of what happens to interest him; or for the chronicler, who may tell what is going on and what people are saying about it—in either case without concern for a general view of things in their right proportions. The historian, who must feel that very concern, needs the perspective which only time can give. For if history teaches anything it is that, in the everlasting flux and reflux of fashion and taste, contemporary opinion is but a fallible index to literary vitality. Even international repute, which has been called the surest indication of posterity's verdict, tends to become a less and less trustworthy sign.

An enormous literary production; sharp antagonisms of doctrine and practice; contending schools and sects

and isms; old idols cast down and new ones set up, to
be in their turn repudiated of many; a small army of more
or less meritorious novelists, poets, and playwrights, a
very few of whom have become objects of international
interest, but none of whom can yet be recognised as
embodying pre-eminently the soul of his epoch—such is
the picture presented by the recent past in Germany. It
is too soon yet for an attempt to determine the literary
resultant of the conflicting forces, if there be any such
thing; all one can do is to describe them and connect them
with what goes before.

The war of 1870, which in a way realised the long-
cherished dream of national unity, was not followed by
anything like a literary renascence. Indeed, with all the
quickening of national pride and hope, the first decade
of the new Germany was a period of literary backwardness, except, indeed, in the way of prose fiction. The
old lines of effort projected themselves into the new era,
poetry becoming a less and less important factor of the
national life. This is a world-wide phenomenon, for
which it would be futile to seek a special cause in German
conditions. In Germany, as elsewhere, the recent past is
rich enough in good verse—verse which often seems to be
better than some of that which has become classical.
There is no lack of technical cunning, no lack of serious
purpose and deep regard for the poetic art. But the volumes appear, make peradventure a nine days' theme of
discussion in the journals, and then are forgotten. The
great public takes but little interest in them. A large proportion of the recent novelists, playwrights, and journalists have published *Gedichte* by way of avocation; but they

make, on the whole, less impression by their verse than by their prose. Is it, as some think, that there is a surfeit of verse which is fairly good without being highly significant, or is it that the temper of the age is unfavourable to that particular form of artistic self-expression? At any rate, the fact remains that the new Germany has produced no poet of great distinction whose fame rests solely or chiefly on his verse.

The fiction of the Bismarck era was largely purveyed by writers who had already won distinction in the fifties. Freytag brought out the six parts of the *Ancestors* (1872–80), a cycle of tales intended to show the evolution of the German social character by describing the form and pressure of life at selected epochs ranging from the fourth century to the nineteenth. Spielhagen published the strongest of his novels, *Storm Flood* (1876), an effective though overdrawn picture of the social depravation—crass materialism, greed of gain, reckless speculation—which followed the payment of the French milliards. Heyse also made his best contribution to fiction of the more elaborate sort in the *Children of the World* (1872), which dealt with contemporary urban life in emancipated, free-thinking and free-living circles. The art of Storm, as a portrayer of still life in Schleswig-Holstein, culminated in *Aquis Submersus* (1877), a much more virile story than the lyric-sentimental *Immensee* of his earlier years.

Aside from these eminent names, to which that of Keller might be added, there were several writers who, by the date of their birth, belonged to the older generation, but did not emerge into literary prominence till after the war. One of them was the highly esteemed Swiss novelist CONRAD FERDINAND MEYER (1825–98), the author of a number of historical novelettes that have hardly been surpassed in their kind. Then there was THEODOR FONTANE (1819–98), who began with romantic balladry, but presently, as journalist and war-correspondent, received the schooling which converted him into an uncompromising realist. His field was to be the novel of Berlin life—a specialty in which, at the time of his death, he was the acknowledged master. The village tale was cultivated by WILHELM RAABE (1831–), who belongs to the literary line of Richter and Immermann. His sympathetic pictures of humble life, with their fantastic humour and mild pessimism, have won him many friends. More convincing to a realistic taste, however, are the tales and plays of Austrian peasant life by LUDWIG ANZENGRUBER (1839–89), and the winsome stories of the Styrian Alps by PETER ROSEGGER (1843–).

As for the drama, the first fifteen years of the new empire brought forth little that now seems particularly noteworthy. Most important, perhaps, was the early work of ERNST VON WILDENBRUCH (1845–), whose *Karlovingians* (1881) was played with great success by the famous Meiningen company, and contributed to a revival of interest in historical tragedy. In general, the stage of the period was held mainly by society plays of the kind just then fashionable in Paris.

In the meanwhile various influences had been preparing the way for a literary insurrection—one that has often been likened to the " storm and stress " of the eighteenth century. The analogy holds good in that the new movement, like the earlier one, was an emphatic protest of youthful radicalism against the tyranny of tradition. But there is an important difference. The young Goethe and his satellites revolted against an outworn literary canon which had never evolved naturally on German soil from the practice of great writers, but had been taken over bodily from France. Theirs was an insurrection against an exotic pseudo-classicism. But the reformers of twenty years ago made war on an indigenous tradition which had its origin in the best period of German literature. It began to be felt that German writers had lived all too long on their classical patrimony. Reverence for the past, it was urged vociferously, had become a fetter which it was necessary to throw off, in order that the living present might come into its natural rights. The old idealisms and forms had done their work and must make way for the literary expression of actualities. In fine, the ever-recurring demand was heard once more that literature come back to life. Like the earlier Young Germany of the thirties, the new school was much influenced by foreign writers. They found the main elements of their gospel recorded in Zola, Dostoyefsky, the earlier Tolstoy, and especially in Ibsen and Björnson.

The philosophic basis of the new naturalism—so far as it can be said to have one, and is not simply a fresh phase of the everlasting conflict between the has-been and the would-be—must be sought in certain conceptions of modern science: namely, the struggle for existence, the effects of heredity and environment, the biologic equality of the sexes. If the law of the world dooms the great mass of mankind to a ceaseless, pitiless struggle for the means of keeping alive, then life is hard, and its hardness is the great overshadowing fact of our social existence. The new creed will have it that literature must recognise this hardness, look it squarely in the face, and describe it as it is. Why, it is asked, should we blink the truth, or try to forget it, or run away from it? From this point of view the old notion of poetry as a refuge from vulgarity—the giver of the beauty and the solace which life denies—becomes unscientific and cowardly. And then, again, if a man is not what he wills, but what he is made by heredity and environment, two conclusions seem to follow. In the first place, heredity and environment are of momentous importance and must be minutely studied and described. Secondly, the real tragedy of life for the modern man must be looked for, not in a fatal clash of towering wills, but in the corrosive and thwarting power of circumstance. Finally, if woman is the equal partner of man in the great life-process, then she can no longer be regarded either as a temptress, or as a slave, or as a plaything. Her right to education, freedom, self-expression, becomes no less exigent, no less important, than his own.

Such is the scientific basis of the new demand for a " revaluation of values "—a demand which was everywhere fortified, and nowhere more than in Germany, by the progress of socialism. If life is hard and ugly for the many—so runs the socialistic argument—then the great duty of the hour lies in the direction of active effort to make it less hard and ugly. This duty presses on the men who write no less than on philanthropists, employers, and social workers of every kind. It is not for them to purvey amusement, or dream pretty dreams, or occupy themselves with the frivolities of the frivolous, but to bear a hand in the great work of social amelioration. This they can best do by describing life just as it is. The truth must not be sophisticated either by an artificial plot or by making men appear better or worse than they really are. If the picture they draw is loathsome and depressing, so much the worse for the society which permits the conditions to exist.

All these ideas have found expression to some extent in the work of the naturalists, but not consistently and harmoniously. As was remarked of the mid-century period, there are cross currents and refluent eddies. Moreover, there is a large stream of tendency running in the opposite direction and proceeding from the writings of FRIEDRICH NIETZSCHE (1844–1900), whose influence on the new school has been considerable. Modern socialism, while it has largely broken with the Christian church, is at one with primitive Christianity, so far as it is a doctrine of brotherly help and of pity and sympathy for the poor. It does not undertake to settle the ultimate question whether life be good, but is content to rest on the practical certainty that the conditions of life can be made indefinitely better. This meliorism is in a way opposed to Schopenhauer, who was born to be the philosopher of romanticism. If life is bad, and the wise man's part is to subdue his will to live and ease the pain of existence by taking such æsthetic pleasure as may come in his way, then there is no room in the world for active benevolence or social effort of any kind. Life being bad at the root, it will be so after a thousand years: why, then, should any one strive and cry? To overcome Schopenhauer's pessimism, restore the joy of living, and find a philosophic groundwork for it, was the central problem of Nietzsche's thinking. He was gradually led to a complete repudiation of Christian ethics and of all morality based on self-control or sympathy for the weak and poor. He detested socialism. The world is for the strong man, the " blond beast " who lives " on the other side of good and evil." The life-process is for the evolution of a wonderful superman whose manifold powers and perfections we can now but dimly imagine.

That such doctrines can long influence the sober thought of Germany is hardly to be expected; but the speculative audacity of Nietzsche, combined with the wonderful rhythm and impassioned eloquence of his style, has proved very fascinating to a generation already predisposed to a general revaluation of values.

By general consent the leading exponent of German naturalism is GERHART HAUPTMANN (1862–). It is certainly to him, if to any imaginative writer, that we must turn for a vindication of the new creed. But he vindicates it very imperfectly. Whatever may be the merit of the doctrine when stated abstractly, in his hands it has usually yielded a clinical diagnosis rather than an artistic treat. Take his first play, *Before Sunrise*. A brutish and besotted farmer has suddenly become rich by the discovery of coal on his premises, and has surrounded himself with the externalities of wealth. He is married to a second wife, who is a vulgar adulteress. By his first wife, who was addicted to drink, he has two daughters, one of whom, a married woman, is also a

27

tippler. The other daughter is a winsome girl who has been away at school and learned enough of decency and refinement so that she realises in a helpless way the wretchedness of her surroundings. A young socialist scholar comes to the place to investigate the labour conditions in the coal-mine. He falls in love with Helene, engages himself to her, and she is deliriously happy. Presently he learns from a medical man of the family proneness to drink. Fearing that the taint may descend to his children if he marries Helene, he runs away like a poltroon; whereupon the girl commits suicide. All this is presented by Hauptmann with the utmost life-likeness. The peasant folk are a depraved set, and the mirror is held up mercilessly to nature. No repulsive detail is spared. It all makes a remarkable illusion of vulgar actuality; but the total effect is very much the same, save for its greater vividness, as if one had read the wretched story in a newspaper. It is not the effect of tragedy, as the world has always understood it, hardly the effect of art at all. It is more like a three-hour survey of actual human conditions. There is little in the play to make one wish to see it or read it again and again.

And here we touch upon the weakness of naturalism as it has developed of late in Germany. The most of its champions have been led, either by temperament or by socialistic proclivity or by personal limitation, to identify "life" with the seamy side of life, albeit health and decency, virtue and high aspiration are just as real, just as "natural," as depravity and vice. Some of the later plays of Hauptmann are less dismally clinical than *Before Sunrise*, but in general what he gives us, whenever he holds fast to the naturalistic faith, is some distressing picture of social wretchedness, family discord or personal infirmity. And that sort of thing soon palls on people whose taste has been trained by the masterpieces of the past. They may acclaim it as a novelty for a season or two, but they presently discover that there is little in it in the way of pleasure, edification, or emotional uplift; then they avoid it and look elsewhere for those eternal desiderata. Authors who wish to give the public medicine in the form of plays and novels may always do so, and may convince themselves by argument that their dose is needed and will ultimately prove beneficial: the difficulty is that people always refuse to take it as soon as they find out what it is.

It is well known, however, that Hauptmann has not always followed the line on which he originally set out as dramatist. In 1896 he surprised his admirers with the *Sunken Bell*, which is a blend of naturalism and romantic symbolism—the two forms between which he has since oscillated. His eerie play of the bell-founder who deserts wife and child and breaks away from parochial morality, in order to pursue a fatuous dream of impossible achievement under the spell of a bewitching elf-maid, remains thus far his masterpiece. In the *Sunken Bell* there is poetry, romantic charm, and imagination not fettered to the clod, even if the symbolism is at times a little baffling.

Another prominent representative of the revolutionary tendencies which so stirred literary Germany some twenty years ago is HERMANN SUDERMANN (1857–), a better playwright than Hauptmann, according to all the old standards, but not so good a poet. Sudermann was never a naturalist of the stricter sect. Like Ibsen, he is first of all a critic of the social order, but he has concerned himself more with polite society than with the proletariat or the humbler *bourgeoisie*. His characteristic scene is the drawing-room of the well-to-do; or perhaps, as in his first play, *Honour*, he moves back and forth between mansion and hovel. The tragic potentialities of a too-strenuous and old-fashioned conception of honour; the calamitous workings of caste feeling or of family pride and prejudice; the corrosive effects of vice on talent; the ugly truth under the glittering surface—such are some of his themes. It is said, with some justice, that he has now and then sacrificed the truth to his well-calculated stage effects. Nevertheless, his best work in play and novel seems likely to endure as presenting a fairly just picture of German social conditions at the close of the nineteenth century.

BIBLIOGRAPHIC NOTE

A COMPLETE bibliography of German literature would fill many volumes. In this " note," which is just what its name implies, I give only a small selection, generally without comment, of works that for one reason or another seem most important. There is a *Handy Bibliographical Guide to the Study of the German Language and Literature*, by K. Breul, London, 1895, which is very useful. The German scholar's great reliance, in matters of bibliographic detail, is Goedeke's *Grundriss zur Geschichte der deutschen Dichtung*, of which vol. 8, covering the period 1815–30, appeared in 1905 at Dresden. The invaluable Goedeke is usefully supplemented by the successive *Jahresberichte für neuere deutsche Literaturgeschichte*, beginning in 1892. Vol. 14, covering the publications of the year 1903, is the latest (now published at Berlin). For authors no longer living consult the *Allgemeine deutsche Biographie* (53 vols., of which the latest, published in 1907, contains *Nachträge* to 1899). For living authors see the annual volumes of Kürschner's *Deutscher Literatur-Kalender*, published by Göschen of Leipzig. Vol. 30 covers the year 1908.

COLLECTIONS OF GERMAN AUTHORS

Kürschner's *Deutsche Nationalliteratur* (Stuttgart, 1882–99, 163 vols.) may be put first. The selections range from the 9th century to the 19th, in critical editions. The work of the many sub-editors varies considerably in point of literary insight, but the collection as a whole is extremely valuable. The same may be said of the *Bibliothek des literarischen Vereins in Stuttgart*, which now numbers 242 vols. (mainly post-mediæval reprints). The more important mediæval poets can be conveniently studied in the *Deutsche Classiker des Mittelalters, begründet von F. Pfeiffer* (12 vols., 1865–81), and the supplementary *Deutsche Dichtungen des Mittelalters,* edited by K. Bartsch (5 vols. 1872–77). Of the most of the volumes there are later revised editions. The two last-named sets are published by Brockhaus of Leipzig. The same house publishes, under the editorship of K. Goedeke and J. Tittmann, *Deutsche Dichter des 16. Jahrhunderts* and *Deutsche Dichter des 17. Jahrhunderts.* Of great value for the study of the 16th and 17th centuries are the critical reprints published by Niemeyer of Halle, under the general editorship of W. Braune, and commonly called *Braune's Neudrucke.* Thus far there are 221 numbers. Many important books of the 18th and 19th centuries have been made more generally accessible by the *Literaturdenkmale des 18. und 19. Jahrhunderts,* begun at Heilbronn in 1881 under the general editorship of B. Seuffert, and afterwards continued at Leipzig and Berlin under other editors. No. 140 has just appeared (1908). Much out-of-the-way material, finally, is contained in *Quellen und Forschungen zur Sprach- und Kulturgeschichte der germanischen Völker,* published by Trübner of Strassburg under the general editorship of W. Scherer, E. Martin, and others. Thus far 101 numbers.

GENERAL HISTORIES

The earliest treatise of any importance was A. Koberstein's *Grundriss zur Geschichte der deutschen Nationalliteratur,* which appeared in 1827 as a book of 299 pages. The 5th ed., issued in 1872–74 by K. Bartsch after Koberstein's death, comprises five volumes that are very erudite but not very readable. Next in order came the *Geschichte der poetischen Nationalliteratur der Deutschen,* by G. G. Gervinus (1835–42). After the author's death this work was likewise edited by K. Bartsch (5 vols., 1871–74). Important in its day but now superseded.

The work of W. Wackernagel, *Geschichte der deutschen Literatur* (1848–55), commendable for its conciseness, has been edited and continued by E. Martin (vol. 1, Basel, 1879; vol. 2, from the 16th century to the present time, 1885–94). The well-known *Geschichte der deutschen Nationalliteratur,* by A. F. C. Vilmar, first published in 1845, still meets with favor; the 26th edition, edited by A. Stern, having lately appeared (1906). The Berlin school of German scholarship is ably represented in the *Geschichte der deutschen Literatur* by W. Scherer (Berlin, 1883, 10th ed. in 1905), of which there is an English translation in two vols. by Mrs. Conybeare (Oxford, 1885). It ends with the death of Goethe. Scherer is always brilliant and suggestive, but often incautious in treating theories of his own as if they were facts. The best of the general histories is that of Vogt and Koch, *Geschichte der deutschen Literatur von den ältesten Zeiten bis zur Gegenwart* (Leipzig 1897; 2d ed. in 2 vols., with excellent bibliography, 1904). Admirable illustrations. Of the more popular illustrated histories, that of R. König, first published in 1878, seems to have found the most readers (29th ed. in 2 vols., 1903). It has solid merits in the way of description and analysis, but is not strong on the critical side. The more recent works of E. Engel (2 vols., 1906) and of A. Biese (vol. 1, 1907, to be completed in 2 vols.) both aim at *Volkstümlichkeit.* Of histories written in English, the most important are those of J. G. Robertson, *A History of German Literature* (London and New York, 1902), and K. Francke, *Social Forces in German Literature* (New York, 1896; later editions with title changed to *History of German Literature as Determined by Social Forces*).

SPECIAL HISTORIES

(a) *From the Earliest Times to Luther*

Allgemeine Geschichte der Literatur des Mittelalters im Abendlande, von A. Ebert (3 vols., Leipzig, 1874–87). Vol. 3

deals with the beginnings of the national literatures and with the Latin literature to the middle of the 11th century.— *Geschichte der deutschen Literatur von der ältesten Zeit bis zum 13. Jahrhundert,* von J. Kelle. Vol. 1, Berlin, 1892, ends with the middle of the 11th century; vol. 2, 1896, covers the period 1056–1190. A highly meritorious work, so far as it goes.—*Geschichte der deutschen Literatur bis zum Ausgang des Mittelalters,* von R. Koegel. Unfinished. Vol. 1 (Strassburg, 1894–96, 652 pages) ends with the middle of the 11th century. It is a work of very minute philological research.— *Geschichte der deutschen Literatur von den ersten Anfängen bis zum Ausgang des Mittelalters,* von W. Golther. Forms the first part of vol. 163 of Kürschner's *Deutsche Nationalliteratur.* The best special history covering the whole mediæval period.

(b) Period of the Renascence

For the 16th and 17th centuries there are no special histories comparable in fulness of detail to those above mentioned. An interesting phase of the subject is treated by K. Borinski in *Die Poetik der Renaissance und die Anfänge der literarischen Kritik in Deutschland* (Berlin, 1886). The same author's *Geschichte der deutschen Literatur seit dem Ausgang des Mittelalters,* forming the second part of vol. 163 of Kürschner's *Nationalliteratur,* is readable but brief. A valuable comparative work is C. H. Herford's *Studies in the Literary Relations of England and Germany in the 16th Century* (Cambridge, Eng., 1886).

(c) The Eighteenth and Nineteenth Centuries

Geschichte der deutschen Literatur von Leibniz bis auf unsere Zeit, von J. Schmidt. Four vols., the last ending with the year 1814, appeared in 1886–90.—*Die deutsche Nationalliteratur im 18. und 19. Jahrhundert, historisch und æsthetisch-kritisch dargestellt* von J. Hillebrand (3d ed. in 3 vols. Gotha,

1875).—*Geschichte der deutschen Literatur im 18. Jahrhundert,*
von H. Hettner. This is Part III of Hettner's excellent *Literaturgeschichte des 18. Jahrhunderts,* of which Part I is devoted to England, Part II to France. Latest edition of Part
III in 2 vols., 1894.—*Hauptströmungen der Literatur des 19.
Jahrhunderts,* von G. Brandes. The first German edition, translated from the Danish by Strodtmann, appeared in 1872–76 (4
vols.). A later revision, begun by the author himself, bore the
title *Die Literatur des 19. Jahrhunderts in ihren Hauptströmungen dargestellt.* Vol. 2 deals with the Romantic School in
Germany, vol. 6 with Young Germany. There is an English
translation of all six vols. (New York, 1901–1905).—The most
elaborate treatment of the 19th century is found in *Die deutsche
Literatur des 19. Jahrhunderts,* von R. M. Meyer (Berlin, 1900,
966 pages 8vo).

MISCELLANEOUS

CHAPTER I. — *Kirchengeschichte Deutschlands,* von A.
Hauck; 2d ed., Leipzig, 1900.—*Handbuch der germanischen
Mythologie,* von W. Golther; Leipzig, 1895.—*Germanische
Heldensage,* von B. Symons; Strassburg, 2d ed., 1905.—*Altger-
manische Metrik,* von E. Sievers; Strassburg, 2d ed., 1905.—
*Denkmäler deutscher Poesie und Prosa aus dem 8. bis 12.
Jahrhundert,* von Müllenhoff und Scherer; 3d ed. by Stein-
meyer, Berlin, 1892. (Text of *Lay of Hildebrand* and the
Merseburg Charms.)

CHAPTER II.—The minor texts are mostly to be found in
the *Denkmäler* (see above).—*Heliand*: ed. by E. Sievers,
Halle, 1878; O. Behaghel, Halle, 1882; M. Heyne, with glos-
sary, Paderborn, 1883.—*Old Saxon Genesis*: See the *Neue
Heidelberger Jahrbücher,* vol. 4 (1894); also *Die neuentdeckte
Bibeldichtung,* von F. Vetter, Basel, 1895.—Otfried: ed. by P.
Piper, Freiburg, 1878, and by O. Erdmann, Halle, 1882.

CHAPTER III.—*Waltharius*: Latin text by H. Althof, Leipzig, 1899; hexameter translation, Leipzig, 1902.—Hrotsvith:

Latin text by K. A. Barack, Nürnberg, 1858, and by P. Win-
terfeld, Berlin, 1902; translation of plays by O. Piltz in
Reclam's *Universalbibliothek* (Leipzig, no date).—*Ruodlieb*:
Latin text by F. Seiler, Halle, 1882; translation by M. Heyne,
Leipzig, 1897.—Ezzo's *Lay of Christ* and the Arnstein *Hymn
to the Virgin* are both in the *Denkmäler.*—*Lay of Anno*: ed. by
M. Rödiger in the *Monumenta Germaniae historica* (1895).—
Heinrich von Melk: ed. by R. Heinzel, Berlin, 1867.—*Lay of
Alexander*: ed. by K. Kinzel, Halle, 1884.—*Lay of Roland*: ed.
by K. Bartsch, Leipzig, 1874.

CHAPTER IV.—*King Rother*: ed. by K. von Bahder, Halle,
1884.—*Duke Ernst*: ed. by K. Bartsch, Leipzig, 1869.—*Nibelung Lay*: the latest and best bibliography will be found in R.
von Muth's *Einleitung in das Nibelunglied*, 2d ed. by J. W.
Nagel, Paderborn, 1907. The subject is too large to be dealt
with here. The fundamental recensions are those of K. Lachmann (5th ed., Berlin, 1878) for manuscript A; K. Bartsch,
Leipzig, 1870–80, for B; and F. Zarncke, 6th ed., 1887, for C.
The most popular German translation is that of K. Simrock
(56th ed., 1902); the best English translation that of G. H.
Needler, New York, 1904.—*Gudrun*: ed. by K. Bartsch, 4th ed.,
Leipzig, 1880; B. Symons, Halle, 1883; E. Martin, Halle, 1901.
—Poems of the Dietrich-saga: ed. by O. Jänicke and others in
Das deutsche Heldenbuch, Berlin, 1866–70, 5 vols. The *Rose-
garden*, not contained in the *Heldenbuch*, has been edited by G.
Holz, Halle, 1893.

CHAPTER V.—Heinrich von Veldeke's *Eneide*: ed. by O. Behaghel, Heilbronn, 1882.—Hartmann von Aue: ed. by F. Bech,
Leipzig, 1893, 2d ed., 3 vols.—Wolfram von Eschenbach: ed.
by K. Bartsch, Leipzig, 1875–77 (2d ed.), and by A. Leitz-
mann, Halle, 1902. Good translation of *Parzival* by W. Hertz,
Stuttgart, 1898.—Gottfried von Strassburg: ed. by L. Bech-
stein, 3d ed., Leipzig, 1891. Good translation by W. Hertz,
Stuttgart, 1901.—For the minor romancers consult the bibliography in Koch and Vogt, I, 336–37.

CHAPTER VI.—The most complete collection of the minnesingers is that of F. H. von der Hagen, Leipzig, 1838, in 4 large vols. The best selections are those of K. Bartsch, *Deutsche Liederdichter des 12. bis 14. Jahrhunderts*, 4th ed. by W. Golther, Berlin, 1901, and F. Pfaff, *Der Minnesang des 12. bis 14. Jahrhunderts*, Stuttgart, 1892. Pfaff has also edited *Die grosse Heidelberger Liederhandschrift*, Heidelberg, 1899–1907. The precursors of Walter can best be studied in Lachmann and Haupt's *Des Minnesangs Frühling*, 2d ed., Leipzig, 1888. *Old German Love Songs*, by F. C. Nicholson, Chicago, 1907, contains a good selection in English translations, together with a useful essay on the minnesingers. The literature of Walter is extensive. There are lives of him by W. Wilmanns, Bonn, 1882; A. E. Schönbach, Berlin, 1895 (2d ed.), and K. Burdach, Leipzig, 1900. The best editions are those of K. Lachmann (6th, Berlin, 1891), F. Pfeiffer (6th, Leipzig, 1880), W. Wilmanns (2d, Halle, 1883) and H. Paul (2d, Halle, 1895).

CHAPTER VII.—Thomasin: ed. by H. Rückert, Leipzig, 1852. —Freidank: ed. by H. E. Bezzenberger, Halle, 1872.—*Meier Helmbrecht*: ed. by F. Keinz, 2d ed., Leipzig, 1887.—*Parson Ameis*: ed. by H. Lambel in *Erzählungen und Schwänke des 13. Jahrhunderts*, Leipzig, 1883.—*Reinhart Fuchs*: ed. by K. Reissenberger, Halle, 1886; Reynke de Vos: ed. by F. Prien, Halle, 1887.—Berthold von Regensburg: ed. by Pfeiffer and Strobl, Vienna, 1862–80.—On the drama of the period consult *Das Drama des Mittelalters*, by R. Froning, Stuttgart, no date (1891). It is vol. 14 of Kürschner's *Nationalliteratur*. See also *Die Oster- und Passionsspiele*, by G. Milchsack, Wolfen-büttel, 1880, and *Die Oster- und Passionsspiele*, by L. Wirth, Utrecht, 1889.—A large number of early shrovetide plays are assembled in *Fastnachtspiele aus dem 15. Jahrhundert*, ed. by A. Keller (vols. 28–30 of the publications of the Stuttgart Verein).—Brant's *Narrenschiff*: ed. by F. Zarncke, Leipzig, 1854, and by K. Goedeke, Leipzig, 1878.—*Teuerdank*: ed. by K. Goedeke, Leipzig, 1878.

CHAPTER VIII.—On German humanism consult *Vom Mittel-alter zur Reformation*, by K. Burdach, Halle, 1893, and *Renais-*

sance und Humanismus in Italien und Deutschland, by L.
Geiger, Berlin, 1882.—Luther: the best life is that by J. Köst-
lin, 4th ed. by G. Kawerau, Berlin, 1892. The great Weimar
edition of Luther, of which some 30 vols. have been published, is
still far from complete. There is a new popular edition, by G.
Buchwald and others, Berlin, 3d ed., 1898. Reprints of certain
important works will be found in Braune's *Neudrucke.* There
are also two good selections for students: one by R. Neubauer,
Halle, 1900–3 (vols. 2 and 3 of Part III of Bötticher and Kinzel's *Denkmäler*); the other by W. H. Carruth (*Auswahl aus
Luthers deutschen Schriften*), Boston, 1899.—Hutten: ed. by
Boecking, Leipzig, 1859–70, 5 vols.; selection by Balke in vol.
17 of Kürschner's *Nationalliteratur.* The same volume contains selections from Murner.

CHAPTER IX.—For the Protestant drama see Creizenach,
Geschichte des neueren Dramas, vol. 2 (Halle, 1893–1904).—
The Swiss plays referred to will be found in *Schweizerische
Schauspiele aus dem 16. Jahrhundert,* by J. Bächtold, Zürich,
1890–93; Rebhun's *Susanna* in *Schauspiele aus dem 16. Jahr-
hundert,* by J. Tittmann, Leipzig, 1868.—Braune's *Neudrucke*
contain the shrovetide plays of Hans Sachs, *Eulenspiegel,* the
German *Grobianus,* the Faust-book of 1587 and the most impor-
tant works of Fischart.—The works of Hans Sachs, Wickram,
Duke Heinrich Julius, and Ayrer have been reprinted by the
Stuttgart Verein.

CHAPTER X.—A useful survey of the century following
Opitz will be found in *From Opitz to Lessing,* by T. S. Perry,
Boston, 1885. See also the interesting essay of E. Schmidt
*Der Kampf gegen die Mode in der deutschen Literatur des 17.
Jahrhunderts* in *Charakteristiken,* vol. 1, 2d ed., Berlin, 1902.
—Weckherlin, Opitz, Fleming, Logau, Gryphius, Gerhardt,
Dach and Spe are all represented in Goedeke and Tittmann's
Deutsche Dichter des 17. Jahrhunderts.—The *Aristarchus* and
Poeterei of Opitz have been well edited by G. Witkowski,
Leipzig, 1888.—The works of Weckherlin, Logau, Dach, and
the tragedies and short poems of Gryphius, appear in the pub-

lications of the Stuttgart Verein.—The Second Silesian School
is quite sufficiently represented in Kürschner, vols. 36 and 37.

CHAPTER XI.—On Grimmelshausen in relation to the earlier
fiction see Bobertag's *Geschichte des Romans,* vol. 2, Berlin,
1884. *Simplicissimus* appears in the *Neudrucke,* nos. 19–25;
also, together with other *Simplicianische Schriften,* in Kürschner, vols. 33–35.—Moscherosch, Weise, Canitz, Neukirch, Günther, Brockes, Haller, Hagedorn, Gellert, Bodmer and Gottsched are all represented in Kürschner.—The trail of *Robinson
Crusoe* in Germany can be studied in H. Ullrich's *Robinson
und Robinsonaden,* Weimar, 1898.—On the English invasion
see M. Koch's *Über die Beziehungen der englischen Literatur
zur deutschen im 18. Jahrhundert,* Leipzig, 1883.—Of recent
Gottsched-literature suffice it to mention *Gottsched und die
deutsche Literatur seiner Zeit,* by G. Waniek, Leipzig, 1897,
and *Gottsched der Deutsche,* by E. Reichel, Berlin, 1901.—Bodmer is best treated in J. Bächtold's *Geschichte der deutschen
Literatur in der Schweiz,* Frauenfeld, 1892.

CHAPTER XII.—On the quickening of national spirit see
Nationalität und Nationalliteratur, by M. Koch, Berlin, 1891;
also *Friedrich der Grosse und die deutsche Literatur,* by A. E.
Berger, Bonn, 1890.—The best life of Klopstock is that by F.
Muncker, Stuttgart, 1888; the most convenient edition of his
more important works that of F. Hamel, in Kürschner, vols.
46–48.—Up to date there is no good biography of Wieland, no
good critical edition of his works. The need is presently to be
supplied by the Berlin Academy. Meanwhile the Hempel edition, 40 vols., Berlin, 1879, with biographic sketch by H. Dünt-
zer, is the best available.—For the Göttingen poets see Kürschner, vols. 49–50; for Bürger, vol. 78.

CHAPTER XIII.—The best book on Lessing is E. Schmidt's
Lessing, 2 vols., 2d ed., Berlin, 1899; it contains a well-
digested Lessing-bibliography. The definitive edition of Lessing is that of Lachmann (1838), as revised by Muncker, 21
vols. (including the letters), Stuttgart and Leipzig, 1886–1907.
—The best life of Herder is that by R. Haym, 2 vols., Berlin,

1880–85. See also *Herder's Leben,* by E. Kühnemann, München, 1895. The definitive edition of Herder's works is that by B. Suphan, 32 vols., Berlin, 1877–99.

CHAPTERS XIV–XVI.—The 202 pages of Goethe-bibliography in Goedeke's *Grundriss,* vol. 4, ends with the year 1891. For the subsequent years consult the *Goethe-Jahrbuch* and the annual *Berichte des freien deutschen Hochstifts* (Frankfort). Of the many biographies of Goethe none is indisputably "the best." The well-known English book of G. H. Lewes (London, 1856) leaves much to be desired. Fascinating in style, but sometimes intemperate, is H. Grimm's *Vorlesungen über Goethe,* Berlin, 1875 (English translation by S. H. Adams, Boston, 1879). Two excellent books are A. Schöll's *Goethe in Hauptzügen seines Lebens und Wirkens,* Berlin, 1882, and V. Hehn's *Gedanken über Goethe,* 4th ed., Berlin, 1900. Illustrated biographies of solid merit are those by K. Heinemann, 2 vols., 3d ed., Leipzig, 1903, and the much briefer one by G. Witkowski, Leipzig, 1899. Much praised in Germany, but often overpraised, is the work of A. Bielschowsky, München, 1896–1904 (English version by W. A. Cooper, New York, 1905–8). For the works of Goethe, including his letters, the definitive edition for all critical purposes is the great Weimar edition, of which 127 vols. have thus far appeared. More convenient for general use are the Hempel edition (36 vols., Berlin, 1868–79), the Kürschner edition (vols. 82–117 of the *Nationalliteratur*), and the Cotta jubilee edition, 40 vols., Stuttgart, 1902–5.— For the minor "storm and stress" writers see *Stürmer und Dränger* in Kürschner (vols. 79–81).

For Schiller-literature down to 1893 consult Goedeke's *Grundriss,* vol. 5 (140 pages); since then, the annual *Berichte des Frankfurter Hochstifts.* The best *complete* biographies in German are those by J. Wychgram, 3d ed., Leipzig, 1898 (well illustrated and sanely "popular"); E. Kühnemann, München, 1905, and K. Berger, 2 vols., München, 1905–9. Thorough and exhaustive in scholarship, but somewhat overloaded with philological detail, are the unfinished works by R. Weltrich, vol. 1,

Stuttgart, 1885–99, vol. 2, 1908, and J. Minor, 2 vols., Berlin, 1890.—There is a good English life of Schiller by C. Thomas, New York, 1901.—For the text of Schiller consult Goedeke's *historisch-kritische Ausgabe*, 15 vols., Stuttgart, 1867–76. But there are many other more convenient editions, such as that in Kürschner (vols. 118–129), that of Bellermann, 14 vols., Leipzig, 1895–98, and the Cotta *Säkularausgabe*, 16 vols., Stuttgart, 1904–5.—The lettters of Schiller have been critically edited by F. Jonas, 7 vols., Stuttgart, 1892–96.

CHAPTER XVII.—The most solid work on the earlier romanticists is R. Haym's *Die romantische Schule*, Berlin, 1870. The two volumes of R. Huch, *Blütezeit der Romantik* and *Ausbreitung und Verfall der Romantik*, Leipzig, 1901–2, are fascinating in style and penetrating in analysis. See also vol. 2 of G. Brandes's *Hauptströmungen der Literatur des 19. Jahrhunderts*; S. Born's *Die romantische Schule in Deutschland und in Frankreich*, Heidelberg, 1879, and C. E. Vaughan's *The Romantic Revolt*, Edinburgh, 1907.

CHAPTERS XVIII–XX.—For the bibliography of nineteenth-century writers it must here suffice to refer, once more, to Goedeke's *Grundriss*, vols. 6–8; to the excellent bibliography in vol. 2 of Koch and Vogt; and, where these fail, to R. M. Meyer's *Grundriss der neuern deutschen Literaturgeschichte*, Berlin, 1902.

INDEX

28   423

(1)

LITERATURES OF THE WORLD.

Edited by EDMUND GOSSE,

Hon. M.A. of Trinity College, Cambridge.

A series of attractive volumes dealing with the history of literature in each country. Each volume will contain about three hundred and fifty 12mo pages, and will treat of an entire literature, giving a uniform impression of its development, history, and character, and of its relation to previous and to contemporary work.

Each 12mo, Cloth.

NOW READY.

Ancient Greek Literature. By GILBERT MURRAY, M.A., Professor of Greek in the University of Glasgow. $1.50.

French Literature. By EDWARD DOWDEN, D.C.L., LL.D., Professor of English Literature at the University of Dublin. $1.50.

Modern English Literature. By EDMUND GOSSE. $1.50.

Italian Literature. By RICHARD GARNETT, C.B., LL.D., Keeper of Printed Books in the British Museum. $1.50.

Spanish Literature. By J. FITZMAURICE-KELLY, Member of the Spanish Academy. $1.50.

Japanese Literature. By W. G. ASTON, C.M.G., M.A., late Acting Secretary at the British Legation, Tokio. $1.50.

Russian Literature. By K. WALISZEWSKI. $1.50.

Sanskrit Literature. By A. A. MACDONELL, M.A., Deputy Boden Professor of Sanskrit at the University of Oxford. $1.50.

Chinese Literature. By HERBERT A. GILES, A.M., LL.D. (Aberd.), Professor of Chinese in the University of Cambridge. $1.50.

Arabic Literature. By CLÉMENT HUART, Secretary-Interpreter for Oriental Languages to the French Government. $1.25 net.

American Literature. By Prof. W. P. TRENT, of Columbia University. $1.40 net.

Hungarian Literature. By FREDERICK REIDL, Professor of Hungarian Literature in the University of Budapest. $1.50 net.

In Preparation.

Latin Literature. By MARCUS DIMSDALE, M.A., Cambridge.
German Literature. By CALVIN THOMAS, LL.D., Columbia.
Hebrew Literature. By Prof. PHILIPPE BERGER, Institut de France.

D. APPLETON AND COMPANY, NEW YORK.

LITERATURES OF THE WORLD.

Edited by EDMUND GOSSE,
Hon. M.A. of Trinity College, Cambridge.

Ancient Greek Literature.

By GILBERT MURRAY, M.A., Professor of Greek in the University of Glasgow. 12mo. Cloth, $1.50

"An illuminating history of Greek literature, in which learning is enlivened and supplemented by literary skill, by a true sense of the 'humanities.' The reader feels that this is no book of perfunctory erudition, but a labor of love, performed by a scholar, to whom ancient Greece and her literature are exceedingly real and vivid. His judgments and suggestions are full of a personal fresh sincerity ; he can discern the living men beneath their works, and give us his genuine impression of them."—*London Daily Chronicle.*

"A fresh and stimulating and delightful book, and should be put into the hands of all young scholars. It will make them understand, or help to make them understand, to a degree they have never yet understood, that the Greek writers over whom they have toiled at school are living literature after all."
—*Westminster Gazette.*

"Mr. Murray's style is lucid and spirited, and, besides the fund of information, he imparts to his subject such fresh and vivid interest that students will find in these pages a new impulse for more profound and exhaustive study of this greatest and most immortal of all the world's literatures."
—*Philadelphia Public Ledger.*

"The admirable perspective of the whole work is what one most admires. The reader unlearned in Greek history and literature sees at once the relation which a given author bore to his race and age, and the current trend of thought, as well as what we value him for to-day. . . . As an introduction to the study of some considerable portion of Greek literature in English translations it will be found of the very highest usefulness."—*Boston Herald.*

"Professor Murray has written an admirable book, clear in its arrangement, compact in its statements, and it is one, we think, its least scholarly reader must feel an instructive and thoroughly trustworthy piece of English criticism."—*New York Mail and Express.*

"Professor Murray has contributed a volume which shows profound scholarship, together with a keen literary appreciation. It is a book for scholars as well as for the general reader. The author is saturated with his subject, and has a rare imaginative sympathy with ancient Greece."
—*The Interior, Chicago.*

"Written in a style that is sometimes spasmodic, often brilliant, and always fresh and suggestive."—*New York Sun.*

D. APPLETON AND COMPANY, NEW YORK.

LITERATURES OF THE WORLD.

Edited by EDMUND GOSSE,
Hon. M.A. of Trinity College, Cambridge.

Japanese Literature.

By W. G. ASTON, C.M.G., M.A., late Acting Secretary of the British Legation at Tokio. 12mo. Cloth, $1.50.

" A volume of unique erudition, wide research, clear discrimination, and excellent design. Mr. Aston has wrought a memorable service not only to those interested in Japan and Japanese studies, but to the world of letters at large."
—*Sir Edwin Arnold in Literature.*

" Mr. Aston has written the first complete narrative from early times to the present of the history, the rituals, the poetry, the drama, and the personal outpourings of thoughts and feelings which constitute the body of the literature of Japan."—*Baltimore Sun.*

" Mr. Aston has unquestionably enabled the European reader for the first time to enjoy a comprehensive survey of the vast and ancient field of Japanese literature, of which we have had hitherto only furtive and partial glimpses."
—*London Times.*

" His work is a model of what a manual of this character should be. While it constitutes an admirable guide-book to anyone who cares to go deeper into this special subject, it is sufficiently comprehensive to meet the requirements of the average reader or the general student of literature."
—*Brooklyn Daily Eagle.*

D. APPLETON AND COMPANY, NEW YORK.

Italian Literature.

By RICHARD GARNETT, C.B., LL.D., formerly Keeper of Printed Books in the British Museum. 12mo. Cloth, $1.50.

"Finished and graceful, at once delicate and strong, and never relapses into prosiness."—*The Dial.*

"Dr. Garnett is lucid in arrangement, agreeable and correct, and often powerful and felicitous in style. He has done a real service to both English and Italian literatures."
—*Literature.*

"The manual is a worthy companion of its predecessors, and will be found useful by each one who desires to refresh or enlarge his acquaintance with the magnificent achievements of Italian genius."—*Public Ledger, Philadelphia.*

"A most interesting book, written from a full knowledge of the subject, but without pedantry. The style is simple, graceful, and readable; the erudition is easily discovered by those who seek for it, but it is not ostentatiously displayed. Scholars will appreciate it at its worth; the general reader will be grateful for the charity of the text, and for the labor that has made his path one of pleasure only"
—*Saturday Evening Gazette.*

D. APPLETON AND COMPANY, NEW YORK.

Spanish Literature.

By J. FITZMAURICE-KELLY, Member of the Span-ish Academy. 12mo. Cloth, $1.50.

"Mr. Kelly has written a book that must be read and pondered, for within its limits it has no rival as 'A History of Spanish Literature.' "—*The Mail and Express*.

"The work before us is one which no student can hence-forth neglect, . . . if the student would keep his knowl-edge of Spanish up to date. . . . We close with a renewed expression of admiration for this excellent manual; the style is marked and full of piquancy, the phrases dwell in the memory."—*The Spectator*.

"A handbook that has long been needed for the use of the general reader, and it admirably supplies the want. Great skill is shown in the selection of the important facts; the criticisms, though necessarily brief, are authoritative and to the point, and the history is gracefully told in sound lit-erary style."—*Saturday Evening Gazette*.

"For the first time a survey of Spanish literature is pre-sented to English readers by a writer of ample knowledge and keen discrimination. Mr. Kelly's work rises far be-yond the level of the text-books. So good a critic does not merely comment on literature; he makes it himself."
—*New York Bookman*.

LITERATURES OF THE WORLD.

Edited by EDMUND GOSSE,
Hon. M.A. of Trinity College, Cambridge.

French Literature.

By EDWARD DOWDEN, D.Litt., LL.D., D.C.L.,
Professor of English Literature in the University of
Dublin. 12mo. Cloth, $1.50.

"Certainly the best history of French literature in the English language."
—*London Athenæum*.

"This is a history of literature as histories of literature should be written.
. . . A living voice, speaking to us with gravity and enthusiasm about the
writers of many ages, and of being a human voice always. Hence this book
can be read with pleasure even by those for whom a history has in itself little
attraction."—*London Saturday Review*.

"Remarkable for its fulness of information and frequent brilliancy. . . .
A book which both the student of French literature and the stranger to it will,
in different ways, find eminently useful, and in many parts of it thoroughly
enjoyable as well."—*London Literary World*.

"A book readable, graphic, not overloaded with detail, not bristling with
dates. . . . It is a book that can be held in the hand and read aloud with pleasure as a literary treat by an expert in style, master of charming words that
come and go easily, and of other literatures that serve for illustrations."
—*The Critic*.

"His methods afford an admirable example of compressing an immense
amount of information and criticism in a sentence or paragraph, and his survey of a vast field is both comprehensive and interesting."
—*Philadelphia Public Ledger*.

"Thorough without being diffuse. The author is in love with his subject,
has made it a study for years, and therefore produced an entertaining volume.
Of the scholarship shown it is needless to speak. . . . It is more than a cyclo-
pedia. It is a brilliant talk by one who is loaded with the lively ammunition
of French prose and verse. He talks of the pulpit, the stage, the Senate, and
the *salon*, until the preachers, dramatists, orators, and philosophers seem to
be speaking for themselves."—*Boston Globe*.

"Professor Dowden's book is more interesting than we ever supposed a
brief history of a literature could be. His characterizations are most admirable
in their conciseness and brilliancy. He has given in one volume a very thorough
review of French literature."—*The Interior, Chicago*.

D. APPLETON AND COMPANY, NEW YORK.